Forty Years of Sport and Social Change, 1968–2008

1968 was a year of protest in civil society (Prague, Paris, Chicago) and a year of protest in sport. After a world-wide campaign, the anti-apartheid movement succeeded in barring South Africa from the Olympic Games, while US athletes from the Olympic Project for Human Rights used the medals podium to decry the racism of North America. Meanwhile, students in Mexico City demonstrated against social priorities in Mexico, the host of the 1968 Games. These events contributed significantly to the rejection of the idea that sports are apolitical, and stimulated the scholarly study of sport across the social sciences.

Leading up to the Beijing Olympic Games, similar dynamics were played out across the globe, while a campaign was underway to boycott the 'Genocide Olympics'. The volume, Forty Years of Sport and Social Change, 1968–2008, considers together sports, human rights and social change in the forty years after Mexico City and the lead up to the Beijing Olympic Games.

The contributions to this volume capture the memories of activists who were "on the ground" using sport as a site for the struggle for human rights and provide scholarly examinations of past and current human rights movements in sport.

This book was previously published as a special issue of *Sport in Society.*

Russell Field is assistant professor in the Faculty of Kinesiology and Recreation Management at the University of Manitoba, whose current research examines the contested meanings of global sporting events.

Bruce Kidd is professor of physical education and health at the University of Toronto. During more than forty years, Kidd has combined careers as an internationally ranked athlete, coach, sports administrator, professor and dean with critical scholarly and popular writing about sport, often on the issues in which he has been directly involved.

Forty Years of Sport and Social Change, 1968–2008

"To Remember is to Resist"

Edited by Russell Field and Bruce Kidd

Routledge
Taylor & Francis Group

LONDON AND NEW YORK

First published 2011 by Routledge
2 Park Square, Milton Park, Abingdon, Oxon, OX14 4RN

Simultaneously published in the USA and Canada
by Routledge
270 Madison Avenue, New York, NY 10016

Routledge is an imprint of the Taylor & Francis Group, an informa business

This book is a reproduction of *Sport in Society*, vol.13, issue 1. The Publisher requests to those authors who may be citing this book to state, also, the bibliographical details of the special issue on which the book was based

Typeset in Times New Roman by Value Chain, India
Printed and bound in Great Britain by CPI Antony Rowe, Chippenham, Wiltshire

British Library Cataloguing in Publication Data

ISBN13: 978-0-415-48854-9

Contents

Sport in the Global Society – Contemporary Perspectives

Series Editor: Boria Majumdar

Forty Years of Sport and Social Change, 1968–2008

"To Remember is to Resist"

Sport in the Global Society – Contemporary Perspectives

Series Editor: Boria Majumdar

The social, cultural (including media) and political study of sport is an expanding area of scholarship and related research. While this area has been well served by the Sport in the Global Society Series, the surge in quality scholarship over the last few years has necessitated the creation of *Sport in the Global Society: Contemporary Perspectives*. The series will publish the work of leading scholars in fields as diverse as sociology, cultural studies, media studies, gender studies, cultural geography and history, political science and political economy. If the social and cultural study of sport is to receive the scholarly attention and readership it warrants, a cross-disciplinary series dedicated to taking sport beyond the narrow confines of physical education and sport science academic domains is necessary. Sport in the Global Society: Contemporary Perspectives will answer this need.

Other Titles in the Series

Australian Sport
Antipodean Waves of Change
Edited by Kristine Toohey and Tracy Taylor

Australia's Asian Sporting Context
1920s and 1930s
Edited by Sean Brawley and Nick Guoth

'Critical Support' for Sport
Bruce Kidd

Disability in the Global Sport Arena
A Sporting Chance
Edited by Jill M. Clair

Diversity and Division – Race, Ethnicity and Sport in Australia
Christopher J. Hallinan

Documenting the Beijing Olympics
Edited by D. P. Martinez

Football in Brazil
Edited by Martin Curi

Football's Relationship with Art: The Beautiful Game?
John E. Hughson

Global Perspectives on Football in Africa
Visualising the Game
Edited by Susann Baller, Giorgio Miescher and Raffaele Poli

Global Sport Business
Community Impacts of Commercial Sport
Edited by Hans Westerbeek

Governance, Citizenship and the New European Football Championships
The European Spectacle
Edited by Wolfram Manzenreiter and Georg Spitaler

Indigenous People, Race Relations and Australian Sport
Edited by Christopher J. Hallinan and Barry Judd

Reviewing UK Football Cultures
Continuing with Gender Analyses
Edited by Jayne Caudwell

South Africa and the Global Game
Football, Apartheid and Beyond
Edited by Peter Alegi and Chris Bolsmann

Sport – Race, Ethnicity and Identity
Building Global Understanding
Edited by Daryl Adair

Sport and the Community
Edited by Allan Edwards and David Hassan

Sport, Culture and Identity in the State of Israel
Edited by Yair Galily and Amir Ben-Porat

Sport in Australian National Identity
Kicking Goals
Tony Ward

Sport in the City
Cultural Connections
Edited by Michael Sam and John E. Hughson

The Changing Face of Cricket
From Imperial to Global Game
Edited by Dominic Malcolm, Jon Gemmell and Nalin Mehta

The Containment of Soccer in Australia
Fencing Off the World Game
Edited by Christopher J. Hallinan and John E. Hughson

The Flame Relay and the Olympic Movement
John J. MacAloon

The Making of Sporting Cultures
John E. Hughson

The Politics of Sport
Community, Mobility, Identity
Edited by Paul Gilchrist and Russell Holden

The Politics of Sport in South Asia
Edited by Subhas Ranjan Chakraborty, Shantanu Chakrabarti and Kingshuk Chatterjee

The Social Impact of Sport
Edited by Ramón Spaaij

Who Owns Football?
The Governance and Management of the Club Game Worldwide
Edited by David Hassan and Sean Hamil

Why Minorities Play or Don't Play Soccer
A Global Exploration
Edited by Kausik Bandyopadhyay

ABSTRACTS

The conservative vision of the amateur ideal and its paradoxical whitening power: the story of Valerie Jerome in 1950s and 1960s Canadian track and field

Valerie Jerome and Stuart Parker

Valerie Jerome was a member of Canada's team at the 1959 Pan American Games where as a 15-year-old she placed 4th in the 100m. She was also a member of Canada's 1960 Olympic and 1966 Commonwealth Games teams. After leaving competitive sport, Valerie continued to serve as a track and field coach and official, serving as Chief Judge for Horizontal Jumps at the 1976 Montreal Olympics and Jumps Referee for the 1978 and 1994 Commonwealth Games and World Indoor (1993) and Outdoor (2001) Championships. She is also a fixture in Vancouver civil society, serving on such diverse boards of directors as the Achilles Athletics Foundation, the Goh Ballet Academy, Vancouver Youth Theatre and the British Columbia (BC) Association of Black Educators. She has been nominated seven times to run for public office beginning with her 1978 candidacy for The Electors Action Movement through to her 1996 candidacy for the Green Party of BC.

The athlete as Sisyphus: reflections of an athlete advocate

Ann Peel

As a 12-year-old living in Moscow in 1973, I watched Canada's Glenda Reiser win the 1,500m at the World University Games, and, as children do, decided that would be me. Raised to believe I could do whatever I set my mind to, off I went. But the journey was to be far more complicated than I could ever have anticipated.

Each time I felt I was making progress in my quest for excellence, a barrier would appear. I felt like Sisyphus who was sentenced to roll a rock up a hill. Each time it reached the top, the rock rolled back down again. His crime had been to challenge Zeus. Mine was much less grandiose: I wanted only to reach my maximum potential free of restrictions created by the sport system.

Athletes are still rolling their rocks up hills. They shouldn't be. The role of the system should be to flatten the barriers, to ease the way, to widen the path. Unfortunately, much of the time that is not what happens. But it could be, and what follows is the story of an effort to help athletes get to the top of the hill a little more easily, with less interference from the system.

My thesis is a simple one: athletes want to perform. Their performance, and the supports needed to create it, should be the focus of the sport system. To ensure that focus, athletes and their coaches must get involved. If, as athletes, we do not shape and support the systems we need, we will roll our rocks for evermore.

Tony Suze's reflections on the importance of sport in the struggle to end Apartheid

Chuck Korr

For 15 years, Tony Suze was a political prisoner on South Africa's notorious Robben Island. He was one of the driving forces behind a campaign to obtain the right to play football (soccer) and he helped to create an organized league that met all the requirements of FIFA, the international governing body for the sport. Football was much more than just a game for the prisoners – it was one of the ways in which they confirmed their dignity as individuals and asserted their right to run at least a part of their lives despite the brutal conditions of the prison. It was a way they trained themselves to participate in governing South Africa and it was one of the few times they could enjoy something they did on the Island. Tony's first time outside of South Africa (a conference in Toronto) gave him the opportunity to give a personal account of how sport on Robben Island helped pave the way to the creation of a free, democratic, and non-racist South Africa.

The untold story of Robben Island: sports and the anti-Apartheid movement

Anthony Suze

Anthony Suze was born in 1942, in a small township northwest of Pretoria. By his own admission, a more avid sportsman than student, he participated in a number of sports and played second-division soccer with Methodist FC. His political awareness emerged in Apartheid-era South Africa 1960 when he was recruited by the Pan Africanist Congress. In 1963, Suze was one of members instructed by party commanders to mobilize and indoctrinate other students. Upon Suze's resulting arrest, he was one of 14 men, most in their early-20s, who were sentenced in May 1963 to a combined 185 years on the infamous Robben island prison. Suze spent the next 15 years on the island. While there he participated in a remarkable movement of sport resistance, as the political prisoners agitated for and won the right to organize their own soccer league. The resulting Makana Football Association was a multi-team, two-division league – featuring formal team administrative structures, referees trained according to FIFA standards, and a leaguewide disciplinary committee – that allowed the participants to be physically active while honing their organizational skills as the government-in-waiting.

'In good conscience': Andy Flower, Henry Olonga and the death of democracy in Zimbabwe

Callie Batts

Just before their first match of the 2003 Cricket World Cup, Zimbabwean cricketers Andy Flower and Henry Olonga issued a statement explaining their decision to protest the ongoing human rights abuses waged by the oppressive regime of Robert Mugabe. By donning black armbands, Flower and Olonga engaged in a political gesture designed to mourn the 'death of democracy' in Zimbabwe and draw attention to the social, political and economic problems of their homeland. For Flower and Olonga, the act of expressing their feelings represented an exercising of basic human rights denied to many of their fellow countrymen and women. In response, the authorities castigated the two athletes, reiterated the myth of apolitical sport, and tightened the connection between the government and the national team. While the protest failed to catalyse direct social change, it raised awareness of human rights issues in Zimbabwe and illustrated the relevance of sport in even the most beleaguered societies.

Social change and popular culture: seminal developments at the interface of race, sport and society

Harry Edwards

Outstanding achievement is enabled by the example of outstanding forerunners transmitted by traditions of community. This essay argues that the post-Second World War pattern of racial integration within the United States was one-way and selective, splitting the black community along class lines, giving the middle-class new access to the established institutions while leaving those left behind in deteriorating circumstances. These changes have been reflected in popular culture – including sports and feature films – and the escalating violence of many urban communities. The essay argues that this split has ruptured the cultural support for excellence in the black community. Reinforced by other changes within the US college and professional sport structures and exacerbated and accelerated by globalization, it has led to a spiralling decline in the number of black athletes in US sport.

Anti-apartheid boycotts and the affective economies of struggle: the case of Aotearoa New Zealand

Malcolm MacLean

One of the major manifestations of sport-centred activist political struggles in the latter half of the twentieth century centred on the demand for the sporting and broader cultural, social, economic and political isolation of South Africa during the apartheid era. The struggle saw apartheid-endorsed South African sports organizations expelled from international bodies beginning in the 1950s, with the South African National Olympic Committee being the only one ever to be expelled from the IOC. The sports boycott was one of the major successes of the international anti-apartheid campaign, yet the existing literature on boycotts is only marginally relevant to cultural (including sports) boycotts. Furthermore, the existing literature dealing with sports boycotts, with its focus on the multilateral politics of Olympic boycotts, is of minimal use in explaining mass activist campaigns such as the anti-apartheid movement. This essay centres on the campaign against the 1981 South African rugby tour of Aotearoa

New Zealand to explore the multiple significances of sport in the target (South Africa) and sender (Aotearoa New Zealand) states, and the character of the mass movement to argue that the cultural significance of both sport and the politics of 'race' and colonialism are vital to an effective understanding of mass movement supported bilateral cultural boycotts.

It's not just sport: Delhi and the Olympic torch relay

Boria Majumdar and Nalin Mehta

This essay studies the 2008 Tibetan protests in Delhi over the Olympic torch relay as a case study to understand the political and social symbolism attached to the rituals of the Olympic relay. It analyses the impact of the political tightrope walked by the Government of India as it sought to balance its diplomatic priorities, in pursuing the recent thaw in Sino-Indian relations, with the imperatives of a democratic public culture. India has been host to the Dalai Lama since the 1950s and the Beijing Olympics provided the trigger for a renewed focus on the Tibetan question. The Delhi leg of the Olympic flame relay emerged as an important cog in the global chain of pro-Tibetan protests that the Games ignited. This essay studies the local manifestations of the Delhi protests, the organization and mechanism of the agitation, the countermeasures adopted by the state, the national and international implications of the protests and its broader meaning for the institution of the flame relay itself.

Between small everyday practices and glorious symbolic acts: sport-based resistance against the communist regime in Czechoslovakia

Dino Numerato

This essay presents a socio-historical interpretation of sport-based resistance against the communist regime in Czechoslovakia. It argues that the sphere of sport was never absolutely subordinated to the prevailing political order and it maintains that sport provided a space for expressions of resistance. Such resistance is not just evident in cases of large demonstrations during which Czech and Slovak sport celebrities reinforced public protests with grand symbolic and mass-mediated gestures. The same level of importance to opposition against the dominant power can be attributed to small everyday practices. Hence, while considering glorious acts of resistance and protest with a large-scale impact, the study simultaneously explores subtle and everyday subversive strategies that have appeared in public participation in sport. The study is based on a secondary analysis of documents and on semi-structured interviews with a number of representatives from the Czech sport movement.

The ambiguities of development: implications for 'development through sport'

David R. Black

This essay brings the perspective of the academic sceptic to bear on Development Through Sport (DTS) – an area of rapid growth and burgeoning enthusiasm in the theory and practice of international development and organized sport respectively. It highlights some of the challenges and dangers of engaging in the development 'enterprise' for this comparatively new and hopeful field. While acknowledging the valuable contributions that may be made to development through sport, it identifies some core ambiguities in the idea and experience of development, and therefore some cautionary implications for those who come to development through this prism. Indeed, one of the key advantages of DTS advocates and actors is that they are latecomers to the development enterprise, with the opportunity to learn from the dangers and missteps that have befallen more 'mainstream' development practitioners through its post-Second World War history. Three key themes are explored: the ambiguous meanings and experiences of development; some of the core challenges they give rise to, particularly in the post-Structural Adjustment era of the late 1990s and beyond; and some key issues and possibilities for the DTS community in this context.

One day, one goal? PUMA, corporate philanthropy and the cultural politics of brand 'Africa'

Michael D. Giardina

This essay addresses lifestyle sport brand PUMA and its recent activist endeavours with respect to 'Africa'. Charting a path different from those of transaction-based philanthropic affairs such as (Product)RED, PUMA, the author suggests, has deployed a transformation-based strategy organized around messages of peace and social justice in which supporters are charged with affecting change themselves in concrete interactions rather than impersonally or from a distance. Likewise, the author discusses the role of Cameroonian footballer Samuel Eto'o and his location to PUMA's mediated efforts with respect to PUMA's brand footprint on the continent. The essay concludes by noting that while such efforts are a step in the right direction, the story is necessarily a work-in-progress.

'No Olympics on stolen native land': contesting Olympic narratives and asserting indigenous rights within the discourse of the 2010 Vancouver Games

Christine M. O'Bonsawin

The Olympic movement is a powerful industry and resistance to it is often deemed unnecessary, and at times is considered to be criminal. The campaign calling for 'No Olympics on Stolen Native Land' is perceived to be a radical crusade calling for the cancellation of the 2010 Vancouver Olympic Winter Games. However, the reality is these Olympic Games will take place and they will be hosted on unceded and nonsurrendered indigenous lands. The British Columbia land question remains unanswered, and the very presence of the current Olympic structure on contentious indigenous lands has the potential to temporarily silence, and perhaps permanently alter, the immediate needs of indigenous peoples within British Columbia, Canada. This essay contributes to the ongoing narrative of the 2010 Vancouver Olympics as it provides an historical framework for understanding the fragile tensions that exist between present-day Olympic programming and indigenous activism.

Epilogue: the struggles must continue

Bruce Kidd

In the epilogue to this special issue, the co-editor reflects upon recent efforts to bring about social change in and through sport, the contributions of scholarship to those efforts and the current terrain. He argues that while sport has power to effect progressive change, we should not exaggerate the extent of that power. Moreover, sport activists rarely make effective coalitions with progressive groups outside of sport, to the detriment of both. He concludes that the most pressing need today is to shore up public opportunities for sport and physical activity. To that end, he suggests four contributions scholars can make: document and publicize the contradictions between promise and reality, conduct critical research, engage students and support open source publication.

Foreword

1968 and all that:[1] social change and the social sciences of sport

Peter Donnelly

Faculty of Physical Education and Health, University of Toronto, Toronto, Canada

It is always a problem to fetishize a particular year. It is both ahistorical and asociological, taking a year out of the context of history and the processes of social change. I am quite self-conscious of the fact that – as someone who is old enough and was usually conscious enough to remember the events of 1968 – I may also be indulging in some wilful nostalgia here. And I am aware that the events of 1968 may only now appear significant because we know what happened since. But, there was something quite singular about 1968, and a volume on *40 Years of Social Change* has to start somewhere. That singularity places 1968 at the centre of momentous social changes, many of which were associated with sport. And, as social scientists, it is fitting to consider the processes of social change.

In 2003 Jeffrey Hill argued that the state of sport history at the beginning of the millennium could be compared to that of social history in the 1970s. Using Hobsbawm's critique of social history, he proposed that sport history needed 'a recognition of the totality of society, and an ability to explain [as Hobsbawm claimed that the companion disciplines of economics and sociology had not satisfactorily explained] the processes of social *change*'.[2]

Despite Hobsbawm's dismissal, it is clear that the disciplines of history, political economy and sociology have, in combination, developed some insights into the processes of social change. These are not complete. There is no grand and widely accepted theory of social change. Modernization theories, those passive notions of social change as grounded in some inevitable and evolutionary process of human development, are no longer given much credence. These are being replaced by the view that processes of social change occur as a result of two overlapping conditions.

The first is technological change – emerging most recently from the scientific revolution that has been developing since the eighteenth century. The shift from a world view rooted in fatalism and superstition to one governed by reason and rationalism led to changes ranging from the agricultural and industrial revolutions of the eighteenth and nineteenth centuries, to the information and communications revolutions of the twentieth and twenty-first centuries. These have had profound effects, both intended and unintended, on social change.

The second involves the struggle between two opposing forces. On the one hand is a human tendency to want to hold on to power and material wealth, to increase those resources whenever possible, and to transfer them to one's offspring. Numerous social formations and forms of social organization have been developed to ensure this, ranging from caste systems and arranged marriages (including marriages to ensure the continuity of aristocratic dynasties), to class systems and other forms of social exclusion. Our understanding of the processes of social reproduction provides insights into this tendency. On the other hand is the human tendency, among those without power and wealth, to attempt to achieve fairness and social justice by implementing systems of social equality and equity.

Thus, those representing the first tendency attempt to turn the benefits of technological revolutions to their own advantage, and prevent or regulate social changes that may cause them to share their wealth and power more equitably; while those representing the second tendency engage in struggles which take a number of forms, and which are not always evident, to achieve greater equity. Williams reminds us that hegemony:

> does not just passively exist as a form of dominance. It has continually to be renewed, recreated, defended, and modified. It is also continually resisted, limited, altered, challenged by pressures not all its own... That is to say, alternative political and cultural emphases, and the many forms of opposition and struggle, are important not only in themselves but as indicative features of what the hegemonic process has in practice had to control.[3]

The great struggles against slavery, and for women's suffrage and workers' rights, provide clear examples of these opposing forces.

The emergence of a sense of shared humanity, and the resulting concept of human rights that began in the eighteenth century, has had a profound impact on the change towards more equitable societies. Hunt argues that, 'human rights are still easier to endorse than to enforce'.[4] However, once the genie of *human rights* was out of the bottle, it was impossible to replace. The ultimate success of human rights lies in the fact that it is no longer possible to ignore them – it is no longer possible to pretend that some humans are less human than others: 'you know the meaning of human rights because you feel distressed when they are violated. The truths of human rights might be paradoxical in this sense, but they are nonetheless self evident.'[5]

1968

The year 1968 was a landmark in the struggles for social change – for freedom, equality and human rights. What ended in 1968, or thereabouts? The assassinations of Martin Luther King and Robert Kennedy were so shocking because so much hope was attached to the two Americans. They represented continuity for the social changes that were occurring in the US and around the world. Similarly, the Soviet invasion of Czechoslovakia marked the end of the 'Prague Spring'. But what ended for so many young people was their innocence, their political *naïveté*, and their unquestioning deference to 'authority'.

So many things started in 1968, or thereabouts. As if to symbolically characterize the differences between Canada and the United States, Pierre Trudeau and Richard Nixon were elected to the highest office in their respective countries in 1968. Students, the poor, ethnic minorities, and ethnic majorities in colonial societies took to the streets in Paris, Prague, Mexico City, Algiers, Montréal, Detroit, Chicago, and many other cities around the world. The year 1968 marked the 20th anniversary of the International Declaration of Human Rights (IDHR), and protestors were asserting their rights to peace (the Vietnam War, the Cold War, nuclear disarmament, etc.), justice, equality and independence.

In 1968, the dismantling of the British Empire was just about complete – who could have imagined in 1938 that an Empire upon which 'the sun never set' would disappear in 30 years? The struggle against apartheid in South Africa was well under way, and South Africa would not appear at the 1968 Mexico City Olympics because the international campaign against apartheid sport, backed by the Soviet Union and its allies, persuaded the International Olympic Committee to withdraw its invitation. And, in the United States, the civil rights movement quickly gathered momentum, reminding us that movements for social change are not dependent on one person. Just six months after King's assassination, on 16 October 1968, two courageous African American Olympic medalists, Tommie Smith and John Carlos, stood on the medal podium in Mexico City, bowed their heads, and raised their gloved fists during the playing of the US national anthem; the third medalist, Australian Peter Norman, showed solidarity by wearing the button of their 'Olympic Project for Human Rights'.

The civil rights movement in the US was distinct from, and yet parallel to, anti-colonial and independence movements around the world, and it foreshadowed so many other social liberation struggles, including the movements for women's liberation, aboriginal rights and gay rights. It is important to recognize that Title IX in the US, that key moment in the democratization of girls' and women's sport, was part of the 1972 Education Amendments to the 1964 Civil Rights Act. Aboriginal rights movements were maturing in various parts of the world, but it was not until the 1970s that sport became a part of that movement (e.g. the Saskatchewan Indian Summer Games started in 1974). Gay and lesbian rights were just beginning to be recognized, although the Stonewall Riot that symbolically marked the start of the gay liberation movement did not occur until 1969, and it was another 13 years before the first Gay Games in 1982.

In terms of the rights of persons with a disability, Eunice Kennedy Shriver had been developing camps for children with an intellectual disability in the US since 1962 and, sustained by Frank Hayden's research carried out at the Universities of Toronto and Western Ontario, organized the first Special Olympics in Chicago in 1968. Paralympic Games were better established by 1968, having made a connection with the Olympics in Rome (1960) and Tokyo (1964). However, the Mexico City Olympics organizers backed out of their commitment, and Tel Aviv stepped in to host the 1968 Paralympics as part of the celebrations of Israel's 20th anniversary. The Paralympics were not able to re-establish their connection with the Olympics until Seoul (1988).

In many ways these successes are in step with recognition of the civil and political rights enshrined in the IDHR – none are fully realized, but progress has been made. Even the struggle for prison reform achieved some momentum following Johnny Cash's famous Folsom Prison concert in 1968, but no one would argue that it has gone very far, or that there have not been reversals. However, even less progress was made in the struggle for the economic, social and cultural rights outlined in the IDHR. Lyndon Johnson won a few small battles in his 'war on poverty', but poverty demonstrations in Mexico City two weeks before the 1968 Olympics led to the massacre of over 300 students by government troops. The students were demonstrating for social justice, protesting the lavish expenditure on the Olympics in the face of so much poverty. More than 30 years later the United Nations was obliged to make the struggle against poverty (and the related deprivations in health and education) central to its Millennium Development Goals. There is every indication that the Goals will not be achieved by their target date of 2015. The Sport for All movement began to appear in the late 1960s, but despite the successes of the various democratizing movements outlined here, poverty is still the greatest barrier to participation in sport and physical activity.

The struggles examined in this volume had much to do with the development of the formal study of sport in the social sciences. Athletes, coaches, journalists and other participants were caught up with, and contributed to, these movements, and many of them sought answers in academic research to the questions they raised and faced. While the sociology of sport began a few years earlier, the events of 1968, in the context of a broad current of liberal curricular reform, led many universities and colleges to offer their first courses in sport studies and give some of the more established contributors to this volume their first academic jobs. The outpouring of scholarly and popular critical writing about the events of 1968 formed the bulk of the first course reading lists. Much of the social scientific study of sport has been devoted to the critical analysis of these issues ever since.

Social change and the social sciences of sport today

The ways in which sport is implicated in the struggles for social change outlined above have been recognized since the earliest days of the sociology of sport. Writing in 1978, Pierre Bourdieu pointed out that:

> sport, like any other practice, is the object of struggles between the fractions of the dominant class and also between the social classes ... the *social definition of sport* is the object of struggles ... the field of sporting practice is the site of struggles in which what is at stake, *inter alia*, is the monopolistic capacity to impose the legitimate definition of sport practice and of the legitimate function of sporting activity.[6]

Five years later, in a defining work, Rick Gruneau showed precisely how these struggles were involved in the origins and development of Canadian sport.[7]

However, although we are able to observe social change, and have some sense of the struggles involved in bringing it about, the understanding of social change could and should be better developed in the social sciences of sport. Hill argues that 'what is lacking ... is any sense of sport being in itself something capable of exerting social and cultural influence; of being a process, a language, a system of meaning through which we know the world'.[8] Coalter's categories of 'sport for all' (the right of citizens to participate in sport) and 'sport for good'[9] (the use of sport to achieve wider social benefits) provide a useful starting point for theoretical developments in the area of sport and social change.

The struggles outlined above bear primarily on 'sport for all', and relate to achievement of the right to participate in sport, struggles to overcome barriers to participation, and ongoing struggles to determine and define the form and meaning of participation in sport.

Our understanding of 'sport for good' is far more limited. Many individuals involved in sport recognize intuitively that sport can be implicated in bringing about progressive social change, but theorizing is still largely at the 'black box' stage. There is a need to develop coherent theories of *change* to attempt to account for the ways in which sport may be involved in, for example, 'promoting health, supporting community development and the educational and social development of young people, preventing crime, and generating economic development benefits'.[10]

The legacies of 1968 are alive and well. The conference on which this volume is based took place in 2008, the year of the Beijing Olympics. Those Games were a vivid reminder of how far we have come since 1968 – for example, at the 1968 Olympics only 14.2% of the participating athletes were women; in Beijing, 42.4% of the participating athletes were women. However, the Beijing Games were also a powerful reminder of how far there is to go in terms of achieving freedom, equity and human rights.

Notes

[1] With apologies the Sellar and Yeatman, *1066 and All That*.
[2] Hill, 'Introduction', 356. See, also, Hobsbawm, 'From Social History', and Hobsbawm, 'Labour History'.
[3] Williams, *Marxism and Literature*, 112–13.
[4] Hunt, *Inventing Human Rights*, 208.
[5] Ibid., 214.
[6] Bourdieu, 'Sport and Social Class', 826.
[7] Gruneau, *Class, Sports*.
[8] Hill, 'Introduction', 361.
[9] Coalter, *A Wider Social Role*.
[10] Veal, 'Review', 467.

References

Bourdieu, Pierre. 'Sport and Social Class'. *Social Science Information* 17, no. 6 (1978): 819–40.
Coalter, Fred. *A Wider Social Role for Sport: Who's Keeping the Score?* London: Routledge, 2007.
Gruneau, Richard. *Class, Sports and Social Development*. Amherst, MA: University of Massachusetts Press, 1983.
Hill, Jeffrey. 'Introduction: Sport and Politics'. *Journal of Contemporary History* 38, no. 3 (2003): 355–61.
Hobsbawm, Eric. 'From Social History to the History of Society'. *Daedalus* 100 (Winter 1971): 20–45.
Hobsbawm, Eric. 'Labour History and Ideology'. *Journal of Social History* 7, no. 4 (1974): 371–81.
Hunt, Lynn. *Inventing Human Rights: A History*. New York: W.W. Norton, 2007.
Sellar, W.C., and R.J. Yeatman. *1066 and All That: A Memorable History*. London: Methuen, 1930.
Veal, A.J. 'Review of *A Wider Social Role for Sport: Who's Keeping the Score?* by Fred Coalter'. *Leisure Studies* 27, no. 4 (2008): 467–70.
Williams, Raymond. *Marxism and Literature*. Oxford: Oxford University Press, 1977.

'To remember is to resist': an introduction

Russell Field

Faculty of Kinesiology and Recreation Management, University of Manitoba, Winnipeg, Canada

It was an event full of poignant moments. One in particular seemed perfectly framed, both visually and historically. On stage, Tony Suze stood behind a podium almost as tall as he is. A soft-spoken man, reluctant to thrust himself into the spotlight, his story of spending more than 15 years as a political prisoner on Robben Island in apartheid-South Africa – and the highly organized soccer league that he and his fellow prisoners created and competed in on the Island – transfixed an audience of 150 post-lunch conference-goers. Nearing the end of his tale, wearied by illness, jet lag and the weight of the story he was telling, Tony paused, put his head in his hands, and gave in to his own overwhelming emotions. The discussion on the anti-apartheid movement and sport for which Tony was the final act also included American scholars Richard Lapchick and Charles Korr who recounted their own engagements with sport and South Africa's apartheid regime. The panel was moderated by Abdul Moola, a South African expatriate who remained active in the African National Congress (ANC) while raising a family in Canada. As Tony wavered, Abdul walked quietly but purposefully across the stage and silently put his arm around Tony, a lifelong member of the Pan-Africanist Congress (PAC). With the audience hushed, unsure of how to honour the raw emotions so unfamiliar to academic meetings, another invited guest strode towards the podium. Opening keynote speaker Harry Edwards, the founder of the Olympic Project for Human Rights, moved towards the front of the room. Standing below the stage, Harry offered Tony a bottle of water, his six-foot, eight-inch frame nearly eye-to-eye with the two South Africans on stage. And so the moment was captured: resistors and activists; protestors and the punished; ANC and PAC; the north and the south; the past in the present.

The occasion which led to this remarkable moment was a gathering of historians and sociologists of sport along with leisure studies and disability studies scholars for a three-day conference – 'To Remember is to Resist': 40 Years of Sport and Social Change, 1968–2008 – hosted by the University of Toronto and Humber College in May 2008. This event was important for bringing together some too-often disparate sub-disciplines in the study of sport, physical activity and recreation, as well as for remembering and celebrating the achievements of some of the men and women who fought for progressive change both within and through sport.

The timing of this event was not coincidental, recognizing as it did the 40th anniversary of the high-profile protest of African-American sprinters Tommie Smith and John Carlos and their black-gloved raised fists on the victory podium of the 200m sprint (and the less-prominent protest of Australian Peter Norman, the silver medallist in that race) at the 1968 Mexico City Olympics. As has been well chronicled, 1968 was a year of significant social protest throughout the world – from Paris and Prague to Mexico City and Chicago. Without forgetting the deaths of student protestors in Mexico City on the eve of the Olympics, little of this unrest was directly linked to sport and sporting events. Forty years later, the growth of the commercial sport industry and its interconnections with the global media make sporting events a high-profile site for human rights activists and protestors, only some of whom promote agendas that are concerned with making progressive changes within sport and physical activity. Well in advance, these groups targeted the then-still-upcoming 2008 Beijing Olympics and the issues raised by the global sport community opting to celebrate its highest-profile event in the People's Republic of China, with concerns that included the status of Tibet, human rights in China, and press freedom during the Games. This 40-year period, bookended as it is by two significant points in the history of sport and social protest, served as the motivation for academics interested in sport and physical activity to gather and debate issues of scholarship at a moment of heightened awareness.

The intent behind the event and this collection has been captured in both literary and visual shorthand. The visual iconography was established in a painting by John Boyle. Commissioned for a set in the play 'The Athlete's Show' by Toronto's Theatre Passe Muraille and Bruce Kidd, which was performed at the Arts and Culture Festival of the 1976 Montreal Olympics, Boyle's 'Ethel' drew upon a photograph of Canadian high jumper Ethel Catherwood. A member of the 1928 Canadian Olympic team – the first IOC Games to feature women participating in athletics competitions – Catherwood, nicknamed 'The Saskatoon Lily' after the flora of her prairie birthplace, was celebrated by the Canadian media as a member of the 'Matchless Six', the collection of women who won the Olympic points table for Canada in Amsterdam. The photograph from which Boyle drew inspiration featured Catherwood clearing the high-jump bar; nearly 50 years later, his stylized 'Ethel' attempted to clear a more daunting bar of barbed wire. Captured in a single painting are the challenges women in the northern hemisphere faced to participate in sport and physical activity during both first- and second-wave feminism.

Figure 1.   "Ethel" by John Boyle (Courtesy: Bruce Kidd).

The need to historicize such struggles – one example among many – is captured in the title of this collection: 'To Remember is to Resist'. Taken from an essay by the Toronto-based writer, educator and anti-apartheid activist, Lennox Farrell, it is worth acknowledging the relevance of this epigraph in the context of Tony Suze's remarkable biography. For without the sleuthing of historian Charles Korr, the story of Tony Suze and the Makana Football Association – the Robben Island prisoners' league – would have remained hidden in dusty unsorted boxes at the University of the Western Cape in Cape Town and be largely unknown outside of the small community of former inmates. Regardless of Korr's involvement, the Makana and Suze narratives would still be significant stories in the history of South Africa's emergence from apartheid rule and the role that the process of organizing and managing sporting institutions played in the lives of prisoners who were maintaining and honing their governing skills while incarcerated. But the intervention of the historian enables a wider audience to engage in the struggle and to understand how the resistance of peoples in one place and time can also be encouragement to act in other places and at other times.

'What can we do?' Having composed himself and finished his remarks, Tony Suze took questions from the audience. Amid the applause and the tears – two accomplished scholars, both veterans of the athletes' rights struggles of the 1960s, clasped hands as Tony concluded his remarks – one graduate student rose and asked the question that should have been, and quite possibly was, on everyone's mind: 'What can we do?' She was not asking for direction on how to aid Tony and his imprisoned colleagues – he had made clear that the Makana footballers knew how to help themselves. No, this young scholar was asking about the future. How can we move forward? What can people – young or not, self-identified scholars or not, those within or beyond sport – do to participate in the fight for justice and human rights?

This collection is but one small answer to such questions. While spawned by an academic meeting, what follows is not a conference proceedings but a stand-alone volume. It is an attempt to collect scholarship that reflects both an activist sensibility and a commitment to understanding the history of such struggles. A conscious effort has also been made to recognize the desire of young scholars to engage with these issues and include in this volume both emerging and established authors. It is worth distinguishing this scholarship on sport and social change from the 2008 Obama-mania dominance of the word 'change'. The essays that follow and the research that informs them acknowledge that 'change' is not a buzzword or fodder for memorable sound-bytes, but that all social change has a material and personal history that needs to be understood, chronicled and learned from; the authors advocate change that is substantive and meaningful, and seek, where possible, to deconstruct the commercialization of modern protest. Despite this, and with a slight nod to the American president, there is an instructive aphorism that dates to his earlier career as a 'community organizer', an appellation celebrated by some and dismissed by others during the 2008 campaign. Saul Alinsky, the doyen of the Chicago organizing scene and a man whose work influenced the young Obama, once noted: 'Evolution is the non-participant's word for revolution'.[1]

While 'to remember is to resist' does not necessarily need a companion catch-phrase, Alinsky's words are another useful starting point. They are a further reminder to historicize our understanding of shifting social realities, to recall the 'history' with some veracity so as not to mistake (or, as Alinsky intended, dismiss) revolutionary and hard-fought-for changes for evolutionary and inevitable processes. More than this, though, Alinsky honours the people in the trenches who are endeavouring to address inequity and change social structures at the grassroots. It is not easy to translate into prose an activist spirit – especially the sense of communal engagement that pervaded many of the discussions at the University of Toronto during the conference that resulted in this volume. One means of bridging a gap between the emotional individual narrative, recounted in person, with the potentially dispassionate academic article and its printed type is to acknowledge the scholarly value of personal reminiscences. These therefore are the starting point for this collection. While three such narratives have been included in this volume, it is important to recognize the other people who shared their stories, many of which are published elsewhere, in May 2008: Raul Alvarez Garin, Abby Hoffman, Richard Lapchick, David Meggysey, Allen Sack, Robert Steadward and Mark Tewksbury.[2]

Three personal narratives begin this collection's emphasis on 'Remembering'. Valerie Jerome and Stuart Parker recall the former's career as a member of the Canadian national track-and-field team in the late 1950s and early 1960s. Blended into this sporting narrative is the story of a young African-Canadian woman – the sister of the best-known Canadian sprinter of the era, world-record holder Harry Jerome – growing up in a predominantly white neighbourhood in Vancouver. Jerome and Parker weave a sensitive narrative that highlights the important intersections between race, gender and social class in the Canadian sport system of the 1950s and 1960s. A generation later, Ann Peel found herself on the same Canadian track squad facing a different set of struggles. She recounts how she worked to transform unfavourable athletic circumstances into campaigns that ultimately paved the way for women's access to better competitive opportunities and equitable sport funding, not only for herself but for many others. These campaigns were fought within the context of a women's liberation movement that found itself increasingly more committed to, and aware of, sport than the feminist battles of the early twentieth century. This initial section concludes with the reminiscences of Tony Suze, whose powerful memories offer a first-hand account of the historic struggles surrounding sport. Introduced by Charles Korr, the historian who brought this tale to Western readers, the story of the Makana Football Association created by the political prisoners on Robben Island is a stirring reminder of the capacity of sport to be a site of social change and of the utility of resistance.

The ways in which sport became a valuable tool for the anti-apartheid movement are also examined in the second section of this volume, 'Resisting', which offers a collection of historical case studies that detail moments of unrest, protest and resistance both within and beyond sport. It is difficult to conceive of a special issue on sport and social change during the last 40 years without reflecting upon the role of sport in the long struggle against apartheid. Malcolm MacLean offers a theoretically rich re-appraisal of what was probably the most sustained protest against a South African tour outside of South Africa, one that engaged and polarized Aotearoa New Zealand and transformed the Commonwealth. And yet, at a time when there is much talk of the power of sport, MacLean also provides a telling reminder of the limits of such mobilizations. While the anti-apartheid activism in Aotearoa New Zealand captured international attention and threatened to shut down an entire nation, protest was and is not always so visible. Dino Numerato distinguishes between what he calls 'glorious symbolic acts' and 'small everyday practices' of resistance, arguing for a greater consideration of the power of the latter. His examination of acts of dissent in communist Czechoslovakia offers a useful context for discussions of resistance and the politics of sport in this region.

More recent explorations of individual and large-scale protest are undertaken by Callie Batts, and Boria Majumdar and Nalin Mehta. The latter pair focus on the protests during the Delhi leg of the 2008 international Olympic torch relay. They frame their understanding of the significance of this event with reference to the Indian response in 1964 as the Olympic torch made its way to Tokyo for the first Asian Olympic Games.

They make a case for the international Olympic torch relay at a time when the received opinion among the western media and the Olympic movement seems to be that the international relay may be too risky to continue. Majumdar and Mehta, however, also go beyond the archives, and provide an on-the-ground diary as protesters in Delhi mobilized and the authorities responded. Batts, in turn, details the silent but dramatic moment when Zimbabwean cricketers Andy Flower and Henry Olonga donned black armbands for their country's opening fixture at the 2003 Cricket World Cup. Her case study of this protest against the Mugabe government and the social conditions and political freedoms of early twenty-first-century Zimbabwe also adds to the literature on collective memory by debating how this moment of athlete protest will be remembered.

The most prominent in-competition athletic protest, however, remains the black power salute of Carlos and Smith and one of its instigators, Harry Edwards, offers a thought-provoking reflection upon the trajectory of American sport during the last few decades when community-based, organic forms of cultural transmission have been interrupted and distorted by capitalistic cherry-picking, the hyper-celebration of athletic feats in the mass media, the immiseration of urban neighbourhoods, and the radical incarceration of black males, with dire consequences for participation in sport among African-American males. As with the authors of the reminiscences that begin this collection, Edwards too acknowledges his own participation in these processes with an account of his work with commercial American football and basketball franchises. Edwards links the well-known history of civil rights struggles in the United States with ongoing social crises and challenges in a telling indictment of social policy in the United States.

The third section of this volume, 'Continuing', recognizes that the debates over justice, human rights and progressive change within which the global sport community have found itself embroiled have not ended. As Edwards demonstrates, in an era of presumed greater tolerance and respect, the struggles around sport and physical activity are no less relevant. In fact, scholars will continue to reflect upon, and turn their analytical lens to, the increasingly prominent examples of sport cultures being mobilized, and at times commodified, to 'do good'. David Black tackles the rapid growth and high visibility of international projects that use sport programmes to achieve their development objectives. His is a thought-provoking examination of the ambiguities of 'development through sport' initiatives. Michael Giardina, by contrast, considers a more corporatized approach to African development. He examines the attempts at corporate philanthropy by the international sporting and lifestyle goods manufacturer, PUMA, in the context of the politics of branding in Africa and the increasing international popularity of commercialized, purchase-driven activism, or 'casumerism'. Finally, in anticipation of the 2010 Vancouver Winter Olympic Games, Christine M. O'Bonsawin critically assesses the Olympic Movement's attempts to engage indigenous peoples and the extent to which the Vancouver organizing committee has enabled or constrained the contestation of colonial narratives and the assertion of indigenous rights. Her activist scholarship makes a case for reconsidering the relationship between the hosting of international sporting events and the continuing struggle for the recognition of native land claims. It is the merging of activism and scholarship by all the contributors to this volume that this collection celebrates, honouring the accomplishments of those who have struggled to effect change in and through sport – at times successfully, though just as often not – gleaning instructive lessons from the past while remembering to keep a vigilant eye on future struggles.

Notes

[1] Eustis, 'Notes', no page. This shorthand for the Alinsky aphorism appeared in the artistic director's program notes to 'The Good Negro', which was staged at The Public Theater in New York in early 2009. Alinsky himself offered a more developed notion: "There are people who say that it is not revolution, but evolution, that brings about change – but *evolution is simply the term used by nonparticipants to denote a particular sequence of revolutions as they synthesized into a specific major social change*" (Alinsky, *Rules for Radicals*, 3–4, emphasis original).

[2] See Hoffman, 'Running for Gold'; Lapchick, *Broken Promises*; Meggyesy, *Out of their League*; Sack, *Counterfeit Amateurs*; Tewksbury, *Inside Out*.

References

Alinsky, S. *Rules for Radicals: A Practical Primer for Realistic Radicals.* New York: Random House, 1971.

Eustis, O. 'Notes' ['The Good Negro', Public Theater]. *Playbill* (March 2009).

Hoffman, A. 'Running for Gold'. *Maclean's* 88, no. 2 (February 1975): 30–33.

Lapchick, R. *Broken Promises: Racism in American Sports.* New York: St. Martin's/Marek, 1984.

Meggyesy, D. *Out of their League.* Berkeley, CA: Ramparts Press, 1970.

Sack, A. *Counterfeit Amateurs: An Athlete's Journey through the Sixties to the Age of Academic Capitalism.* University Park, PA: Pennsylvania State University Press, 2008.

Tewksbury, M. *Inside Out: Straight Talk from a Gay Jock.* Mississauga, ON: J. Wiley and Sons Canada, 2006.

The conservative vision of the amateur ideal and its paradoxical whitening power: the story of Valerie Jerome in 1950s and 1960s Canadian track and field

Valerie Jerome[a] and Stuart Parker[b]

[a]Vancouver, Canada; [b]Department of History, University of Toronto, Toronto, Canada

Valerie Jerome was a member of Canada's team at the 1959 Pan American Games where as a 15-year-old she placed 4th in the 100m. She was also a member of Canada's 1960 Olympic and 1966 Commonwealth Games teams. After leaving competitive sport, Valerie continued to serve as a track and field coach and official, serving as Chief Judge for Horizontal Jumps at the 1976 Montreal Olympics and Jumps Referee for the 1978 and 1994 Commonwealth Games and World Indoor (1993) and Outdoor (2001) Championships. She is also a fixture in Vancouver civil society, serving on such diverse boards of directors as the Achilles Athletics Foundation, the Goh Ballet Academy, Vancouver Youth Theatre and the British Columbia (BC) Association of Black Educators. She has been nominated seven times to run for public office beginning with her 1978 candidacy for The Electors Action Movement through to her 1996 candidacy for the Green Party of BC.

Usually, when I tell a story about my involvement in the history of Canadian sport, I appear in the background, as a corollary to the much more impressive athletic achievements of my older brother Harry Jerome; Harry, after all, represented Canada in three Olympics (1960, 1964 and 1968), whereas I only competed in one. Harry, after all, set five world records whereas I set none. My usual presentation also focuses on the disturbing ways that my family's blackness limited our opportunities and placed us at the margins of Canadian society in the 1950s and 1960s, even as we were winning medals. This essay seeks to complicate this story by examining some of the peculiar and positive unintended consequences of Canada's intersecting systems of race, class and gender.

The year after the 1950 Red River flood inundated two thirds of Winnipeg, and following years of harassment from his employer because of his part in the struggle to unionize his fellow railway workers, my father decided to move our family to Vancouver. The railway police had made just one too many raids of our home, supposedly looking for contraband. After a few weeks in the Stratford, the only hotel in the city that would accommodate blacks, we moved to the suburb of North Vancouver. A petition had been circulated in the neighbourhood prior to our arrival and every family on the street signed the petition except one.

Despite, or perhaps because of, their parents' failure to bar us, the neighbourhood kids formed the next line of defence. My siblings (Harry, Carolyn and Barton) and I never actually made it onto the school grounds for the first week of school that fall. The staff at

Ridgeway Elementary School had no interest in constraining the rock-throwing mob of children chanting 'nigger' until my father took time off work to escort us to school a few days later. At that point, the principal was shamed into telling the students that they could not keep us off the grounds indefinitely, yet even as he failed to react, students continued kicking stones at us as he spoke with my dad.

This was what I might term Jim Crow Vancouver. This was the city where, during our house fire in 1953, I was sent, as the lightest-skinned member of my family to plead with a neighbour, who had refused to speak to us for two years, to use her telephone to call the fire department, as the other neighbours watched passively from their windows. Unlike similar communities in Chicago or Detroit, working-class Lonsdale was not a neighbourhood based on white flight; there were almost no black people to flee. Indeed, we were the only black family living in any of Vancouver's three north-shore suburbs.

As a result, our annual respite from the all-white world in which we lived was, ironically, provided by the discriminatory racialized hiring practices of Canada's national railway. The same discriminatory contract that barred my father from any promotion on the basis of his race, also ensured that the CNR porters' Christmas party was always an all-black affair.

At school, of course, no acknowledgment was made of Canada's non-white citizens and acknowledgment of blackness came only in music class, where my fellow students and I were required to sing songs from the Stephen Foster corpus about the 'happy darkies' working in the cotton fields of the lost utopia of America's slave south, complete with caricature illustrations.

Later, after John Diefenbaker[1] proclaimed Canada's Bill of Rights, my father and his friend Bob Jackson would stage two-man sit-ins in Vancouver's downtown cafés, weekend after weekend, year after year, filing complaint after complaint with Vancouver's passive and disinterested police department.

Canada in the 1950s and 1960s was a more conservative nation than its neighbour to the south in a number of ways. And our Olympic movement was no exception. Canada's amateur sports ideals continued to conform to the vision of IOC President Avery Brundage, a man whose 1912 decathlon medal was made possible only through the disqualification of a poor, non-white competitor. The Olympics, in the view of both Brundage and Canada's amateur sports establishment, were games for gentlemen of means. The vaunted amateurism of sport was not merely about preventing the contamination of sports with commercialism and endorsements; it was a pretext for ferreting-out those undesirables in sport who used their bodies in their day-to-day work.

This spirit of elitism had nearly barred my grandfather Army Howard, the first black man to compete for Canada, from participating in the 1912 Stockholm Olympics, because in 1909 he had been asked to purchase the prize listed in the programme at a shop across the street from the track. Despite having beaten all of America's sprinters prior to the Olympics, Army was still publicly mocked and insulted not only by the Canadian media but also by his coach and teammates. He was withdrawn from competition and reinstated only at the last minute, but remained segregated from his teammates. The umbrage he took at this only served to label him, in the words of the press, 'a coloured boy, outspoken and disobedient'. Ironically, similar words, 'an arrogant, dusky boy' would be used to describe my brother in the 1960s when he contested the media's attempts to label him a 'quitter' after suffering a muscle injury so severe that it required unprecedented surgery and nearly a year of convalescence and rehabilitation.

This spirit of amateurism left me chronically insecure about my own career; when I was 12 and again at the age of 13, I had participated in a long-distance walk as part of the

Lynn Valley Days country fair and won $30. I remained worried my whole career that this prize might be exposed and I would be stricken from Canada's teams and record books.

I recall doing a double-take in 1984 when I walked past a TV in a store window and saw that every single runner in the 100m in Canada's national Olympic trials was black. When Harry and I won the national championships in Winnipeg in 1959, we had been the only black people on the track.

It was in this amateur sport community, which saw itself embodying the ideals of gentlemanliness, whiteness and privilege, that my brother and I first became involved in track and field in 1958. Although our coach was a young Italian man of humble background, our club, the Optimist Striders, soon came to conform more closely to Canada's Olympian ideals. Our training moved from Vancouver Technical High School in the east end to Brockton Oval in Stanley Park. And our team was soon joined by the likes of Jock Reid, the son of Jack Reid, an Upper Canada College[2] alumnus and Vancouver's premier cardiac surgeon.

More impressively still, the president of our club was a professor of physics at the University of British Columbia (UDC), and it was only due to his considerable social status that my increasingly abusive mother capitulated and allowed me to begin competing. And so I was able to join my brother Harry on the track and together we went to the national championships. At the Pan American Games trials in 1959, a few weeks after my 15th birthday, I placed first in the 60m, 100m and long jump and was third in the high jump. Our BC relay team won gold as well, giving me five medals. Harry won the

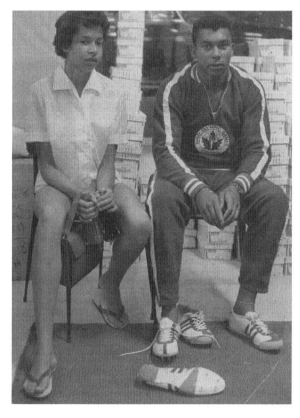

Figure 1.   Valerie and Harry Jerome (Courtesy: Valerie Jerome).

100m and 200m and was also on a winning relay team. We were written up from coast to coast as the 'dusky duo'.

In August both Harry and I travelled to Chicago for this our first international competition. I was recently informed by a sports journalist that I remain the only Canadian athlete to be entered into five individual events at an Olympic, Commonwealth or Pan American Games. I did get a fourth place finish in the final of the 100m, two places behind my hero Wilma Rudolph. But what was even more interesting to me that day was the offer I received from Wilma's coach who was very disappointed that I was only 15 and still three years away from the scholarship that he was offering me at Tennessee State University.

I was flattered by the offer and was glad I could turn it down without revealing my true concerns. If Vancouver was bad, I could not imagine surviving in the violent segregated environment of the American South, a place I still have never visited to this day. And even though Harry was just at that time deliberating over the many US scholarship offers that were pouring through our mail slot, I knew there were no others that were going to come my way. Girls did not get sports scholarships. But I do think about how my track career might have turned out differently in Tennessee – Wilma and some of the Tigerbelles were not that far ahead of me in 1959. But by the 1960 Olympics, she beat me in the sprints by huge margins.

My own disappointing performance at Rome was not just occasioned by the difference in resources between me and my American competitors. At those games, Canada was not a large enough country to warrant its own dining room in the village and so we had the choice of either the American or the British. That was absolutely no problem for me. I had never before seen so many tall handsome gregarious black men. I could hardly tear myself away. Spending so much time in the dining hall to chat with the likes boxing gold medalist Cassius Clay, and others, caused a weight gain from 128 to 151 pounds.

This was overshadowed by the tragedy of my brother's 100m semi-final result[3] which gave license to Canadian journalists and strangers on the street to tell this 19-year-old world record holder that he was a quitter, and the 'biggest bastard in this country'. The racism of the staff and the official delegation on that Olympic team was indescribable. Some of them were quoted in the press saying that they had bet that Harry would fold even before he ran. They did not see fit to provide my brother with a doctor and so it fell to the British and German teams' physicians to diagnose a torn tendon at the top of his hamstring.

Fortunately, the hard-nosed University of Oregon track coach Bill Bowerman, founder of Nike, was more interested in medical fact than media sensationalism and recruited my brother to run for the University of Oregon. But adjusting to life in Oregon was difficult with the state's conservatism and proud 'Don't Californicate Oregon' bumper stickers protesting the rising tide of racial liberalism in America. His white Canadian acquaintances who preceded him to Eugene adapted quickly to the local racial dynamic, cutting off all social contact with him, refusing even as much as a passing word in the library or cafeteria. He watched as blacks were refused service in restaurants while he, recognized as member of the NCAA champion Oregon Ducks, would be served. Of course his 'English accent', as the Americans termed it, helped.

But neither did he hang out with other blacks on the team; they found his accent alien and patrician. While Bowerman encouraged the proud Otis Davis to abandon his scholarship and finish out his schooling at Oregon State, he liked Harry because his deportment was not like that of the other blacks on campus. By Canadian standards, Harry's demeanour was too proud; but in the environment of 1960s America, where black people were acquiring a newfound confidence and agency, his deportment seemed, by comparison, a welcome throwback to the Brundage ideal.

Harry's 'scholarship' was not what we might think of as an athletic scholarship today. Arthur Ashe observes that for black athletes, 'scholarship'[4] was a euphemism for a guaranteed on-campus menial job. And so my brother worked as a janitor, due in part no doubt to the university's fear that his amateur status would be compromised but, given the diversity of on-campus jobs, equally motivated by the need to reinforce that Harry's status as an athlete was not portable to the social or economic sphere.

This contrasted, curiously, with my experience. While Harry struggled to achieve academically, his departure from my family home, followed shortly thereafter by my older sister, intensified and focused the abuse I suffered at the hands of my mother. After yet another physical assault and exhortation that I begin supporting the family by working as a prostitute, my coach determined that something had to be done. And so it was agreed that I would take up temporary residence not with a foster family the government picked out but with the president of the track club, Dr Harry Cannon.

While Harry had been sucked into the emerging system of racialized sport patronage in the US, I began to be absorbed into social and economic aspects of Canada's relic of British imperial amateurism. Harry might be patronized by a university sport coach yet, ironically, I completed my grade 11 year in high school living with the family of an erudite and well-connected tenured professor.

I trained on the track with future Supreme Court justice Bill Smart and future vascular specialist Jock Reid. I ate dinner every night in the Cannons' dining room with white linen tablecloths and napkins and service items and utensils I had never seen before. Mrs Cannon, an expert seamstress, sewed for me Vogue couture design clothing and encouraged me to wear fashionable hats and kid gloves. And although initially shocked by the formality of life at my foster home, I soon adapted to the radically different social interactions that could not have been more different from that of my upbringing.

But the Cannons' home was far away from North Vancouver and so, reaching out through their connections in the Cooperative Commonwealth Federation (CCF),[5] they found another family, the Thompsons, who were much more deeply involved in supporting the Student Nonviolent Coordinating Committee (SNCC) and other anti-racist causes south of the border. The Thompsons took me in sight-unseen, adding to my expanding social repertoire an appreciation for the Canadian Broadcasting Corporation (CBC)'s weekly live opera cast and discussions of literature and politics. The Thompsons also fixed my grammar in a matter of weeks.

In 1962 I met Ron Parker as I watched my brother set a world record of 9.2 seconds in the 100 yards at Empire Stadium in Vancouver. His father was a partner in West Coast Securities, a major firm trading on the Vancouver Stock Exchange (VSE), and two years later we were married. But even as accolades poured in for Harry's incredible time, he and his wife were unable to rent an apartment anywhere in the city of Vancouver. Vacancy signs would remain posted for days after they were turned away. In the end, Dr Thompson rented an apartment for them from which they had been turned away only hours before.

Although initially crushed by the fact that her son was dating a black woman, my future mother-in-law did eventually make adjustments. We picked out the diamond solitaire engagement ring at the OB Allan jewellery store that rivalled Birks[6] in status. And Jessie Parker hosted an elegant tea to show me off to her friends whose husbands were major shareholders in VSE-listed companies, after paying to have my hair straightened, of course.

The kid gloves, straightened hair and carefully-trained grammar and etiquette allowed me to pass a Vancouver School Board job interview in 1964 with flying colours. This was confirmed for me decades later when I met the man who had interviewed me once again; he was so very impressed with my deportment and especially those gloves.

Ironically, the class dynamics that kept Canadian amateur athletics a patrician backwater and the gender dynamics that kept me out of American universities had placed me on a course towards that ever-elusive dream of black respectability.

By the mid 1960s I had dropped out of athletics, and my husband and I had rented an apartment in the same neighbourhood of South Granville that had turned away my brother in 1962 and my father later in 1965. While Harry was running some of the most impressive races of his career, setting his legendary record of 9.1 seconds in the 100 yards, I was enjoying success in teaching, taking up a position at the prestigious Quilchena School, serving the south end of Vancouver's wealthiest neighbourhood, Shaughnessy. But I do not want to suggest that the class mobility I experienced somehow erased my continuing experience of systemic racism; rather I simply want to present this mobility as a counter-weight to the routine experiences of being excluded, insulted, persecuted or mistaken for someone's servant.

I briefly returned to competition in 1966 to participate in the British Empire and Commonwealth Games in Kingston, Jamaica, where I was able to observe the local pigmentocracy in action. In 1968, I joined Canada's national team on tour and found myself running at the same track in Stockholm where they had attempted to bar my grandfather from competing 56 years earlier. But by the mid-1960s, my remaining interest in athletics had been refocused on coaching, more an extension of my teaching career than a continuation of my competitive one. In 1968, it finally seemed that the respectability (as contrasted with fame and accolades) that had been conferred on me was finally coming to my brother. The new Prime Minister, Pierre Trudeau,[7] had attended the 1968 Mexico City Olympics and asked my brother to come to Ottawa and help him create a new Department of Sport for the Ministry of Health and Welfare.

By the time Harry returned to Vancouver in the mid-1970s after Trudeau's New Democratic Party (NDP) partners in governing[8] mothballed his most ambitious programme for youth involvement in sports, I was living in the upscale neighbourhood of Kerrisdale with my husband in a house his mother had bought us to lure him back to Vancouver after an attempted separation. It was a house my father always feared visiting: if working-class Lonsdale residents were content to stone his children off the school grounds and watch impassively as his house burned, how might people in the centre of white, bourgeois privilege react to his presence?

Meanwhile, enraged by the actions of the NDP federally, Harry became a key ally of Grace McCarthy, the former cabinet minister who masterminded the reconstitution of BC's Social Credit Party[9] from 1972–75. Social Credit, a working-class, populist, right-wing movement had lost power in 1972 due to the fragmentation of its coalition and the exodus of its better-educated urban voters to the resurgent provincial Liberals.

But after years of placating urban patricians, McCarthy was eager, after retaking power in 1975, to shore up Social Credit's working-class base. What better candidate to contest the Vancouver East by-election, where the former NDP premier was attempting to regain a seat, than Harry Jerome, the tough-talking self-made man who had set a world record in that very riding? Ultimately, after a very public flirtation, Harry declined to run but he remained a fixture of the Social Credit movement until his premature death seven years later.

In the 1970s, I too was asked to seek public office, albeit for a movement quite different from the one my brother supported. In 1978, The Electors' Action Movement (TEAM), the party that had ruled Vancouver for the previous six years, nominated me as a candidate for Parks Commissioner.[10] And while my brother and the other self-styled 'self-made men' with whom he was associated in Social Credit certainly supported my campaign, TEAM was no Social Credit. Indeed, Social Credit's less patrician but more conservative municipal allies, the Non-Partisan Association, ended up winning the election because TEAM could not hold onto its privileged West Side base.[11] In campaign literature, my recent award as the Kerrisdale Community Centre Volunteer of the Year overshadowed my record as an Olympian.

When I returned to politics in 1988, seeking the same office for the Green Party, I was astounded to discover the degree of legitimacy my candidacy conferred on the Greens, an obscure fringe party at the time.[12] Indeed, outside of election writ periods, the only coverage the Green Party received between 1989 and 1995 in the *Vancouver Sun*, the city's main daily paper, were my appearances in Malcolm Parry's society column.[13]

Of course, many things changed during the 1980s. My brother was eventually able to purchase a house in working-class East Vancouver in 1981. But he died unexpectedly a year later. Although he was also survived by a daughter, two other sisters and a brother, I became the logical choice to function as Harry's proxy at public events. Certainly my own record as an athlete was an important factor, but the deportment I had been taught and the social standing I had gained elevated my involvement in such things from a logical choice to an unthinking assumption. And so I came to open the Harry Jerome International Track Classic each year and represent the family at Toronto's Harry Jerome Awards.[14]

It was at these awards that I met Conservative cabinet minister Barbara McDougall who worked hard to recruit me as the party's candidate in Vancouver Centre, a seat being vacated by Energy Minister Pat Carney.[15] After my adamant and repeated refusals, the party went with their second choice, former school board chairperson and backbench member of the legislature, Kim Campbell who would, five years later, become Canada's first female Prime Minister.

Once upon a time, I used to think about the irony of how Jim Crow segregation created a black public sphere that gave my rival and hero, Wilma Rudolph, the support necessary to make her the world champion she became, a space that did not exist in egalitarian Canada. But in examining my own life, I see ironies every bit as deep and contradictory.

I do not mean to suggest that there was some virtue in a Canadian athletic establishment that was so sexist that the women's washroom at my track practices was seized each week by a men's rugby team, or that there existed no athletic scholarships for me at the nation's universities. I do not mean to suggest that there was some virtue in a Canadian athletic establishment so patrician that entering the homes of my teammates and club president was like stepping into a wholly different world. I do not mean to suggest that there was some virtue in a racialized Canadian labour system that kept my father out of the house, unable to protect me either from rampant discrimination or systematic abuse at the hands of my mother. I simply want to observe the irony that my brother, the world champion, found himself cleaning toilets and pushing a broom while I, with my uncultivated talent and unreached athletic potential, was listening to opera and eating my dinner on white linen tablecloths.

This essay is not, I hope, a self-congratulatory narrative of self-made success. The good fortune I have enjoyed is neither wholly earned nor wholly unearned; mine was, however, in track terminology, a wind-assisted victory. It is about an upwelling of privilege within an environment of systemic oppression. It is about, in the words of historian Kenneth Mills, 'the messy edges of human experience'.[16]

As Evelyn Brooks Higginbotham observes, the American system of race typically serves to collapse differences of gender and class into a racial metalanguage; more practically, in my experience, a women's blackness typically deprives her of the protections and opportunities enjoyed by white women.[17] But this absurd and inconsistent system sometimes goes the other way too. And for no special reason, I have been lucky enough to benefit, intermittently, from that inconsistency through my association with Canadian organized sport at a particular moment in time.

Notes

[1] John G. Diefenbaker, Canada's first Conservative Prime Minister since 1935, headed three governments from 1957 to 1963.

[2] Upper Canada College was the most prestigious private Canadian educational institution for boys.

[3] Harry was severely injured due to a pulled muscle and unable to finish the competition.

[4] Ashe, *A Hard Road*.

[5] The CCF was Canada's first national social democratic party existing between 1933 and 1960.

[6] Birks remains the most prominent Canadian retailer of watches and jewellery.

[7] Liberal Party leader Pierre Trudeau, the most internationally prominent prime minister in Canadian history, served continuously (except for nine months in 1979–80) from 1968 to 1984.

[8] In the 1972 general election, Trudeau's Liberals won the most seats but failed to obtain a parliamentary majority. They were therefore forced to enter into a parliamentary alliance with Canada's social democratic third party, the New Democratic Party.

[9] British Columbia's Social Credit Party was a coalition party formed by members of the Liberal and Conservative Parties to concentrate their vote and prevent the election of the very popular BC wing of the leftist New Democratic Party. It governed the province uninterrupted from 1952 to 1972 and then again from 1975 to 1991.

[10] Vancouver is the only jurisdiction in Anglo America to directly elect its Parks Commissioners.

[11] Until the early 1990s, Vancouver municipal elections pitted its west side, populated by its wealthier, better-educated residents against its east side, populated by its white, working-class residents and visible minorities.

[12] Not until the 2001 BC provincial and 2008 federal elections did the Green Party receive more than 5% of the popular vote in an English Canadian jurisdiction. In 1988, the party had just won 0.36% of the vote in the previous federal election and 0.23% in the BC provincial election.

[13] Vancouver has two daily newspapers, a tabloid (the *Province*) and a broadsheet (the *Sun*). Since 1984, all of Vancouver's newspapers have had only one society column among them; since 1990, it has been written by Malcolm Parry.

[14] The Harry Jerome Awards are Canada's national black community awards run by the Black Business and Professional Association.

[15] The federal Conservatives had returned to power in 1984 under the leadership of Brian Mulroney who led them to their first majority government since 1958. In 1988, he would become the first Conservative Prime Minister to win back-to-back majorities since Robert Borden in 1917.

[16] Personal communication, October 2008.

[17] Higginbotham, 'African-American Women's History'.

References

Ashe, Arthur. *A Hard Road to Glory*, volume 3. New York: Warner Books, 1988.

Higginbotham, Evelyn Brooks. 'African-American Women's History and the Meta-language of Race', *Signs* 17 (Winter 1992): 251–74.

The athlete as Sisyphus: reflections of an athlete advocate

Ann Peel

Toronto, Canada[1]

As a 12-year-old living in Moscow in 1973, I watched Canada's Glenda Reiser win the 1,500m at the World University Games, and, as children do, decided that would be me. Raised to believe I could do whatever I set my mind to, off I went. But the journey was to be far more complicated than I could ever have anticipated.

Each time I felt I was making progress in my quest for excellence, a barrier would appear. I felt like Sisyphus who was sentenced to roll a rock up a hill. Each time it reached the top, the rock rolled back down again. His crime had been to challenge Zeus. Mine was much less grandiose: I wanted only to reach my maximum potential free of restrictions created by the sport system.

Athletes are still rolling their rocks up hills. They shouldn't be. The role of the system should be to flatten the barriers, to ease the way, to widen the path. Unfortunately, much of the time that is not what happens. But it could be, and what follows is the story of an effort to help athletes get to the top of the hill a little more easily, with less interference from the system.

My thesis is a simple one: athletes want to perform. Their performance, and the supports needed to create it, should be the focus of the sport system. To ensure that focus, athletes and their coaches must get involved. If, as athletes, we do not shape and support the systems we need, we will roll our rocks for evermore.

My story starts in Moscow for a reason. Our family lived there from 1972 to 1974 at the height of the Cold War, a time of ideological conflict between the United States and the Soviet Union, and their respective allies.[2] The conflict was expressed through military alliances, propaganda, espionage, space exploration, the nuclear arms race and sport.

My father was posted in Moscow with the Canadian Embassy. We moved to Moscow just three weeks before the Canada–Russia Hockey series began in September 1972. The series was an example of ideological competition through sport. We were certain that we would beat the Russians hands-down. Our arrogance was curtailed somewhat when the Russians played brilliantly, and we headed into the final game with the series tied three games to three.

My brother and I watched that game in our apartment on television. Just as Paul Henderson's winning goal shot toward the net, the TV signal went dead. The authorities had decided not to show the Russian defeat. We only learned when our parents came home that Canada had won. Living in Moscow was the ultimate totalitarian experience. It was an ironic place to launch a dream.

I didn't start out with dreams of greatness. I just loved to run. I loved to racewalk even more. The physical demands were matched by technical demands which engaged my mind.

There was something to think about other than the pain. That was important because, more than anything else, I loved to win. And you can't win if you can't get past the pain.

I enjoyed a long and rewarding international career as a racewalker from 1977 to 1992. The racewalk is an event in track and field (athletics) and is hugely popular outside North America. It has a fascinating history in the eighteenth-century British sport of pedestrianism. Pedestrians walked in indoor arenas over long distances while spectators bet on the outcome. I have never managed to learn when and how the sport evolved to become the heel/toe progression that is the modern racewalk, which first appeared in the 1908 Olympic Games for men. I started racing internationally in 1977 and qualified for my first World Cup in 1978 in Valencia, Spain where I finished seventh. In 1980 I won the Olympic Trials ... and encountered my first hill.[3] I would not be a member of the Canadian Olympic team because there was no women's racewalk in the Olympic Games.

Encounters with the system: the hills on the horizon

I learned that year that pain was not the only obstacle to performance. Sport's attitude to gender was also in the way of my progression. The women's racewalk was not yet an Olympic event. In fact, by 1984 only 22% of the competitors at the Olympic Games were women. Given that the founder of the Olympic Games, Baron Pierre de Coubertin, had declared, 'Women have but one task, that of crowning the men with garlands', that is not really surprising. What was surprising to me was how little had changed.

I returned to the University of Toronto where I was studying Political Science and Economics, and asked Professor Bruce Kidd to help me out. In courses given by Bruce, he had inspired me to think critically, and to be an agent of change. I learned that sport's attitude to women both reflected and reinforced that of society at large. The limits put on female athletes were a social issue of tremendous importance. It was time to add my voice to the struggle for women's rights.

I had never advocated for anything before and had no idea where to turn or what to do. I only knew that it was unacceptable to be shut out of the Olympic Games because of my gender. Bruce suggested a postcard campaign addressed to the International Amateur Athletic Federation (IAAF), the international governing body for athletics (track and field). I took the postcards to every competition and mailed them in bulk to racewalkers around the world. We managed to flood the IAAF offices with over 1,000 postcards. At the time this was an unprecedented show of support. We also lobbied the International Olympic Committee (IOC), focusing our campaign on Richard Pound and James Worrall who were the IOC's members in Canada.

By 1987 female racewalkers were competing in the IAAF World Championships, and in the Pan Am Games. In 1990, we had our first opportunity to compete at the Commonwealth Games. In 1988 the IOC made the decision to include the women's racewalk in the 1992 Olympic Games in Barcelona. We had arrived.[4]

The focus of our campaign had been to create equitable opportunities for all athletes, regardless of gender, to participate in major international competitions. In Canada, opportunities for female athletes were expanding rapidly in the 1970s and 1980s. The first pan-Canadian conference for women in sport was held in 1974, funded by Sport Canada. The Canadian Association for the Advancement of Women in Sport (CAAWS) was founded in 1981. The Legal Education and Action Fund (LEAF), founded in 1985 to support women's claims under the new *Charter of Rights and Freedoms*, was supportive of women's rights to compete. However, sport policy in Canada was not yet fully evolved.

In 1986, it took legal action by Justine Blainey to change Ontario human rights legislation. Until she fought for, and won, the right to compete at the highest levels in hockey (which meant competing in the men's leagues), Ontario law had explicitly permitted gender discrimination in sport. It was also only in 1986 that Sport Canada developed a 'Women in Sport' policy to address inequitable opportunities for women. The focus of the policy addressed outright discrimination against women's participation, but did not fully recognize systemic barriers that conflicted with the equitable treatment of female athletes.

As in the larger feminist movement, there were conflicts between those women who thought equality in sport was to be treated the same as men, and those who thought that women's make-up is unique and that uniqueness must be taken into account when considering equality. These differing interpretations of equality continue today in the debate between equality as sameness and equality as equity of outcome. The latter attempts to recognize systemic and social barriers encountered by a group of people – in that respect, simply requiring that the law treat everyone the same does not go far enough.

The narrow view of equality dominated Sport Canada's approach, and may have been why I lost my financial support under Sport Canada's Athlete Assistance Program (AAP) when I became pregnant in 1990. Sport Canada's policy at the time was to claw back one third of the monthly AAP stipend (which for an A card athlete was $650 per month) on the basis that pregnancy was 'a conscious attempt to jeopardize one's high performance status'. Successive pregnancies resulted in greater clawbacks, almost as punishment.

The policy failed in fact (pregnancy may not be intentional and, in many cases, enhances later performance), in policy (by discouraging female participation in sport), and in law. Section 15 of the *Charter of Rights and Freedoms* had finally come into force in 1985. The legislation specifically recognized that equality of outcome, or substantive equality, was to be protected. Law and policy which had an unequal impact on women would be struck down as contrary to the *Charter*. This generous and progressive interpretation of equality as equitable impact was the outcome of a decision by the Supreme Court of Canada in the 1989 case of *Brooks v. Canada Safeway Limited*. The Court determined that discrimination against pregnancy was, in fact, discrimination against women.

As a practising lawyer I was in a good position to fight Sport Canada's policy. I brought an action forward to the Canadian Human Rights Commission on the basis that Sport Canada's maternity policy discriminated on the basis of gender. I had done the research, the law was on my side, and the timing was right. I was not the first female athlete to protest the policy. In making my arguments I worked closely with Clint Ward, then the President of Waterski Canada, and with athletes from waterskiing and badminton who had previously lost their carding benefits while pregnant. However, their cases had preceded section 15, so the external pressures on Sport Canada simply hadn't been there.

As is often the case when the law is on your side, the final solution was a negotiated one. By sheer coincidence, James Christie, a sports reporter with Toronto's *Globe and Mail*, learned that I was planning to race the Indoor Nationals in February 1991, right after my child was due. He knew about that because his wife was expecting at the same time. I was racing to restore my access to the Athlete Assistance Program. The policy that had reduced my stipend also specified that the full stipend would be restored when I returned to competition. Oddly enough, I didn't have to meet any performance criteria, I just had to compete.

Jim got my picture and the case on the front page of the *Globe and Mail* the next day. At the opening of the Ontario Winter Games later that week, the Ontario and federal

Ministers of Sport were stating their pride that women in Canadian sport had equal opportunities to men. Jim challenged them both, pointing to my case. While male athletes continued to receive AAP in full when their careers were interrupted, women whose careers were interrupted by pregnancy were discriminated against.

Shortly thereafter, I began to receive calls from the office of the Minister of Sport and from Sport Canada. I was asked to recommend policy changes. I did so, and recommended that all interruptions to an athlete's career be treated alike. I opted for equality as sameness, rather than taking a more assertive stance that an athlete should be supported through her pregnancy and the early years of motherhood. I think I was concerned about pushing the point too far and losing any ground we had gained.

About three weeks later the policy was changed. Pregnancy is now considered a normal life event for the female athlete. Any interruption in training and competition is treated as would be injury or illness. Whether interruptions due to pregnancy might benefit from a more generous policy which takes into account such associated impacts as childcare costs, is an open question. Hopefully, another athlete will take that on someday.

The critical lesson I had learned as an activist was to do my research and to be prepared with policy alternatives, as well as with arguments about policy failure. There was so much more to the pursuit of sport than I had ever imagined!

I learned other lessons in activism while advocating for equal prize money on the IAAF Mobil Indoor Grand Prix circuit held in North America during the winter. Because opportunities for prize money were largely determined by each meet director, we decided to apply marketing strategies, rather than lobby the IAAF. To generate interest in the women's racewalk, we decided to approach races strategically. We had two goals: the first was to get out of the 6.00 p.m. pre-meet time slot and into prime time; the second was equal prize money, an important source of income. The strategy we initiated in 1987 accomplished both these goals (until the circuit lost the Mobil sponsorship in 1989 following Ben Johnson's positive test and the resulting move of corporate sponsorship away from track and field). Behaving cooperatively, we raced in a pack until 400m to go, at which point we would split and sprint to the finish. This made for fun and exciting races, and the women's racewalk became a prime event. Our prize money reflected our new bargaining power.[5]

I remember with fondness a conversation at the time with one of the IAAF racewalk judges. He thought that men should get more prize money 'because they race for a longer time'. I suppose he meant that the men raced longer distances. I don't think he shared my take on it when I replied that, based on his logic, the last place finisher should win the most money. I think that at that point I felt I was finally at the top of the hill and could smile.

But I wasn't. While the marketing approach had benefited our event, it did nothing for other women on the circuit. And there were still lots of other hills to climb.

Discovery: the rock begins to move

Thinking that if athletes were in the places where decisions were made, they would be made with more awareness of the realities of competitive excellence, I had joined the Board of the Canadian Track and Field Association (CTFA) in 1986 as the athlete representative. It was a fascinating exercise to discover the minutiae of governance. As the only athlete on the Board at the time, my views were received with a respect that was gratifying. I became convinced that all we needed was more athlete voices, and the system would change.

Then Ben Johnson tested positive for performance-enhancing substances at the 1988 Olympic Games. As well as being the athlete representative on the Board of the CTFA, I was on the Executive of the Canadian Olympic Association's (COA) Athletes Council.

To express the athlete point of view on doping, the COA Athletes Council decided to organize athletes in cities across the country in regional groups. Our task was to respond to the Dubin Commission that had been established by the Canadian government to investigate Ben's case and the practice of using banned substances in sport. The Commission was led by Justice Charles Dubin, and so became known as the Dubin Commission.

As international competitive athletes, we knew that Ben's case was not an aberration. The athletes' submission to the COA was to the effect that doping was systemic in international sport, and that this had a number of impacts on Canadian athletes, including the pressure to dope to meet standards to compete in the Olympic Games.

When the COA ignored our report and chose to submit to the Dubin Commission that Ben was a unique case, we were extremely frustrated. The rejection of our views gave us the spur we needed to act on the other most consistent belief in each of the regional athlete groups – that athletes needed our own, independent voice to express our views and advocate for the changes to the sport system that we thought necessary to enable performance.

Canada had a long history of athlete activists – Bruce Kidd, Abby Hoffman, and lawyers such as Mary Eberts, were the first wave. Bruce and Mary published the book *Athletes' Rights in Canada* in 1982.[6] It was the first formal study of the state of the Canadian athlete from a human rights perspective ... and their conclusion was that we were not doing very well.

Athlete activism took the next step when the Canadian Athletes Association was created. This was the second wave.

The Canadian Athletes Association: more hands on the rock

After a year of athletes meeting around my kitchen table, the first CAA Athletes Forum was held at The Talisman Inn near Toronto in October of 1993. The Forum marked the creation of the first independent athletes association in the world. The organizing group consisted of athletes from a wide range of sports, and a wide range of experiences.[7] Our collective experience included participation in the existing structures of sport – in other words, we had all tried hard to work within the system and had been successful to varying degrees. Our drive to create our own organization was fuelled by our belief that the sport system would improve if athletes had a recognized, formal, collective voice.

We were supported in this belief by the findings of several reports on Canadian sport, including the Dubin Report (1990) and 'Sport: The Way Ahead' (1992). The latter was the report of the Canadian Minister of Sport's Task Force on Federal Sport Policy. Its recommendations supported the concept of an athlete-centred system, and sought to realize the concept by recommending that sports be required to demonstrate a commitment to athletes' rights, and that the federal government support the CAA for four years. It also recommended the establishment of a neutral dispute resolution process in sport, a key platform of the CAA.

We received funding from Sport Canada for our first Forum. Direct athlete participation was now considered core to an inclusive system dedicated to achieving performance. At the Forum, 25 athletes ran for nine positions on the Board. It was an astounding rebuttal to those who had told us athletes weren't interested in sport leadership. Our founding Board included Charmaine Crooks, who moved on to a career with the International Olympic Committee, including a term on the IOC Athletes Commission. Liljana Ljubisic and Carla Qualtrough represented Paralympic athletes and still do. Carla is now the President of the Canadian Paralympic Committee. Dano Thorne represented the new Aboriginal Sport Circle. Susan Auch became a multiple Olympic medalist. Dan Thompson, who had captained the Canadian swim team at the 1978 Commonwealth Games and missed the 1980 Olympics due to the boycott, co-chaired with me a Board of engaged, educated, intelligent activist athletes. It was an exciting time.

The first four years: rolling the rock to the top

The mission of the CAA (which became Athletes CAN in 1996) was to work with others in leadership, advocacy and education to ensure a fair, responsive and supportive sport system for athletes. In doing so, we were committed to accountability, equity, inclusiveness and mutual respect.

Our strategy was to focus systematically on what athletes had expressed as their major concerns: funding (the Athlete Assistance Program of Sport Canada), legal rights (fair selection, discipline and dispute resolution procedures), communication, leadership and self-marketing skills.

We advocated for what 'Sport: The Way Ahead' had offered as the signature characteristics of athlete-centred sport within the National Sport Organizations – elected athletes councils, athletes on the Board, neutral and fair internal dispute resolution processes, a system-wide alternate dispute resolution system, and athlete agreements that benefited and supported athletes. Athletes CAN's athlete leadership workshops, held across Canada, and the manual *Effective Athlete Leadership* were demonstrations of our commitment to the effective participation of athletes in the system.

In my mind, none of this was radical. Our efforts only signalled the maturation of the Canadian athlete from subject of the system to full and equal participant with rights and responsibilities, from child to adult. However, many found this maturation threatening, and we often had to deal with backlash and barriers from the established interests.

We knew this and were prepared. At the annual Forums we set the year's priorities. We left room for opportunistic action, but we realized early that discipline and a rigorous approach to change were keys to success. We knew what we had to do and we stayed the course. We were not reactive and we set the agenda. On every issue we did our research, worked to understand the perspectives of all parties, prepared our arguments and offered potential solutions. We did not hesitate to work with the media who are experts at taking complex issues to the public (and sponsors) in ways that can be easily understood. We also identified and worked with like-minded allies in the sport system on every issue.

It was not easy. We took a lot of heat at various times, and put in hours and hours of our time travelling to Ottawa to meet with Ministers and sit on various sport committees, preparing policy, researching, networking with athletes, building consensus and holding our group together through all the struggles. We know we made mistakes; we could often be quite assertive and probably annoying. However, we learned and evolved, always committed to excellence, as athletes are.

Taking this approach, by 1996, the CAA had changed its name to Athletes CAN and had established:

1. A 25% increase in AAP (the first increase since the programme's creation) and the ability of athletes to defer or 'bank' the tuition credit until graduation (a great benefit to winter sport athletes in particular);

2. The Sport Solution – a programme headquartered at the Faculty of Law at the University of Western Ontario by which athletes received free legal advice from law students when dealing with issues such as selection, discipline and access to carding.[8] The programme partnered with Jim Smellie, then of Osler, Hoskin & Harcourt LLP (now of Gowlings LLP), to provide a full range of *pro bono* legal services to athletes.

3. The ACAN Speakers Bureau, in partnership with Dale Carnegie & Associates. Athletes could qualify for Dale Carnegie scholarships to participate in programmes across Canada. Graduates became members of the ACAN Speakers Bureau, supported by Junior Achievement of Canada and the Dairy Bureau of Canada, among other partners.

4. Athletes CAN Connect in partnership with Bell Canada whereby athletes received free mobile phones.

5. Communication was also supported by the Forum, a quarterly newsletter and Canada-wide athlete leadership workshops.

6. Athlete Advocates on the 1994 Commonwealth Games and 1996 Paralympic Games teams.

7. Manulife initiated athlete sponsorships to support training and competition.

8. The Bruce Kidd Athlete Leadership award to recognize an active athlete who has shown leadership in the sport community. The inaugural award in 1995 went to Charmaine Crooks.

9. Sport partnerships with the Coaching Association of Canada, the Canadian Paralympic Committee, the Aboriginal Sport Circle and Sport Canada.

One of our great opportunistic successes occurred in 1996 when we won the important right for athletes to stay until the Closing Ceremonies at the Olympic Games. The fight for this right was very public, very intense and very personal to our incoming Chair, Ed Drakich, who was also a member of the 1996 Beach Volleyball team.

About two months before the Games, the COC announced that athletes who had finished competing would be sent home, ostensibly because they might become disruptive to other athletes still waiting to compete. As athletes, we know that we respect our fellow athletes, and, if there were any issues, we thought they could be dealt with through the Code of Conduct, rather than by sending everyone home. Our view was that participation in the Opening and Closing Ceremonies is an integral part of the athlete experience and an expression of the Olympic ideals. In addition, the COC wasn't saving money by sending athletes home so there was no cost argument.

On CBC Newsworld, Carol Anne Letheren, then CEO of the COC, faced a tough interview on this decision and declared that she had been told that athletes didn't want to stay anyway, so it was a non-issue. Ed, sitting with her in the interview, responded that he did, as did the entire Canadian swim team who had signed a petition to that effect.[9] The media slammed the decision and the COC reversed course within three days. To our knowledge, this was the first time they had so quickly reversed a decision that had been announced publicly.

Ed and I were then invited to participate in monthly meetings with the COC because they did not want to be caught offside again. This was a smart response, as was their decision to hire a communications manager. Of course, no communications manager can make bad decisions into good ones, but at least the heat would be off the senior executives. To this day, we are proud that Canada's athletes have the right to stay throughout the Opening and Closing Ceremonies of the Games.

Our major achievement was to shift the paradigm from participation in sport as a privilege, with the arbitrary and sometimes capricious decision-making that implies, to the recognition that athletes are persons under the law and enjoy the full complement of legal and human rights enjoyed by all citizens of Canada. That includes participation in decisions that affect them either directly or through their elected representatives, due process in selection and discipline, and access to fair dispute resolution procedures.

Unfortunately, these achievements sparked backlash. In our efforts to move a system (and anyone who has moved systems knows the effort and momentum required), we alienated others. We were accused of going too far, too fast and of disregarding other participants in the sport system, such as coaches. Nothing happened in Canadian sport without athlete involvement, we were quoted in the media across the country, and our opinions carried weight. Others, not as successful at making their voices heard, were not happy and felt excluded.

My activist career had also evolved. I had become an active proponent of an independent doping authority on an international level (noting the success of the Canadian Centre for Doping in Sport, now the Canadian Centre for Ethics in Sport) and spoke often in the US on athletes' rights and doping. In 1996, I resigned from Athletes CAN and the torch was handed to Ed. In short order the Chair position went to Lori Johnstone (racquetball) who was perceived as a bridge builder between athletes and others in the sport system, whereas Ed was perceived as continuing on my more aggressive path.

Athletes CAN is now over 15 years old. It is part of the sport system in Canada, and no longer fights for legitimacy. Perhaps because it is now so firmly entrenched in the system, it is no longer an activist organization. The pattern now is that athletes seeking to be sport administrators cut their teeth at Athletes CAN. This means that they cannot be truly independent advocates for athletes whose views on what is needed for success may run counter to the system's need to control the athlete. To enhance the career paths of its members, Athletes CAN cannot ruffle feathers. This is a personal disappointment, but I feel certain that, one day, athletes will find their voice and Athletes CAN will be there.[10] Indeed, there are signs that this is happening under the recently-elected leadership.

We know that Canada lacks infrastructure, that athletes and their coaches still have inadequate resources, that athlete agreements are too often one-sided opportunities to control athlete behaviour (such as attendance at training camps or participation in sport science studies that an athlete may determine are not helpful) rather than to enable performance. I still receive calls from athletes about selection issues and carding agreements. In many ways, it seems that little has changed.

Is the rock falling back down the hill?

There are two frontiers on which progress must be made for athletes to thrive. One is on the frontier of the economic rights of high performance athletes. This will be the third wave, should anyone take it on. The second is to address the way in which Canadian sport is organized.

What I learned as an athlete, and continue to learn as a member of society, is that scale is very difficult to manage. As long as we keep things small and responsive we are able to progress toward shared goals. Once we increase the numbers involved, we increase the likelihood of competing interests, and we often experience a breakdown. As long as athletes are competing at the club level, they and their coaches know what is needed and can usually go find it – be it a trip to Europe, a better built canoe, or a testing session.

The difficulties are immense and not to be understated, but really determined athletes can usually get to where they need to be.

Once athletes begin to compete internationally, different obstacles arise. Now the athlete must work with people not focused on his or her performance. Instead the sport administrator's focus is on the viability of the system. Their progress in their work as administrators depends on policies and procedures that will be applied to all athletes and coaches, regardless of circumstance. All of a sudden, or so it seems to the athlete, the athlete's needs are not the priority.[11]

In these circumstances, athletes succeed in spite of the system. I would argue that unless the system is geared to the needs of each athlete (working with his or her coach), the system cannot enhance performance. Athletes cannot succeed in a system designed to meet the needs of the 'average' high performance athlete, athletes cannot succeed when they cannot race their top competition, and they cannot succeed when they have to spend so much time fighting to be heard.

I believe that athletes must both understand and participate in the business of sport. They cannot trust that those around them will look after their interests. This places a burden on the athlete, and requires that the athlete be educated about the big picture of sport. Athletes must learn both to work together in a community of athletes, and to protect their own interests.

Athletes must be selfish. They succeed only when they know exactly what they need and can count on the people around them to support those needs. Greatness does not fit in a box.

Greatness makes mistakes, it looks awful sometimes, it gets injured, it has bad days, months, even years, it gets angry, and it knows it needs help to get where it wants to go. Most definitely, greatness is individual, even when a member of a team.

I think that is why athletes flock to support Jane Roos' Canadian Athletes NOW Fund. Jane gives funds to aspiring Olympians and Paralympians, no strings attached. One of her major sources of revenue is from athlete donations (athletes supporting athletes). Jane has no bureaucracy and no systems to support. She trusts athletes to know what they need to succeed. Even more significantly, she trusts that success is what athletes want. She doesn't need them to account for their spending because she knows where it is going. And the athletes she supports usually come through. Sometimes they don't, because greatness doesn't always succeed, but Jane keeps funding them because she trusts athletes. Why does she trust them? I think it is because she takes the time to get to know them as individuals with specific needs and aspirations. To Jane, it's not about Jane, it's about the athlete.

We need more Jane Roos stories.

We need them in combination with National Sport Organizations (NSO) that understand their role is to maximize the benefits of economies of scale – support for infrastructure, bulk purchases of plane tickets, shared access to coaching and facilities, successful marketing programmes that actually raise athlete and sport profiles.

Too many of the NSOs still believe their role is to monitor athlete training programes (how do they think the athlete got to that level if the athlete/coach didn't know how to train?); to determine the sport science needs of an athlete; to decide at which competitions an athlete should participate. No wonder athletes become so frustrated.

Athletes must have agency over their own careers. They must be trusted to work with their coaches and other members of their team.

Which leads me to the next frontier: rolling the rock back up again

In any civil rights movement, the legal rights of personhood, and the responsibilities that flow from personhood, come first. They include the right to be at the table, to vote, to have one's interests represented responsibly, together with the right to protection from and under the law.

The next frontier is equitable economic status. When we founded Athletes CAN (then the CAA) we received government funding because governments understood the need to fund voice. Today, that is not the case. The triumph of neo-liberalism has been to marginalize voice. The free market of ideas is not enabled by the state. Somehow, it has become acceptable to ignore the public when making public policy. As a result, one now needs economic independence to have voice.

Athletes are inherently conservative (sport is about the rules, after all), and resources are scarce. When we founded Athletes CAN we received government support and, as individuals, we were retired from sport and economically independent. Consequently, we were able to push the system hard. Now, those who participate in Athletes CAN become sport administrators. They have something to lose. The potential for loss risks restricting independence.

As for economic rights, to participate on national teams, athletes relinquish their intellectual property – their image and performance. The lack of ownership of intellectual property, coupled with the nature of the market, makes it almost impossible for an athlete to market him or herself independently. Those who can are those with multiple medals in high profile sports who can negotiate their own deals with their National Sport Organizations.

Additionally, and unfortunately, most NSOs do not use the pool of athletes' intellectual property well to market either the athletes in their sports or across a category (snow sports, for instance). In the end, athletes have neither their own image to market, nor the benefit of resources raised by sport organizations.

I believe that a truly independent voice for athletes and the attainment of full legal and economic rights will happen only when athletes have the means to be economically independent.

Getting it to the top

I have two suggestions:

Athlete fund

One of the greatest needs of athletes is access to adequate resources to support excellence. World-class Canadian athletes are eligible to benefit from the Athlete Assistance Program (AAP) of Sport Canada, an agency of the Canadian government. The AAP provides a tax-free monthly stipend as well as various financial and training supports, including post-secondary tuition. This allocation is of great benefit to athletes, but is rarely adequate.

Most athletes still face financial obstacles in meeting their goals. Even to receive AAP, athletes must sign an agreement with their NSOs. These agreements often restrict athletes' abilities to determine their own paths by requiring athletes to attend predetermined competitions and training camps. The agreements usually include giving up the intellectual property in his or her image for the benefit of the NSO.

The argument, of course, is that an athlete must be part of the system to benefit from its rewards. Athletes understand this. Clearly, athletes seek to test themselves through the competitive offerings of the national and international sport system. The difficulties arise when the system itself gets in the way of an athlete's abilities. Then we have a problem.

I suggest that each national team athlete, in exchange for his or her image and performance rights (intellectual property) would receive from Sport Canada an unconditional grant sufficient to support 80% of estimated annual training and competition costs. The grant would replace the monthly stipends of the AAP. Funds to support the grants would be raised from government and through the collective efforts of the Canadian sport system, including a multi-year allocation from the Canadian Olympic Committee.

The Fund could be administered by Sport Canada in partnership with the relevant National Sport Organization. On an annual basis, eligible athletes (those on a national team) would submit their estimated training and competition costs to meet goals agreed upon with the Fund's administrators. An annual allocation would be made and the athlete would report at year end. This process would both ensure accountability, and reduce the administrative burden on athletes and their sport organizations.

The National Sport Organizations would be free to do what systems do best – the development of shared resources, the provision of infrastructure, bulk purchases and shared supports (coaching and facility rentals, access to sport science and other services where those can be provided more efficiently to a group of athletes etc). The role of the NSO would also be to enforce the regulations associated with the use of high performance substances and the rules of the associated international federation.

Clearly, this idea is in its infancy and requires more thought. Its main premise, however, that funding should enable performance and be less about the administration associated with performance, is viable.

Venture capital

Athletes are self-starting, resourceful and goal-oriented. Sometimes, however, we have difficulty redefining ourselves after we retire. There are services available to athletes in transition, but I've often wondered if another approach could be possible.

Many athletes have an entrepreneurial approach to the world. Would it be viable to establish a fund for athletes to provide each retiring athlete with seed capital for the future? I would imagine that such a fund would be attractive to the private sector. The fund could be part of a comprehensive support system for transition, including seed capital and other support for business ventures, grants to pursue further education, a showcase of athlete initiatives (Jane Roos uses her gallery to showcase athlete artists) etc. With such a fund, athletes would not be starting another life completely without experience and support. I offer that such a fund would also give athletes a sense of future independence, and enable them to be more active participants in the politics of sport. Again, this requires more thought, but the kernel of the idea of enabling life after sport to fuel an independent life within sport, is viable.

Lessons in hubris and futility

Sport is a wonderful place to be. I think there is no pursuit quite like it. When one wins, one knows that, at least at that moment, and for the moment, she is the best. For those of us to whom that is important at some point in our lives, we couldn't really care less how many times we have to roll the rock back up the hill to get there.

But that is not fair to those who may be slightly less determined or talented or a combination thereof. All of us need support to achieve our goals.

I think that Canada's athletes deserve nothing less than the full support of the system whose *raison d'être* is their performance success. I hope Zeus has learned something, too.

Notes

[1] Ann Peel was a member of Canada's athletics team from 1977 to 1992, during which time she earned numerous international medals and campaigned for the inclusion of the women's racewalk in major Games. In 1992 she co-founded Athletes CAN, the only independent national team athletes association in the world. As a lawyer, and now involved in sport and community development, she continues to play a leading role in advocating for women and children in sport.

[2] The Cold War describes the period of hostility and ideological competition between the United States and the Soviet Union, and their respective allies, from the end of the Second World War through the early 1990s. Throughout this period, conflict was expressed through military coalitions, espionage, propaganda and competitive technological development, including the nuclear arms race and the exploration of space. Conflict was also expressed through sport. Allies of the United States boycotted the 1980 Olympic Games held in Moscow to protest the Soviet invasion of Afghanistan. The Soviet bloc retaliated with a boycott of the 1984 Los Angeles Olympic Games. The tit for tat gave neither bloc a strategic advantage, and destroyed opportunities for athletes on both sides of the conflict.

[3] Of course, for many athletes the 1980 Olympic Games were a nightmare because of our government's decision to boycott in protest of the Soviet invasion of Afghanistan. Not only do I think that was a strategic error in every respect (and my father used to argue against the boycott at the Department of External Affairs because he had first hand knowledge of how hard athletes worked for this four-yearly experience), but it punished our athletes rather than the Soviets. See Boutilier and San Giovanni, *The Sporting Woman*.

[4] There are still female athletes excluded from the Games whose male counterparts can compete, including the female ski jumpers who lost their legal fight to be included in the Vancouver Olympic Games of 2010. They got lost in jurisdictional battles between the IOC and VANOC, while both those bodies ducked the issue and hid behind the other. I hope I am not the only Canadian who finds that an affront to our country's commitment to gender equality.

[5] This strategy may offend some, but remember that Sisyphus was also the most cunning of the gods.

[6] Kidd and Eberts, *Athletes' Rights*.

[7] The founding group included Shelley Steiner (fencing, lawyer), Cheryl Gibson (swimming, chartered accountant), Laura Robinson (cycling, journalist), Denise Kelly (cycling, coach), Steve Podborski (skiing, business), Dan Thompson (skiing, business), Bruce Robinson (freestyle skiing administration), Deirdre Laframboise (equestrian, environmentalist), Heather Clarke (rowing, non-profit administration), Kay Worthington (rowing, investment banker) and Sandra Levy (field hockey, lawyer) as well as me (athletics, lawyer).

[8] I tried to persuade my law firm, Goodmans LLP, to take this on. By 1993, I had over 50 athletes to whom I was giving legal assistance at any given time. In the end, Richard MacLaren, a law professor at Western, and now a member of the Court of Arbitration for Sport, co-created the programme with us and helped us to train the law students. The programme operated as a community legal clinic, which is a usual part of a law student's experience.

[9] I had organized this because I got to know the swimmers at the 1994 Commonwealth Games where I was the athlete advocate. Swimming is always in the first week of the Games so the swimmers knew they would be sent home early if the decision stood.

[10] This may be happening already!

[11] I am sure there are some sports that manage to put athlete and coach first. My apologies to those who are doing a great job. Please ask your athletes to let me know who you are.

References

Boutilier, Mary, and Lucinda San Giovanni. *The Sporting Woman*. Champaign, IL: Human Kinetics Publishers, 1984.

Kidd, Bruce, and Mary Eberts. *Athletes' Rights in Canada*. Toronto: Ontario Ministry of Tourism and Recreation, 1982.

Tony Suze's reflections on the importance of sport in the struggle to end Apartheid

Chuck Korr

Professor Emeritus of History, University of Missouri-St. Louis, USA; Visiting Professor, International Centre for Sport History and Culture, De Montfort University, UK

For 15 years, Tony Suze was a political prisoner on South Africa's notorious Robben Island. He was one of the driving forces behind a campaign to obtain the right to play football (soccer) and he helped to create an organized league that met all the requirements of FIFA, the international governing body for the sport. Football was much more than just a game for the prisoners – it was one of the ways in which they confirmed their dignity as individuals and asserted their right to run at least a part of their lives despite the brutal conditions of the prison. It was a way they trained themselves to participate in governing South Africa and it was one of the few times they could enjoy something they did on the Island. Tony's first time outside of South Africa (a conference in Toronto) gave him the opportunity to give a personal account of how sport on Robben Island helped pave the way to the creation of a free, democratic, and non-racist South Africa.

Tony Suze's remarkable story of courage and perseverance demonstrates how much sports can mean to people, even those in a situation as brutal as that of the prisoners on Robben Island. He presented it as a talk at the 'To Remember is to Resist' conference at the University of Toronto in May 2008; however, the words on the page cannot fully describe the talk he gave. It is the most emotional and heart warming event I have ever seen at an academic meeting – his time behind the platform was framed by his inability to get past the first few lines because of the emotions that overcame him and the spontaneous, extended standing ovation as he concluded his talk. That evening, it took me most of a very long dinner to convince Tony that a response like that was uncommon at conferences. The audience was responding to both the importance of the story and the life experiences that enabled Tony to become the spokesman for untold numbers of former political prisoners – men who have become the anonymous foot soldiers in the struggle that toppled apartheid.

His performance was all the more remarkable since he had been ill in the days preceding it. It was also the first time he had spoken to a gathering of academics, and the only time he had ever been out of South Africa. A few months earlier, when I told him about the possibility of appearing at the conference he said, 'it would mean so much to me, since the farthest I've ever been out of South Africa was to go to Robben Island'.

Tony's purposeful error in political geography was more than a throwaway joke. It brought into focus the unique nature of what Robben Island was and why it was so important for the prisoners to find ways to resist once they were there. The Island was most definitely a part of South Africa, both politically and physically. Almost every day of the year, people driving along the beautiful beaches of Cape Town could look across at the Island that was highlighted by the lighthouse. No one could deny the existence of the Island, even though government censorship mandated that it could never be discussed publicly. It was part of South Africa in a much more sinister way – for centuries, the Island had been a place to which succeeding governments had sentenced dangerous political opponents. The idea of harsh confinement for political prisoners pre-dated the National Party's victory in 1948, but its decision in 1963 to create a maximum security prison for political opponents started a whole new chapter in the struggle for freedom in South Africa.

The Island was meant to punish people for their efforts to change the political circumstances that maintained apartheid. It was meant to serve as an object lesson to everyone else about the dangers of trying to struggle against apartheid. The experience of a fellow prisoner of Tony's, Sedick Isaacs, demonstrates this point. When Isaacs was in detention, his cell mate was a man charged with a number of murders and rapes. When he learned that Isaacs was awaiting trial for 'being involved in politics', this hardened criminal's response was 'politics, that's dangerous stuff, man'. Thousands of men who were imprisoned on Robben Island and the hundreds who were killed by the security forces could attest to the wisdom of this criminal.

The ultimate purpose of the Island was to isolate men from everyday society and to break their will to continue the struggle for change. In turn, the prisoners regarded it as an obligation to find ways to strengthen their resolve and to equip themselves with the skills and determination they would need to create the free, democratic South Africa they thought would exist during their lifetimes.

The willingness of the prisoners to carry on a four-year-long campaign that involved harsh punishments to have the *right* to organize a football league showed how much the sport meant to them. The fact that their petitions always stated that they wanted 'the right to play football' not just 'to play football' demonstrated that they knew the importance of establishing the fact that they had rights. They were politically sophisticated and they knew they were challenging what passed for justice in South Africa to live up to its professed standards. The prisoners took special pleasure in knowing they had used the rules of the prison system to win this battle. The time they spent writing memoranda, letters and minutes, as well as the innumerable committee meetings, showed their attention to detail and 'to do things properly'. It also proved the maxim that in prison one thing they had plenty of was time. The months they spent in judicial reviews about a football related sit-in that was witnessed by hundreds of prisoners showed that they were extending to one another the due process that the judicial system had denied them. The fact that their own football disciplinary committee generated more paper than all the other committees combined showed that however admirable might be the dedication of the prisoners to the cause of freedom, they were human beings with normal flaws.

The Island prisoner community was made up of two major factions in the struggle against apartheid, the PAC (Pan Africanist Congress) and the ANC (African National Congress), along with a number of small groups. The PAC was a group that had separated from the ANC and established itself in April 1959. The two groups disagreed on a number of issues including the future for a multi-racial South Africa and the tactics to be used to confront the increasingly violent enforcement of the apartheid regulations. They did agree on the need to end the system over time and, in the short term, to challenge some of its harshest policies. The obvious target for resistance was the hated Pass Laws which turned Africans into virtual foreigners in their own country and gave the government effective control over their lives. The Pass Book was described by one opponent of apartheid, Adam Malefane, as 'a rough chain on our necks'. The PAC organized peaceful demonstrations against the Pass regulations and on 21 March 1960 the police met one of those demonstrations in Sharpeville with gunfire. Sixty-nine people were killed (most running from the police) and 180 injured.

When Robben Island was opened as a maximum security prison for political rivals of the regime, the PAC and the ANC were operating as totally separate, often hostile opponents to the government. They carried this hostility onto the Island, separating themselves as much as was possible in the close confines of the Island. They were in separate work gangs, they created their own seminars and discussion groups, and the only time they actively cooperated was in their opposition to the prison authorities.

The campaign for football and the need to create an organized structure for that changed the relationship between the PAC and the ANC. It was the first activity upon which the two largest political factions on the Island (at that time, the PAC was the larger of the two) cooperated which showed how much football mattered and that it was possible for the men to act together. They also recognized the need to organize since there were a lot of men who wanted to play and only a short period of time and limited space in which to play. The Makana FA and all of its subsidiary organizations was a way the prisoners recreated within the walls of Robben Island the mundane aspects of the ordinary world they had been forced to leave behind them.

Tony's story makes clear the passion he and others had for football. The chance to play gave them a sense of freedom. It gave them something to look forward to throughout the week. After talking with many of the former prisoners, I am convinced that I have never met anyone who believes more passionately that 'sports builds character'. What a wonderful paradox that the men who were fighting against the consequences of Victorian imperialism accepted one of its cultural norms.

However, sports did something more. As one former prisoner described it, 'you can only have so many seminars and talk about politics so long and then you have to have some fun'.

Football was special for Tony Suze, the student activist. That remained true on Robben Island for Tony Suze, the political prisoner. No surprise that Tony was one of the driving forces behind the creation of football on the Island. He is very proud that he was the leading scorer of the Manong FC, the perpetual champion of the league, even prouder that he wrote a provision in Manong's constitution that made it the first club to recruit across political lines. It was the right thing to do, but it also allowed Manong to recruit good players, regardless of their politics. As Tony often says about football, 'I liked to win!'

My involvement with this story started in 1993 when a colleague of mine at the University of the Western Cape introduced me to scores of archival boxes filled with miscellaneous documents written by the prisoners. The boxes carried the simple label, 'Robben Island – Sports' and contained the story of what might be the most exceptional football league ever organized. From the first day in the archives, I knew that I was dealing with a story that was as important as it was unknown to the public and to other scholars. After I had read most of the documents, I started a series of interviews with former prisoners. Without their involvement, the story of sports on the Island could never be told.

I first met Tony Suze in Pretoria in 1999, along with four of his comrades from the Island. They took turns asking me detailed questions about why I was there and what I expected from them. They couldn't quite figure out why they should help. I recognized the names of Tony Suze and Solomon Mabuse from repeated mentions of them in the papers in the archives. The former had been a star player, often leading the league in goals and had been one of the ringleaders in the Atlantic Raiders Affair, when the club of that name staged a sit-down demonstration that brought football on the Island to a halt for weeks. They were protesting what they thought was bad officiating that cost them a cup match. Forty years later, former prisoners are still angry about what the Raiders did. The latter had been a busy administrator and, as one of the stalwarts of the disciplinary committee, had judged his close friend at the time of the Atlantic Raiders protest.

On a Sunday afternoon in 2000, 14 old friends were at the home of Tony Suze in a tree-lined suburb of Pretoria. They had collectively served well over 230 years in prison on Robben Island. If the apartheid government had not been replaced in a free election, at least two of them would have still been on the Island, having been sentenced to life on the Island. There were two outsiders at the table – myself and a tape recorder.

As the men arrived, almost everyone expressed curiosity about why anyone, let alone an American professor, had come so far to talk to them about sports. After all, in the hundreds of stories they had read about experiences on the Island no one had said much about sports. The conversations amongst the men were lively, punctuated by laughter, exclamations and the shaking of heads. They reminded one another of what had happened decades ago – the 'crimes' that had brought imprisonment, the terrors during interrogation, the harshness of imprisonment and the brutality of some guards – and the fears and hopes they had shared. So much of the talk was about how they had stood up to the authorities and what the prisoners had done to make life tolerable. The conversation was filled with reminiscences about tension-filled matches, great goals, terrible refereeing and everything else you would expect when friends got together to talk about years of watching and playing soccer together. Side conversations broke out constantly and there were arguments about both the details and meaning of what had happened almost 40 years ago.

The world knows about Nelson Mandela, the leading political figure in the prison. None of the men at Suze's home were in the isolation section that housed the prisoners known to the outside world including Mandela, Walter Sisulu, and Govan Mbeki. Tony's comrades knew Robben Island had become a virtual icon in the history of the struggle to end apartheid. They knew how important for the future of South Africa it was that people learned what men had done on the Island. They also knew that the public (including the thousands who visited Robben Island from all over the world) had little knowledge of the totality of the Robben Island experience for the vast majority of the prisoners. They feared that people would never be able to understand something that meant so much to them. Towards the end of the day, Suze turned to me and said: 'Unless you sing your own song, the hymn sheet will be buried away. Your history will disappear, no matter how noble it might be.' What follows is Tony Suze singing the song of the history of his comrades in the Makana Football Association for the first time outside of South Africa.

The untold story of Robben Island: sports and the anti-Apartheid movement

Anthony Suze

Businessman and property developer, South Africa

Anthony Suze was born in 1942, in a small township northwest of Pretoria. By his own admission, a more avid sportsman than student, he participated in a number of sports and played second-division soccer with Methodist FC. His political awareness emerged in Apartheid-era South Africa 1960 when he was recruited by the Pan Africanist Congress. In 1963, Suze was one of members instructed by party commanders to mobilize and indoctrinate other students. Upon Suze's resulting arrest, he was one of 14 men, most in their early-20s who were sentenced in May 1963 to a combined 185 years on the infamous Robben island prison. Suze spent the next 15 years on the island. While there he participated in a remarkable movement of sport resistance, as the political prisoners agitated for and won the right to organize their own soccer league. The resulting Makana Football Association was a multi-team, two-division league – featuring formal team administrative structures, referees trained according to FIFA standards, and a league-wide disciplinary committee – that allowed the participants to be physically active while honing their organizational skills as the government-in-waiting.

Many stories have been told about Robben Island and books have been written about certain aspects and experiences of Robben Island. These have always focused on some parts and sections of Robben Island and not others; and on some people who are significant in the eyes of the world and not others.

The story I am about to tell is significant in more ways than one. It is the untold story of the prisoners in the communal prison on Robben Island. They were the majority of the Island's inmates and bore the brunt of the atrocities meted out by ruthless, illiterate prison guards. A very small group of prisoners (including Nelson Mandela, Walter Sisulu and Govan Mbeki) were kept in a separate section of the prison. These men in the communal section were part of the bulk of those prisoners who are never mentioned in the history of Robben Island. The story of these men and the community they formed is poignant, compelling and exciting.

It is a story of that majority who toiled in the stone quarry, which was created when the prison authorities separated a portion of the island from a very hostile and extremely cold sea. As prisoners, we machined and hammered big boulders from the quarry hole and hauled them up where they were shaped into building slabs or crushed manually with four pound hammers to form concrete stone for building the prison. It was tough, hard 'slave' work.

In the face of such hardships, this is a story about how a whole community managed to shrug off a brutal system, which was determined to dehumanize them and strip them of their dignity; about the triumph of the human spirit and the emergence of a new social order brought about by sport and mainly the game of soccer on Robben Island.

Life before Robben Island

I was born on 24 March 1942 – the third child in a family of three brothers and three sisters – in a small township called Bantuli Location. Bantuli lay about 7–8 kilometres northwest of the centre of Pretoria, closer still to the Indian township of Marabastad. Bantuli is snuggled on the slopes of Magaliesburg Mountain and, standing on the stoep (veranda) of my home, I could see the city centre and Marabastad beckoning. My passion for soccer started here. Although the township was very small, with only two primary schools for the entire township and no high school, it had two highly reputable soccer teams that played in the Pretoria (Bantu-Black) first division and it was there that I started playing soccer when I was about 6 or 7 years old.

In 1956, three years after my mother died of chronic diabetes, we were forcefully removed from Bantuli and relocated to Atteridgeville, 12 kilometres to the west. Thereafter I led a nomadic existence, living with different relatives (my father was a chef for Parliamentary ministers in Pretoria and was rarely at home) and moving from school to school. I completed grade nine in 1960 at Hofmeyer High School in Atteridgeville, in which I enrolled because it was home to most of the senior students who were on their way to becoming soccer legends in Pretoria. My close association with these students not only strengthened my love for sports in general, and soccer in particular, it also helped nurture and expand my socio-political horizons.

I was beginning to experience a sense of restlessness and anger at a number of things. My poverty was one of them. But there was also a general sense that things were not right in and around the school system as well as in society at large. Two circumstances had a very strong influence on my political character: South Africa's Pass Laws (a system of identification that required black people to carry a 30–35 page identity document, which was appropriately nicknamed the Dom [or stupid] Pass) and the Bantu Education Act of 1953, which formally separated races in the South African education system and led to reduced state funding for black schools. I was among the first recipients of this abominable system when I began my Standard Six (grade six in today's terms).

Maybe this was why the Pan Africanist Congress, which was formed in 1959, did not find it hard to recruit me in 1960. I had been venting my anger by defying school rules, primarily those related to punctuality and the school uniform. I was so boisterous and rebellious that I was expelled from three different high schools in the same year. Between 1960 and 1963, I was in and out of school and working. I continued to practice all forms of sports, including bodybuilding, tennis, volleyball and softball, and I played soccer in the second division with Methodist FC, one of Atteridgeville's top clubs.

In 1963, I went back to school. I had decided that the best way to fight the system was to be equipped with an education and not with anger alone. At the same time, PAC leaders had decided that the time had come to expand the movement. We were instructed by party commanders to mobilize and indoctrinate other students. All political parties were already banned at that stage and any form of gathering in the name of a political party was an offence. We did not care. In any case, the justices in our country had become intolerable. So we disregarded the law and held secret meetings at night in secluded locations. The arrests that followed, and the subsequent 'trials', enforced a justice that was swift and relentless.

Arrest and imprisonment

In the early 1960s, hundreds of political activists were rounded up and thrown into South African jails for so-called political crimes relating to subversive activities against the state. Invariably, the majority of those convicted for these political 'crimes' ended up on the notorious Robben Island – the Alcatraz of South Africa. They were men of different ages, the youngest being 15 years old, from different backgrounds: educated, illiterate, lawyers, ministers of religion, sons of paupers and affluent parents.

So it came to pass, that I and 13 others, all nearly the same age – I was 20 years old then – were sentenced to an effective 185 years combined jail term and ended up on Robben Island in May 1963. I was to serve a marathon prison sentence of 15 years. Of that time, I am often asked: how did these people survive these unforgiving prison conditions? Did any of them lose their sanity? If not, why? And are they today bitter people?

When we arrived on Robben Island, we were received as true 'enemies of the state' by a bunch of well indoctrinated and angry warders, who were ready to make us suffer. Robben Island is very cold and wet in winter and extremely hot and dry in summer. In the winter, we were made to wear khaki shorts and shirts, sieve-like jerseys that were open on the back or front, khaki lumber jackets that never fitted, and a pair of open sandals.

Each morning we were fed cold soft porridge with one spoon of sugar and sugarless coffee that seemed to be made from sawdust, boiled maize and a tasteless powdery stuff mixed with water at lunch time, and again soft porridge with a boiled vegetable like onion or beetroot for supper. We had our breakfast at 7.00 in the morning and supper at 5.30 in the afternoon. Occasionally, we would enjoy small pieces of meat or a spoon of mashed fish cooked with water and onion. There was never any variety in the meals we ate and we were always hungry.

Working conditions at the stone quarry and elsewhere were atrocious and unbearable, made worse by being driven not only by the warders themselves but also by hardened criminals, who were used by the warders for this and other purposes as well. These conditions were challenging physically and mentally.

The Robben Island communities

There were three distinct communities on Robben Island. Their only commonalities were the fact that, firstly they were all of the human species and, secondly, they all shared the same space. Other than that, these communities were as dissimilar as chalk and cheese. In their value systems, what they stood for or represented, their hopes and aspirations, long-term and short-term goals, and in many other attributes there were no similarities.

The community of warders

The wardens represented authority and were an extension of the oppressive South African apartheid regime with an unmistakeable mandate to break the morale and spirits of the so-called 'terrorists' by brutalizing and dehumanizing them in whatever manner possible. They seemed to have been carefully chosen from the rank-and-file of the poorest and most illiterate Afrikaner communities, which hated, despised and looked down on black people as sub-humans. In no time, the warders would have the political prisoners cleaning their shoes and begging them for favours.

The community of common low prisoners (hardened criminals)

These were a group of people serving prison sentences of various lengths for a variety of crimes committed against society. These prisoners were individualistic in character and most of them paid their allegiance to whichever gang they belonged to. For them it was survival of the fittest, and the weak survived by serving the strong. Their attitude toward us political prisoners was very inconsistent, always determined by the circumstances of the moment. Some were allies of the warders at the Island's work places, helping the warders to brutalize us, while others were trading partners, privately selling tobacco and newspapers to us in exchange for pieces of meat or whatever they considered to be of value. These prisoners never ceased to be amazed by our courage to stand up to the warders and insist that they treat us with respect.

The community of political prisoners

Although we arrived on Robben Island in batches and at different times, there was never a doubt among any group of political prisoners that the stage was being set for a showdown with the white apartheid government. We believed that being brought to Robben Island only elevated our fight for freedom against the South African regime to another level. Accordingly, we understood that we had to conduct ourselves with those disciplines, morals and principles distinct to people on a mission. We were a close-knit community sharing common values and resolve. Most of us knew each other from home, school, training camps and exile or even from work. The need for us to maintain a high moral ground was not negotiable.

Yet, we were highly vulnerable at the same time. Our physical conditions were intended to undermine our resistance to illnesses such as tuberculosis, asthma, pneumonia and other severe cold-induced illnesses. Psychologically, we were meant to suffer irreparable mental damage. It was clear that we could not allow this to happen. It would have been like losing the fight for freedom if that happened.

Unlike the warders and the common law prisoners (hardened criminals), the majority of us were literate, trained in many areas and, most of all, we shared the common sentiment and conviction that we were going to rule South Africa in the not-so-distant future. So we acted and behaved like leaders at all times, even when the going was very tough.

The ordinary people who comprised this community were men of remarkable conviction. Today, the former Robben Island political prisoners who have been deployed in various spheres of government or are running their own successful business is too long to list in full, but they include:

- Jacob Zuma: president of the African National Congress (ANC) and the new president of the Republic of South Africa (RSA);
- Dikgang Moseneke: Deputy Chief Justice of the Constitutional Court of South Africa;
- The late Steve Tshwete: the first Minister of Sport of the post-apartheid government and later Minister of Safety and Security;
- Panuel Maduna: Minister of Justice in the new government;
- Stanley Mogoba: retired Archbishop of the Methodist Church of South Africa;
- Njongonkulu Ndungane: former Archbishop of Cape Town and Primate of the Anglican Church of Southern Africa;
- Tokyo Sexwale: South African mining and business tycoon;
- The late Eric Mobola: steered Kagiso Trust to its present heights;
- Saki Macozoma: Chairman of Stanlib Bank and a familiar face and name on many boards; and
- Terror Lekota: former Minster of Defence of RSA.

Change on the Island: soccer as a way of life

Change in our social and physical conditions did not take place overnight. The period from 1963 to 1967 was the hardest on the Island. The sadistic prison commander came for his prison inspection rounds only once a week. At first, we feared these inspections because they invariably resulted in wholesale punishments (withholding of meals). But we were in prison for protesting and fighting against a system maintained by more powerful military and police establishments. We were not about to be intimidated for long by this cock-like striding official. The only things he could boast of were his shiny boots and army of illiterate guards.

We soon orchestrated a series of complaints against, at first, the very obvious cruelties perpetrated by the prison guards and the unbearable working conditions. Then we moved on to really important matters: soccer.

We lived a very eventful life on Robben Island. We studied, taught one another and engaged in debates of issues ranging from religion to different political ideologies and economic systems. We played indoor games: rugby, tennis, volleyball and we even organized summer games. Yet the game of soccer seems to dominate as the single most influential sport in the lives of the Robben Island political prisoners.

The campaign for a privilege

Everything on Robben Island, except for prison work and the lousy prison food and attire, was a privilege for which we had to fight before it was granted. It came as no surprise therefore that once the decision was taken that we wanted to play soccer, the authorities turned down our request. This began a relentless four-year-long campaign.

Prisoners were allowed to play soccer for the first time in 1968. Soon thereafter, the political prisoners recognized that the sport needed to be run in as organized a manner as possible. Eight clubs were formed along political party lines: four clubs of ANC supporters, three clubs of supporters of the Pan Africanist Congress (PAC) supporters, and one apolitical club. Soccer was treated as a communal activity and it soon became an all-consuming occupation for the prisoners. Those who didn't participate actively were vocal and vociferous supporters.

Figure 1.   Goalposts on Robben Island, built by Tony Suze (Courtesy: Chuck Korr)

With the arrival of soccer, the social life on the Island underwent very dramatic changes. The life of the prisoners was punctuated by games on Saturday, the weekend game's post mortems (from Saturday to Wednesdays), and planning for the next game (from Thursday to Friday). Incredibly, slowly but surely, the warders and prison guards came to identify with the prisoner's sport, soccer, and began to root for different sides. This allowed us to see their human side. The hardened criminals, or common low prisoners, also started playing soccer and we had a couple of challenging games with them. Some of them even swapped sides and became what were known as Poqo Criminals (loosely translated as criminals who sympathized with the political prisoners or who had become influenced by them and wanted to be part of their community), and they had to come and live on our side of the prison which was considered less privileged.

For the political prisoners, administering and managing soccer became a developmental process for honing administrative and leadership skills. Soccer was a crutch that supported us from mental collapse but it also focused us on who we were, what could happen (if we honed our organizing skills), and what would be! There was never any doubt in our minds that we were a government-in-waiting. And everything we did, including playing, managing and administering soccer, had to be done properly.

Life after Robben Island

I was released from prison in June 1978, apprehensive but confident that I was ready to meet head-on the challenges of joining the mainstream economy. My confidence was misplaced. The regime began a campaign to frustrate the economic interests of the so-called 'enemies of the state'. We could not find jobs or our efforts at finding jobs were deliberately thwarted by the Special Branch Police. Would-be employers, colluding with the system, claimed we were over-qualified, under-qualified or lacked experience.

My first job after leaving prison was teaching. The father of the present Deputy Chief Justice, Dikgang Moseneke, who was then the principal of Dr Nkomo Secondary School in Atteredgeville, risked his own job by offering me a private teacher's position in his school. I loved teaching economics and English but this did not last. After six months, Mr Moseneke, senior, was ordered to get rid of me. Someone had discovered that school children were being exposed to an 'undesirable element'. Despite protests and representations from various quarters, including the school's governing body, and under threat of being fired himself, Mr Moseneke reluctantly let me go.

My roller coaster career in industry then started. In the three decades since, I have run my own supermarket outlets and small cafes and have also occupied positions as a human resources manager, senior empowerment executive and marketing director in various major corporations. Presently, I am involved in major commercial developments as well as ex-political prisoners' assistance projects and programmes.

I feel no bitterness for time I spent in prison because it was there that I grew up to be a man of principles. In any case, I was doing what I had to do. But Robben Island has, thus far, been understood by the world through the experiences and histories of a few select individuals. It is not the fault of the world community that this is the case. Even as I write, the plight of ordinary ex-political prisoners and freedom fighters goes unnoticed, for the same reasons that led to only the stories of the highest-profile former prisoners being told. This community of people has aged and now, robbed of the energy of youth, has resigned itself to the ravages of poverty, disease and often premature death. They have lost the will to continue to fight because they thought that, thanks to their role in ushering in a new political order, their fight was over.

In prison, these same people rose above brutal circumstances and survived a vicious and dehumanizing experience by finding a purpose and meaning in the game of soccer. There are many lessons to be learned from this story and I hope that those of us who identify with these lessons will share them with others. We cannot let the accomplishments of these men fade away. This is the story of ordinary people who survived because they lived with conviction, courage and hope.

Acknowledgements

I would like to thank the organizers of the 'To Remember is to Resist' conference, held in Toronto in May 2008: Dr Bruce Kidd for extending an invitation to me; Russell Field for making sure that I came to Canada; and my countryman Abdul Moola and his family, his daughter Fiona and friend Maggie for making my stay in Toronto memorable and pleasant.

'In good conscience': Andy Flower, Henry Olonga and the death of democracy in Zimbabwe

Callie Batts

Physical Cultural Studies Program, Department of Kinesiology, University of Maryland, Maryland, USA

Just before their first match of the 2003 Cricket World Cup, Zimbabwean cricketers Andy Flower and Henry Olonga issued a statement explaining their decision to protest the ongoing human rights abuses waged by the oppressive regime of Robert Mugabe. By donning black armbands, Flower and Olonga engaged in a political gesture designed to mourn the 'death of democracy' in Zimbabwe and draw attention to the social, political and economic problems of their homeland. For Flower and Olonga, the act of expressing their feelings represented an exercising of basic human rights denied to many of their fellow countrymen and women. In response, the authorities castigated the two athletes, reiterated the myth of apolitical sport, and tightened the connection between the government and the national team. While the protest failed to catalyse direct social change, it raised awareness of human rights issues in Zimbabwe and illustrated the relevance of sport in even the most beleaguered societies.

Introduction

When Zimbabwean cricketers Andy Flower and Henry Olonga wore black armbands during their opening match of the 2003 Cricket World Cup, they engaged in an eloquent political gesture that resonated with the local population yet infuriated the cricketing authorities. By donning the armbands and releasing an explanatory written statement, Flower and Olonga protested the 'death of democracy' in Zimbabwe and spoke out against the ongoing human rights abuses propagated by the oppressive regime of Robert Mugabe. Concerned that millions of Zimbabweans were suffering from starvation, poverty, an escalating rate of HIV/AIDS and political persecution, the two cricketers used the World Cup as a platform to draw attention to these problems and the failure of the government to provide support to the people. Reaction to the protest was swift: the opposition Movement for Democratic Change hailed Flower and Olonga as heroes, while the ruling authorities vilified and chastised them. Having anticipated the consequences of their gesture, both Flower and Olonga ended their international careers at the conclusion of the World Cup and fled Zimbabwe for fear of arrest and prosecution on charges of treason. Within the context of a World Cup marked by commercialization, faulty leadership and political wrangling, Flower and Olonga's protest was a fierce act of empowerment and resistance on behalf of a population regularly denied the right to freedom of expression.

While Flower and Olonga's protest did not spur immediate social change, it is worth remembering for its spirit of resistance and its significance as a piece of collective memory with the potential to be shared by not only Zimbabweans or cricket fans, but by everyone committed to social justice and equality. In addition to highlighting the narrative of the protest, this essay seeks to link it to the ideas of collective and counter-memory in order to explore how it might be remembered in the future. Although a relatively recent event, Flower and Olonga's story is a fruitful example of the capacity of popular culture to function as public history. The memory and meanings of this narrative are open to contestation and revision, particularly since the context within which it was born, that of a troubled Zimbabwe, is itself so open to change. As Mugabe continues to rule and Zimbabwe slips further into crisis, we must question the place that Flower and Olonga's protest has in the collective memory of the Zimbabwean population, and within a larger global consciousness as well. Will it remain a story of resistance to inspire the opposition, or be manipulated to serve the interests of the dominant authorities? Who will ensure that this story is remembered, and for what purposes?

In grappling with these questions, we must not regard memory as a simple record of the past or as a reified recollection of an important event or moment. History is a human construct, and we must accept the challenge of recognizing the contexts in which, and the purposes for which, it is written. As Daniel A. Nathan reminds us:

> Collective memory is a cultural construction, an elaborate network of narratives and texts that represents or explains the past … it is not an autonomous, static force, but is instead a dynamic phenomenon produced and modified by individuals and institutions in specific contexts.[1]

Collective memory is thus contested terrain, a space for debate and interpretation steeped in cultural politics. Memories are constructed and recalled within certain contexts, and they are always selective, fragmentary and provisional. Individual and collective memories are 'socially constructed and anchored in the present',[2] providing as much relevance to current experiences as to those past. Flower and Olonga's protest will thus be remembered differently by individuals and communities depending on such contextual particularities as place, time and social condition.

This essay is not intended to offer a comprehensive analysis of the past and present troubles in Zimbabwe, nor does it attempt to address the controversies surrounding the future of cricket in Zimbabwe. Rather, this essay aims to suggest that the meanings of Flower and Olonga's protest are subject to re-evaluation and reinterpretation as Zimbabwe strives to redefine itself and as the rest of the world attempts to comprehend its ongoing plight. Since 2000, the situation in Zimbabwe has been characterized by a 'downward spiral of the country's social, economic and political sectors'[3] in which government policies and acts of legislation have generated an insular, nationalist and anti-imperialist discourse that restricts and censors the basic human freedoms of Zimbabweans. To understand the capacity of Flower and Olonga's protest to serve as a potent collective memory, it is imperative to recognize the challenges facing Zimbabwe and explore the role of popular culture within such times of turmoil.

In 2003, at the time of the Cricket World Cup, Zimbabwe was facing charges of human rights abuses from the Commonwealth of Nations, nearly half of the population was threatened by starvation due to severe food shortages, and the government passed the Public Order and Security Act in order to increase the powers of the police and criminalize acts of protest and civil disobedience.[4] Two years later, during the summer of 2005, the government initiated Operation Murambatsvina (Shona for 'Clean the Filth'), also known as Operation Restore Order. The government's official agenda was to eradicate illegal settlements and stamp out the black market, but the wholesale demolition of shantytowns also dispersed and displaced large segments of the urban poor who were strong supporters of the opposition political party.[5] Approximately 700,000 people in the cities lost their homes, their source of livelihood or, in some cases, both. A further 2.4 million people were indirectly affected by the Operation through the loss of consumer and commercial opportunities.[6] As of 2007, approximately three million Zimbabweans, out of a total population of 12 million, lived outside the country, mostly as refugees in South Africa, due to a scarcity of food, displacement, unemployment and fear of political persecution.[7]

At the time of writing, in early 2009, the political, social and economic contexts in Zimbabwe remain explosive. The national unemployment rate reached 80%, life expectancy dropped to the lowest in the world, inflation rose on a seemingly daily basis, chronic water shortages led to a deadly cholera outbreak, and the chaotic presidential election pitting Robert Mugabe against opposition leader Morgan Tsvangirai was marred by charges of fraud before ending in a tenuous power sharing agreement.[8] It is in such contexts that the relevance and value of sport might be disregarded, but as the actions of Flower and Olonga illustrate, sport (and other forms of popular culture) occupies an important and potentially powerful place in even the most beleaguered societies.

The act of remembering Flower and Olonga's protest holds additional power, not merely as a quaint memory or a captivating event in history, but as an active and dynamic part of a collective historical imagination grounded as much in the present as in the past. Following Alun Munslow's assertion that 'history is designed and composed in the here and now',[9] we must recognize that the representations and interpretations of Flower and Olonga's protest will change in response to evolving social and political imperatives both within and beyond Zimbabwe. This is not to say that the currents of postmodern theorizing will strip their story of collective meaning and ultimately render it incoherent and hollow;[10] rather, the pliancy of the past allows for the construction of a potentially influential and compelling collective memory infused with cultural significance. The remembering and retelling of Flower and Olonga's narrative will never be a simple matter of recollecting an event fixed in the past, but will instead contribute to the continuous process of shaping a piece of memory grounded in themes of resistance and the struggle for social justice.

A troubled Zimbabwe

Speaking shortly after leading his country to independence in 1980, Robert Mugabe once famously remarked, 'Cricket? It civilizes people and creates good gentlemen. I want everyone to play cricket in Zimbabwe. I want ours to be a nation of gentlemen.'[11] So deep was his belief in cricket that he installed himself as the patron of the Zimbabwe Cricket Union (ZCU), the national governing body for the sport. Little did Mugabe know, however, that the game of cricket would provide the setting for a challenge to his leadership and authority 23 years later. Mugabe, initially hailed as a champion of liberation and freedom, now rules over a government blighted by corruption, oppression and human rights abuses. Ironically, the actions of two cricketers, men who supposedly represented the epitome of Mugabe's gentlemanly model, brought global attention to his crooked regime and illuminated the struggles of the Zimbabwean population.

Saddled with the legacies of British colonialism, Zimbabwe has endured a tumultuous contemporary political and social history. Known as Southern Rhodesia under the ruling influence of Great Britain, the country did not formally adopt the name Zimbabwe until independence was achieved in 1980.[12] Rumblings of political opposition and cries for independence from colonial rule had begun in earnest in the late 1950s, progressing to guerrilla incursions and acts of political sabotage in the early 1960s. In 1963, Mugabe helped form the Zimbabwe African National Union (ZANU), a nationalist political party intent on mobilizing the black majority against the white minority rule. After an 11-year stint in prison for illegal political activity, he joined the guerrilla forces and launched armed assaults against the white, ultra-conservative Rhodesian Front party and its supporters.[13] The black nationalism movement was gaining strength throughout Africa, and Mugabe was eager to bring its messages of freedom, self-rule and reclamation to Zimbabwe.

Upon his release from jail in 1974, Mugabe assumed military and political leadership of the ZANU party. In order to distinguish his party from the similarly named Zimbabwe African People's Union (ZAPU), Mugabe added the suffix of Patriotic Front (PF) to the ZANU party name. Civil conflict and political machinations continued to rage until the principal parties, namely the Rhodesian Front, ZAPU and ZANU-PF, agreed to a progressive peace agreement. Democratic elections were finally held in February of 1980, with ZANU-PF securing a majority of seats in parliament and Mugabe emerging as the country's first freely elected prime minister. Official independence was granted in April, and Mugabe promised to focus on 'forgiveness, reconciliation, and reconstruction'.[14]

Mugabe's peaceful promises did not last long. In 1982, he detained leaders of opposition political parties, ordered the extermination of ordinary citizens who did not support his ruling party, and used the media as a mouthpiece for government propaganda. As many as 30,000 people died at the hands of Mugabe's troops that year, with many more having been tortured and threatened.[15] As a man who 'matured politically at a time when violence was the norm rather than the exception',[16] Mugabe led Zimbabwe into a quagmire of repression, starvation, fear and anger.

By 1999, Mugabe's ruling ZANU-PF party held 148 of the 150 seats in the parliament, including the 30 positions that were filled by presidential appointment. Voter participation was low because of the lack of a viable political alternative, the economy had plummeted, and food was in short supply due to farm seizures and land redistribution. An opposition party, the Movement for Democratic Change (MDC), had been established in 1999 to spur improvements in Zimbabwe's economic conditions and restore a functioning democracy.[17] At the conclusion of the election held in 2000, the MDC succeeded in winning 57 of the 120 elected parliamentary seats, enough to pose a palpable threat to the reigning regime.[18] This tangible display of defiance was also enough to incite an unprecedented level of violence and oppression against those who expressed support for the opposition.

In 2002, nearly half of the country's 13 million people were threatened by starvation due to severe food shortages and unchecked inflation.[19] The food crisis provided Mugabe with an effective political tool, allowing him to manipulate the provision of food supplies in response to a community's political affiliation. Using food as an 'instrument of political pressure'[20] is prohibited by international human rights law, but Mugabe routinely denied access to government food supplies to impel political loyalty and acquiescence. Exacerbating the escalating problem of starvation was the government's unyielding refutation of a chronic food shortage.[21]

Compounding the abysmal economic situation and the lack of basic social freedoms was the culture of impunity suffused through all levels of Zimbabwean society. Broadcasting, including television and radio, was a state monopoly, and the independent newspaper, the *Daily News*, was often subject to government intimidation.[22] The Public Order and Security Act, passed by the parliament in early 2002, increased the powers of the police and criminalized such acts as boycotts and civil disobedience. According to Amnesty International, the Act 'provided the police with a pretext to intimidate, harass, and brutally torture real or perceived supporters and members of the opposition'.[23] Victims of human rights abuses hesitated to speak out for fear of additional reprisals and further abuse. The protection of the law served only the ruling interests, leaving the bulk of the population in a constant state of trepidation. The situation prompted Amnesty International to issue the following statement in a 2003 report:

> Since 2000, the human rights situation in Zimbabwe has undergone a rapid decline … State-sponsored intimidation, unlawful arrests and torture perpetrated by the police, ruling party supporters, youth militia, and other state agents have become commonplace. The main targets for repression have been those most vocal and critical of the government's human rights record.[24]

Such was the local context as Zimbabwe prepared to host six preliminary matches of the 2003 Cricket World Cup. The role of sport in a country so rife with social, economic and political problems was certainly questionable at the time. When seen as merely a form of luxurious leisure, sport appeared to have little importance in a society where starvation is a daily threat. In such a context, sport is often deemed an irrelevant waste of time, energy and resources. As one distressed journalist proclaimed:

> In reality, sporting normality is not possible while Robert Mugabe remains in power. In the meantime, the infrastructure of his country collapses, his opponents are imprisoned without trial and millions of people cannot even afford a loaf of bread. What place has cricket in such a land?[25]

Despite such troubling circumstances, cricket proved to have a very important place in Zimbabwe as the nation readied itself for the international sporting stage. Far beyond providing a superficial source of national pride and temporary escapism, cricket became a symbolic representation of Zimbabwe's struggles resonant with conflict and complexity.

The 2003 Cricket World Cup

From its very beginning, the 2003 Cricket World Cup was an event reflective of the current global conditions surrounding it. Corporate sponsors hawked exclusive products, international media conglomerates transmitted the matches across the globe, and drug testing began for the first time in international cricket. Doping, frantic media coverage, and commercialism are regular features of modern global sport, and the World Cup revealed the extent to which cricket has been shaped by, and contributes to the shaping of, those processes.[26] Perhaps most telling, the World Cup also illustrated the complex and relentless interrelationship between politics and sport, regardless of how diligently the ruling authorities attempt to stifle the interplay between the two.

The International Cricket Council (ICC) initially awarded the 2003 World Cup solely to South Africa, but the South African government made a strategic political move by handing six matches to Zimbabwe and two to Kenya. South Africa claimed it was helping to make the tournament 'more African' by sharing the slate of matches with Zimbabwe and Kenya.[27] Critics remarked that there were no convincing sporting reasons to hold matches in Zimbabwe and Kenya, pointing out that the pitches were in sub-standard condition, the crowds would be small, and the extra travel would be a burden. The South African government, however, insisted on sharing the tournament with its African compatriots, perhaps guided by the hope that its gesture of pan-Africanism would reflect positively on its bid to host the 2010 football World Cup.[28]

Just a few weeks before the tournament was due to begin, the decision to hold matches in Zimbabwe met with intense criticism, particularly from the English and Australian sides scheduled to play preliminary fixtures in the country. Activists supporting the opposition

MDC also expressed their concerns about the World Cup. They campaigned against the decision to hold matches in Zimbabwe, asserting that the World Cup would give credence to Mugabe's regime and divert attention away from the humanitarian crises facing the country and the constant 'terrorization' of the people.[29] In addition, anonymous members of the Zimbabwean squad called for the cancellation of matches slotted for Harare and Bulawayo on moral grounds. Bound by strict contracts and expected to follow the ruling party line that insisted upon maintaining a veneer of normalcy, the players were hesitant to make their private views public. As one team member explained:

> It simply isn't possible to say too much of what you think. But how can I possibly agree with Zimbabwe being portrayed as one big, happy multi-racial society, which is the image Mugabe wants the world to see at the World Cup. How could I shake his hand? England can't come. It would be morally wrong.[30]

The English team, backed by the England and Wales Cricketing Board (ECB), waffled in its moral stance, ultimately threatening to boycott their game against Zimbabwe in Harare due to safety concerns rather than moral apprehension.[31] The ICC established a standing committee to monitor the security situation in Zimbabwe, but the ECB demanded that the match be moved to South Africa.[32] On 6 February 2003, just one week before England's scheduled match in Harare, the ICC refused to move the match. Confident that the security situation was under control, the ICC reiterated its policy that the sole criterion for switching venues was a direct and tangible security threat.[33] Enmeshed in messy political wrangling over the threat of a boycott, the English team dragged out and delayed its decision as the players, the ECB and the government all weighed in on the situation. Eventually the team decided to skip the trip to Harare and forfeit the match, citing lingering safety fears.[34]

Well before the first wicket fell, it was evident that 'politics ran through this World Cup like the zebra-skin logo that bedecked the stands'.[35] Amidst this politically charged atmosphere, the World Cup got underway with an opening ceremony in Cape Town, South Africa. Expectations were high for a tournament in which the game of cricket could transcend the talk of boycotts and the machinations of politics. Soon thereafter, on a pitch in Harare in front of a stunned crowd, those expectations were shattered by two black armbands and a stirring set of words.

Protesting the 'death of democracy' in Zimbabwe

When they took the pitch to face Namibia on the morning of 10 February 2003, Andy Flower and Henry Olonga engaged in a simple political gesture that became the defining moment of the World Cup. With the simple addition of a black armband to their regular kit, Flower and Olonga protested against the 'death of democracy' in Zimbabwe and the continuing human rights abuses levelled by the government.[36] Flower, a white batsman and arguably one of Zimbabwe's greatest cricketers, and Olonga, a fast bowler who was the first black member of the national team, acted as a pair and purposely distanced themselves from the rest of the squad for fear of unduly embroiling them in the inevitable controversy to come. The crowd of 4,000 spectators at the Harare Sports Club reacted strongly in favour of Flower and Olonga, and as the day progressed many of the fans fashioned their own versions of the black armbands.[37] The protest did not disrupt the match, as it proceeded as usual with Zimbabwe gaining the eventual victory. Yet the players and spectators seemed to sense that they had witnessed an 'unprecedented attack by sportsmen who are usually advised to be seen and not heard'.[38]

Just minutes before the match, Flower and Olonga had issued a joint statement to the press explaining their gesture and the reasoning behind it. As a vital component of their overall protest, the written statement specified the nature of their discontent and justified their use of cricket as means to a political end. Flower and Olonga contended that the black armbands were a symbol of mourning, a silent plea for recognition of their fellow compatriots who were suffering from starvation, oppression, torture and other abuses. Taking pride in representing Zimbabwe as athletes, they also admitted feelings of shame and distress at the current condition of their country. In describing their perceived sense of responsibility as concerned citizens, Flower and Olonga declared:

> We cannot in good conscience take to the field and ignore the fact that millions of our compatriots are starving, unemployed and oppressed. We are aware that hundreds of thousands of Zimbabweans may even die in the coming months through a combination of starvation, poverty and AIDS. We are aware that many people have been unjustly imprisoned and tortured simply for expressing their opinions about what is happening in the country. We have heard a torrent of racist hate speech directed at minority groups. We are aware that thousands of Zimbabweans are routinely denied their right to freedom of expression. We are aware that people have been murdered, raped, beaten and had their homes destroyed because of their beliefs and that many of those responsible have not been prosecuted ... Although we are just professional cricketers, we do have a conscience and feelings. We believe that if we remain silent, that will be taken as a sign that either we do not care or we condone what is happening in Zimbabwe. We believe that it is important to stand up for what is right.[39]

Through their thoughtful statement, the two cricketers aligned themselves with the Zimbabwean people and all those disturbed by the current state of affairs. Combined with the visual punch of the black armbands, the emotional force of the written statement suggested that Flower and Olonga had deliberately constructed this political gesture as a blow against Mugabe. In choosing to use the World Cup as their platform, Flower and Olonga became more than 'just professional cricketers' by taking a strong stand and speaking up for the basic rights routinely denied to many of their fellow countrymen and women.

Reaction to Flower and Olonga's gesture was immediate. They became heroes within the Zimbabwean opposition movement and darlings of the international press. Members of the Western media, generally critical of Mugabe's repression of the press, praised Flower and Olonga for their uncompromising words and fearless actions. Described as 'brave, decisive, and dignified',[40] the protest quickly gained notoriety and was regularly compared to Tommie Smith and John Carlos's 1968 black power salute and Muhammad Ali's refusal to fight in Vietnam.[41] It was also viewed by many as a gesture imbued with racial politics and nationalistic sentiments. As Jayanta Sengupta argues:

> The symbolic value of a white and a black cricketer risking their careers simultaneously to defend democracy was immense, and in the media glare surrounding the World Cup, the image of this cross-colour patriotism became the iconic representation of Zimbabwean nationalism, displacing the image of a predatory Mugabe bent upon wreaking vengeance on history by extorting the white minority.[42]

With such a riveting mixture of surprise, courage and solidarity, Flower and Olonga's protest received ample public support and international recognition. Yet the two athletes also faced powerful detractors. While the population of Zimbabwe generally lauded Flower and Olonga, the ruling cricketing authorities were swift to chastise them.

The Takashinga Cricket Club was the first official authority to act in response to Flower and Olonga's gesture. The ZCU had assigned Olonga to play for Takashinga, an all-black club known for its staunch support of the Mugabe government. Immediately following Zimbabwe's match against Namibia, the club moved to suspend Olonga and require him to stand before a disciplinary committee for breach of conduct. Defending Takashinga's rapid decision, the club chairman explained that 'the code of conduct is non-political' and that all club members 'must refrain from making public statements that are political'.[43] With the suspension, Olonga's domestic playing career was effectively over.

In a far less resolute response, the ZCU issued a vague statement indicating that it would convene a special committee to evaluate the situation. As patron of the ZCU, Mugabe took a keen interest in the proceedings of the World Cup but had not attended the opening game in Harare. After watching television coverage of the match and seeing the black armbands, Mugabe apparently reacted 'like a bull incandescent with rage'[44] at the players' gesture. The deep involvement of the government in all aspects of Zimbabwean society, cricket included, gave the ZCU in a delicate dilemma. In deciding how to resolve the problem of the players' politicking, the ZCU could either 'discipline the players and face worldwide condemnation' or 'fail to discipline them and risk government interference'.[45] Stephen Mangongo, a national selector for the ZCU and a former ally of Olonga, promptly denounced the protest:

> What Flower and Olonga did is very wrong. They have jeopardized our reputation when given this once in a lifetime chance to host the World Cup. The ZCU will look at Olonga's contract. He might be stopped from playing. It would be wrong if they wore black armbands again.[46]

After a full day of deliberation, the ZCU informed Flower and Olonga that it was reporting their offence to the ICC and that further action from the ZCU would be delayed until after the World Cup. According to the ZCU, Flower and Olonga would be subject to disciplinary action from the ICC for bringing the game of cricket into disrepute.[47] Failing to settle its own dilemma, the ZCU simply passed the matter to the ICC.

Three days after taking control of the issue, the ICC declared that Flower and Olonga would not be charged with a formal offence. In lieu of official disciplinary action, the ICC requested that the pair stop wearing the black armbands for the remaining duration of the tournament. The statement released by the ICC recognized the political nature of the players' protest and reiterated the organization's commitment to apolitical sport:

> The ICC seeks at all times to avoid using cricket as a platform on which to advance political agendas and its very strong belief is that the players, officials, and administrators within the game should refrain from doing the same ... The players [Flower and Olonga] have blurred the lines between political issues and the sporting arena.[48]

In its rather contradictory decision, the ICC admitted that Flower and Olonga's gesture constituted a political action, but it did not warrant immediate disciplinary action on charges of bringing the game into disrepute. Why then, if the armbands did not dishonour the game, did the ICC request Flower and Olonga to stop wearing them? The ICC also promised to consider stricter punitive measures if Flower and Olonga continued to display the armbands. Rather than make a firm decision, the ICC wobbled on the issue, allowing a politicized act to take primacy over the playing of the game – an ironic and inevitable refutation of the ICC's guiding principles.

Not surprisingly, Flower and Olonga refused to abide by the ICC's request. During Zimbabwe's match against India on 19 February 2003 in Harare, the pair wore black wristbands. More visible than the armbands, the wristbands were a direct continuation of the original gesture and a symbolic challenge to the authority of the ZCU and ICC. Again, Flower and Olonga acted alone and did not attempt to speak on behalf of the entire team. Continuing the protest amid fears of reprisal from the ICC and the ZCU, Flower and Olonga emphasized the personal nature of their decision. This time, their fans arrived at the Harare Sports Club ready for active displays of support. Nearly 200 spectators wore black armbands, while several others held aloft signs that praised the duo's bravery. Many of the spectators were questioned by police and several were ultimately arrested and forced to pay a fine on the grounds of plotting to overthrow Mugabe.[49] For Zimbabweans at least, the spirit of cricket had become politicized. Rather than placating the nation, the game had inspired it to activism.

Refusing to make martyrs out of Flower and Olonga, the ICC did not punish the pair for wearing the wristbands. The inaction of the ICC was perhaps as strong a statement as any disciplinary action. Attempting to extinguish the controversy by ignoring it, the ICC retained its apolitical stance and focused on keeping a tight hold on the tournament. Rather than take the risk of either condoning the gesture or vilifying it, the ICC instead passed the matter back to the ZCU, from whence it originally came a week earlier. This game of authoritative yo-yo embarrassed both the ICC and the ZCU, allowing Flower and Olonga to emerge from the controversy with global commendation and respect.[50] Ultimately, the ZCU had the final say on Flower and Olonga's future in international cricket, but all decisions were postponed until after the World Cup in order to maintain the pretence of safety and normalcy on which the ICC was so insistent.[51]

By the time the squad reached the Super Sixes to face Sri Lanka, Flower and Olonga anticipated serious reprisals. The state press, controlled by Mugabe's minister of propaganda, had issued harsh invectives against the players, calling Flower a 'racist and bitter man' and labelling Olonga an 'Uncle Tom' who acquiesced to the influence of the white man.[52] If public support had been increasing for the pair, then so too had the government's indignation. The match, played in South Africa, resulted in a loss for Zimbabwe and proved to be Flower and Olonga's last for the national team. On the day of that final match, reports circulated that members of Mugabe's secret police were in attendance to escort the two cricketers back to Zimbabwe to face charges of treason under the Public Order and Security Act. With their fears already heightened by death threats and a spate of criticism from the state press, Flower and Olonga took the rumours of arrest and prosecution very seriously.

Immediately following the match with Sri Lanka, Olonga packed his bags, handed a statement of resignation to the press, and fled into hiding in South Africa. In his statement, Olonga declared that he was quitting international cricket because he felt it was too dangerous to return to Zimbabwe.[53] Having already announced his intention to retire from international cricket at the conclusion of the World Cup, Flower removed himself quickly from the team and made preparations to move his family to England.[54] In the course of six weeks, Flower and Olonga went from being sport stars to political refugees.

The complexities of remembering

In reviewing the events of the 2003 World Cup, cricket writer Tim de Lisle identified Flower and Olonga's protest as the single action that defined the tournament and salvaged it from the discouraging elements of commercialization, shaky leadership and mismatched contests. In describing the gesture and its immediate impact on the spirit of the game, de Lisle wrote:

> Their stand was not just brave but shrewd: there were two of them, one black, one white, they were both senior players, and they had not even been friends until this episode made them, in Olonga's words, 'blood brothers'. Together they were responsible for a shining moment in the game's history, which is already on the way to entering its mythology … Two strips of black tape, more potent that any logo, breathed life back into the game's battered spirit.[55]

If the protest is indeed entering into a mythologized space of cricket history, it must also be claimed as a broader piece of collective memory relevant to a global consciousness concerned with social justice and human rights.

For the gesture not only changed Flower and Olonga's individual lives, but also contributed to change within cricket in Zimbabwe representative of shifting social and political contexts. Instead of attempting to depoliticize the game in response to the players' protest, the ZCU became an active agent working on behalf of the state government, a move that concretized the political link between the national cricket team and Mugabe's regime.[56] In June 2003, only four cricketers who played in the World Cup remained members of the national team. Enraged by the perceived embarrassment that Flower and Olonga's protest had caused the country, Mugabe ordered the leading officials of the ZCU to cleanse the squad of any politically active players. As a result, the team was 'politically vetted and gagged to ensure that no player criticizes Mugabe'.[57] The team thus became another victim of political repression and served as little more than a tool of government propaganda.

The political management of the national cricket team continued well after the immediate reaction to Flower and Olonga's protest. In 2004, the ZCU fired captain Heath Streak for demanding changes to the composition of the ZCU selection panel and its guiding directives. Concerned that not all of the national selectors had experience playing at a first-class level, Streak also contended that their unofficial quota policies were racially based and being used to eliminate white players from the national team. Such mobilization of race as a legitimizing force in the fight against historical inequities only serves to cover up the systemic structural problems that actually contribute to an increase in racial inequality. As Brian Raftopoulos notes, one of the most disquieting features of the crisis in Zimbabwe has been the ways in which the Mugabe regime has 'articulated a repressive national politics to a broad anti-imperialist, pan-Africanist appeal, with essentialist notions of race as the central markers of the conflict'.[58] By utilizing racialized quota policies, the ZCU played into this strategy, effectively making the national cricket team a politically and racially vetted tool of the ruling government.

Streak's dismissal prompted 14 other players to walk out on the team, citing discontent and frustration at the increasingly intrusive political influence in the team's operations and selection policies. In addition to petitioning the ZCU for Streak's reinstatement, the 'rebels' called for greater transparency in the selection process, the formation of a player's union, a minimum wage, and more financial support for club cricket.[59] The players boycotted the team until early 2005, when Streak was reinstated to the national side and many of the former rebels returned under a new labour agreement.[60] Upon restructuring, the ZCU became Zimbabwe Cricket (ZC) but the organization was still strongly linked with Mugabe's government. In 2006, under the leadership of chairman Peter Chingoka and managing director Ozias Bvute (both of whom were, and still are, staunch supporters of Mugabe), ZC refused to renew the contracts of several players, eventually leading to a drastic exodus of players from the national team and dropping Zimbabwe's standard of play to such a low level that ZC cancelled the domestic Logan Cup for the first time since its hiatus during the Second World War, and, even more troubling, withdrew Zimbabwe from Test cricket.[61] The team performed poorly at the 2007 Cricket World Cup but scored an impressive and altogether unexpected victory over Australia in the inaugural Twenty20 World Cup later that year. Yet the current state of Zimbabwean cricket continues to be unpredictable at best, as the country yearns to return to full Test status but still wrestles with a management structure that faces worldwide scrutiny and remains indelibly tied to ruling political policies and ideologies.

During a recent interview in which he spoke about the turbulence of Zimbabwean cricket, Flower admitted that his protest with Olonga did not have a transformative impact in Zimbabwe:

> I feel a little guilty that we couldn't follow it up, but I don't know what more we could have done. We didn't change anything and weren't powerful enough to do so, but we got an amazing response from people who felt they'd been jogged out of their apathy.[62]

If the protest did not change anything and Zimbabwe continues to slide further into crisis, then what value does its memory hold? As Flower points out, it raised awareness of the situation and helped catalyse pockets of opposition, but nothing really changed. Will their protest thus be pushed aside to the fringe of memory, recalled perhaps as a brave but futile stand, as an interesting side note in cricket history, or, for their critics, as an inappropriate mixing of sport and politics? Even though the gesture did not result in immediate tangible change, it is worth remembering and re-telling as an example of not only individual resistance and political protest, but of the capacity of popular culture to communicate and confirm the power of agency. Flower and Olonga's narrative has the potential to become a vital part of collective memory within and beyond the borders of Zimbabwe, undoubtedly in different forms for different people, as the country strives for change and redefinition.

In his examination of popular culture and memory, George Lipsitz argues that seemingly innocuous and everyday practices hold immense cultural significance. Although he does not specifically mention sport as part of popular culture, his ideas are certainly applicable to the study of sport and society. He asserts:

> For all their triviality and frivolity, the messages of popular culture circulate in a network of production and reception that is quite serious. At their worst, they perform the dirty work of the economy and the state. At their best, they retain memories of the past and contain hopes for the future that rebuke the injustices and inequities of the present.[63]

The memory of Flower and Olonga's protest could fill either of Lipsitz's scenarios; used by the state as a reminder of the consequences of speaking out against the government, or seized by those who find inspiration to continue the fight for justice and equality. Considering that we 'arouse and arrange our memories to suit our psychic needs',[64] the social production, manipulation and perpetuation of the protest's memory could fill very different needs for different people, communities and institutions.

Accepting that dominant and competing memories can exist simultaneously, it is particularly important to recognize the sensitivity of memory in places of conflict, unrest and trauma. Differentiating between dominant and alternative memories is crucial in shaping a history that includes a multiplicity of pasts and speaks for all. This task is especially significant in former colonial countries, as alternative histories and popular memories struggle against a master narrative constructed, and privileged, by those in power. In such situations, as in Zimbabwe, what is increasingly being contested is 'not simply an upheaval around notions of the past or the role of the past in the present, but a crisis in our imagining of possible futures'.[65] The memories and meanings of Flower and Olonga's protest thus have relevance to comprehending Zimbabwe's past *and* sculpting its future.

The narrative also holds the possibility of functioning as counter-memory, Lipsitz's concept of a 'way of remembering and forgetting that starts with the local, the immediate, and the personal'.[66] By focusing on instances of localized oppression, counter-memories help to challenge and re-evaluate dominant narratives avowing a sense of universal experience and truth. Flower and Olonga spoke out against oppression, yet both ultimately became victims of it. If the memory of their protest becomes part of a master narrative put forth by the ruling authorities, the counter-memory will rise as a means to tap into local and personal experiences of repression and subjugation. As Lipsitz argues, narratives of counter-memory only flourish when they resonate with the direct feelings and experiences of others. For these narratives to succeed completely, they 'must address the part of audience memory in touch with real historical oppressions and memories'.[67] The people of Zimbabwe face real instances of oppression and human rights abuses each day, making the memory of Flower and Olonga's protest a source of connection and shared understanding rather than a tool of a dominant history crafted to serve the hegemonic interests of a corrupt regime.

In discussing the challenges to collective memory stemming from a postmodern context, Brett Hutchins argues that it is a mistake to overestimate the influence of postmodernist theorizing that places the collective under attack from the ideologies and technologies of individualism that drive image-based consumer society.[68] In defending the very existence, and indeed the significance, of shared collective meanings, Hutchins asserts that communal events 'still command collective reflection and emotional response' even though they are mediated, represented and consumed in a multitude of ways across groups and between individuals.[69] As a communal event relevant to a wide range of people, Flower and Olonga's protest continues to gain meaning and elicit emotional reaction even though it was ultimately not the harbinger of change that so many hoped it would be.

For example, when the ECB appointed Flower as the new director of the English national cricket team in April 2009, English newspaper reports of the hiring decried Flower's lack of head coaching experience but celebrated the 'integrity, bravery and honesty'[70] he displayed by donning a black armband back in 2003. Other articles highlighted Flower as 'an honest man who knows the game inside out' and whose 'moral courage ... sets him apart from his peers'.[71] One sportswriter admitted that Flower has a difficult job ahead but argued that his time in Zimbabwe made him a courageous leader who 'can call upon that most valuable of commodities for anyone in the sporting world: respect'.[72] The effects of the protest have followed Flower to England, not only in a physical sense of displacement from his homeland, but also in terms of a meaningful collective memory that crafts his protest as a brave stand emblematic of his overall character. This memory has cultural currency, as Flower was hired as the national team coach decidedly not for his coaching experience but for his management skills, goodwill and international reputation made famous by the 2003 protest. In England, at least, the collective meaning of Flower and Olonga's protest is present and visible, informing how people represent, understand and consume both Flower as an individual and the historical event of which he was an integral part.

Final thoughts

In an essay about memory and forgetting in Indian cricket, Satadru Sen contends that 'it is difficult to deny that as a cultural artefact, cricket has more room for memory than any other sport'.[73] With its statistical measures against the greats of the past, its intrinsic tie to the nation state and movements for independence, and its continuing link to cultural politics, cricket relies on its mutual relationship with history and memory. How particular events, moments and people in cricket history are remembered (or forgotten) depends on a complex web of socially constructed meanings and interpretations of the past.

In the case of Flower and Olonga, their elegant political protest during the 2003 Cricket World Cup is open to reinterpretation as the social, political and economic conditions in Zimbabwe continue to shift, and as Flower and Olonga themselves pursue their lives shadowed by the legacy of their protest. After playing county cricket for Essex, Flower retired in 2007, became an assistant coach for the England national cricket team, and is now the director and head coach.[74] Olonga also settled in England, dabbling in public speaking at sports clubs, coaching school cricket, and occasionally writing newspaper columns. He no longer plays cricket competitively, instead devoting himself to a new career in music and the performing arts.[75] Both Flower and Olonga are often asked to comment upon the latest developments in Zimbabwe, but neither of them plans on returning to their home country while Mugabe is still in power. As default expert voices on the situation in Zimbabwe, Flower and Olonga cannot easily escape the memory of their own protest as it continues to be linked to not only cricket history, but to the ever-evolving history of Zimbabwe as well.

   The 2003 Cricket World Cup was undeniably politicized, used as a political tool by both the Zimbabwean cricket administrators as pretence to normalcy and by Flower and Olonga as a vehicle to express their discontent over the current state of their country. Due to its vibrant political and cultural meanings, the narrative of their protest also has the potential to become an intriguing piece of collective memory that reaches beyond the borders of Zimbabwe and the confines of cricket history, into a larger consciousness shared by all those concerned with human rights and social justice. The direct and tangible impacts of Flower and Olonga's protest might have been negligible, but their actions will certainly become a part of multiple memories and mythologies connected to the troubles of Zimbabwe and the rest of the world's efforts to understand them. As such, the narrative of the protest is relevant to broader histories of human rights and political struggle. The representations and meanings of this narrative are not permanently fixed and remain open to contestation and revision, but the mere act of remembering Flower and Olonga's story suggests that the promise of resistance remains strong and available to all.

Notes

[1] Nathan, *Saying It's So: A Cultural History of the Black Sox Scandal*, 60.
[2] Ibid., 61.
[3] Manase, 'Zimbabwean Urban Grooves', 56.
[4] Ibid.; and Uusihakala, 'Crisis in Zimbabwe'.
[5] Uusihakala, 'Crisis in Zimbabwe'; and Raftopoulos, 'The Zimbabwean Crisis'.
[6] Raftopoulos, 'The Zimbabwean Crisis', 217.
[7] Uusihakala, 'Crisis in Zimbabwe', 2.
[8] See Celia W. Dugger, 'Cholera is Raging, Despite Denial by Mugabe'. *New York Times*, December 12, 2008; and Celia W. Dugger, 'Mugabe Swears in His Rival as Prime Minister of Zimbabwe'. *New York Times*, February 12, 2009.
[9] Munslow, *Deconstructing History*, 162.
[10] Hutchins, 'Sport History'.
[11] Quoted in Chesterfield, 'Zimbabwe Cricket', 131.
[12] Cubitt and Joyce, *This is Zimbabwe*.
[13] Ibid., 28.
[14] Ibid., 29.
[15] Hill, *The Battle for Zimbabwe*.
[16] Ibid., 78.
[17] Ibid., 108.
[18] Ibid., 117.
[19] Andrew Meldrum, 'Is This Really the Right Place to Send a Cricket Team?' *The Observer*, December 29, 2002.
[20] Amnesty International, 'Zimbabwe: An Assessment'.

[21] See *Zimbabwe: The Food Fix*, DVD. Directed by Farai Sevenzo. London: BBC Television Production, November 16, 2004.

[22] Kevin Mitchell, 'On Back Foot Over Mugabe'. *The Observer*, May 23, 2004.

[23] Amnesty International, 'Zimbabwe: Rights Under Siege', paragraph 59.

[24] Ibid., paragraph 1.

[25] Tom de Castella, 'The Last Hope for a Dying Game'. *The Observer*, January 9, 2005, 36.

[26] Majumdar, 'Prologue'.

[27] de Lisle, 'The Age of Speed'.

[28] Ibid.

[29] Philip Sherwell, 'Beaten to Death for Protesting at Cricket'. *The Sun Herald*, February 16, 2003.

[30] Olga Craig, 'A Nation on a Sticky Wicket'. *The Sunday Telegraph*, January 5, 2003, 16.

[31] See Wagg, '"To Be an Englishman"'.

[32] Denis Campbell and Kamal Ahmed, 'Violence May Settle Cricket Row'. *The Observer*, January 12, 2003.

[33] Tong, 'Red Letter Day'.

[34] Sengupta, 'Globalizing Patriotism?', 595–6.

[35] de Lisle, 'The Age of Speed', 16.

[36] Flower and Olonga, 'Statement', 11.

[37] Telford Vice and Andrew Meldrum. 'Olonga Risks His Career with Political Protest'. *The Guardian*, February 11, 2003.

[38] Telford Vice, 'Zimbabwean Players Defy Mugabe'. *The Independent*, February 11, 2003, 28.

[39] Flower and Olonga, 'Statement', 11. The full text of the statement is as follows:

> It is a great honor for us to take the field today to play for Zimbabwe in the World Cup. We feel privileged and proud to have been able to represent our country. We are however deeply distressed about what is taking place in Zimbabwe in the midst of the World Cup and do not feel that we can take the field without indicating our feelings in a dignified manner and in keeping with the spirit of cricket.
>
> We cannot in good conscience take to the field and ignore the fact that millions of our compatriots are starving, unemployed and oppressed. We are aware that hundreds of thousands of Zimbabweans may even die in the coming months through a combination of starvation, poverty and AIDS. We are aware that many people have been unjustly imprisoned and tortured simply for expressing their opinions about what is happening in the country. We have heard a torrent of racist hate speech directed at minority groups. We are aware that thousands of Zimbabweans are routinely denied their right to freedom of expression. We are aware that people have been murdered, raped, beaten and had their homes destroyed because of their beliefs and that many of those responsible have not been prosecuted. We are also aware that many patriotic Zimbabweans oppose us even playing in the World Cup because of what is happening.
>
> It is impossible to ignore what is happening in Zimbabwe. Although we are just professional cricketers, we do have a conscience and feelings. We believe that if we remain silent that will be taken as a sign that either we do not care or we condone what is happening in Zimbabwe. We believe that it is important to stand up for what is right.
>
> We have struggled to think of an action that would be appropriate and that would not demean the game we love so much. We have decided that we should act alone without other members of the team being involved because our decision is deeply personal and we did not want to use our senior status to unfairly influence more junior members of the squad. We would like to stress that we greatly respect the ICC and are grateful for all the hard work it has done in bringing the World Cup to Zimbabwe.

[40] Brian Oliver, 'Lawyers, 1, Sport 0 (After Extra Time)'. *The Observer*, February 16, 2003, 15.

[41] Barnes, 'Brothers in Arms'.

[42] Sengupta, 'Globalizing Patriotism?', 595.

[43] Vice and Meldrum, 'Olonga Risks His Career', 26.

[44] Christina Lamb, 'Black-Armband Cricketers Vow to Keep Up Rebellion'. *The Sunday Times*, February 16, 2003, 29.

[45] Ward, 'No-Win Situation', 50.

[46] 'Fearless Olonga Ready for Another Armband Protest'. *The Mail on Sunday*, February 16, 2003, 113.

[47] Lamb, 'Black-Armband Cricketers'.

[48] Quoted in Owen Slot, 'Flower and Olonga Stand Firm Over Protest'. *The Times,* February 15, 2003, 41.
[49] Jan Raath, 'Placards Show Growing Crowd Support for Players' Defiance'. *The Times*, February 20, 2003.
[50] Ward, 'No-Win Situation'.
[51] Basildon Peta, 'The Cricket Revolutionaries'. *The Independent*, March 26, 2003.
[52] Raath, 'Placards Show Growing Crowd Support', 42.
[53] Nevin, 'Olonga's Last Stand'.
[54] Peta, 'The Cricket Revolutionaries'.
[55] de Lisle, 'The Age of Speed', 18.
[56] Henry Olonga, 'Racism at Heart of Losing Streak'. *The Observer*, April 18, 2004
[57] Andrew Meldrum, 'Mugabe's Cleansing of Zimbabwe Squad'. *The Observer*, June 1, 2003.
[58] Raftopoulos, 'The Zimbabwean Crisis', 212.
[59] Gough, 'Q&A: Zimbabwe Cricket Crisis'; and Chesterfield, 'Zimbabwe: What of the Future?'
[60] For a detailed examination of the boycott see Dabscheck, 'Out on a No Ball'.
[61] Chesterfield, 'Zimbabwe: What of the Future?'
[62] Quoted in John Westerby, 'Flower Admits Lingering Guilt over Problems in Zimbabwe'. *The Times*, February 13, 2008, 69.
[63] Lipsitz, *Time Passages*, 20.
[64] Kammen, *Mystic Chords of Memory*, 9.
[65] Meskell, 'Trauma Culture', 157.
[66] Lipsitz, *Time Passages*, 213.
[67] Ibid., 228.
[68] Hutchins, 'Sport History'.
[69] Ibid., 62.
[70] Mike Selvey, 'All Power to the Pick of Flower as England's Team Director'. *The Guardian*, April 16, 2009, 9.
[71] Mike Walters, 'Bloomin' Flower!' *The Mirror*, April 16, 2009, 53.
[72] Mike Atherton, 'Flower's Main Task Must Be to Blossom into Highly Skilled Man-Manager'. *The Times*, April 16, 2009, 70.
[73] Sen, 'History Without a Past', 94.
[74] Atherton, 'Flower's Main Task'.
[75] Larry Claasen, 'Still Testing the Boundaries'. *Financial Mail*, July 4, 2008.

References

Amnesty International. 'Zimbabwe: Rights Under Siege'. AI Index: AFR 46/012/2003, May 2003.
Amnesty International. 'Zimbabwe: An Assessment of Human Rights Violations in the Run-Up to the March 2005 Parliamentary Elections'. AI Index: AFR 46/003/2005, March 2005.
Barnes, Simon. 'Brothers in Arms'. *Cricketer International*, March 2003, 11.
Chesterfield, Trevor. 'Zimbabwe Cricket: A Challenge Almost Won'. In *Cricketing Cultures in Conflict: World Cup 2003*, edited by Boria Majumdar and J.A. Mangan, 129–46. London: Routledge, 2004.
Chesterfield, Trevor. 'Zimbabwe: What of the Future?' *Sport and Society* 10, no. 1 (2007): 143–61.
Cubitt, Gerald, and Peter Joyce. *This is Zimbabwe*. London: New Holland, 1992.
Dabscheck, Braham. 'Out on a No Ball: Industrial Relations in Zimbabwean Cricket'. *Sporting Traditions* 22, no. 1 (2005): 57–79.
de Lisle, Tim. 'The Age of Speed'. In *Wisden Cricketers' Almanack 2003*, edited by Tim de Lisle, 14–16. Hampshire: John Wisden and Company, 2003.
Flower, Andrew, and Henry Olonga. 'Statement of Andrew Flower and Henry Olonga'. *Cricketer International*, March 2003, 11.
Gough, Martin. 'Q&A: Zimbabwe Cricket Crisis'. *BBC News*, April 19, 2004. http://news.bbc.co.uk/sport2/hi/cricket/3637387.stm.
Hill, Geoff. *The Battle for Zimbabwe: The Final Countdown*. Cape Town: Zebra Press, 2003.
Hutchins, Brett. 'Sport History between the Modern and Postmodern'. In *Deconstructing Sport History: A Postmodern Analysis*, edited by Murray G. Phillips, 55–73. Albany, NY: State University of New York Press, 2006.

Kammen, Michael. *Mystic Chords of Memory: The Transformation of Tradition in American Culture*. New York: Vintage Books, 1991.

Lipsitz, George. *Time Passages: Collective Memory and American Popular Culture*. Minneapolis, MN: University of Minnesota Press, 1990.

Majumdar, Boria. 'Prologue'. In *Cricketing Cultures in Conflict: World Cup 2003*, edited by Boria Majumdar and J.A. Mangan, 1–14. London: Routledge, 2004.

Manase, Irikidzayi. 'Zimbabwean Urban Grooves and Their Subversive Performance Practices'. *Social Dynamics* 35, no. 1 (2009): 56–67.

Meskell, Lynn. 'Trauma Culture: Remembering and Forgetting in the New South Africa'. In *Memory, Trauma and World Politics: Reflections on the Relationship Between Past and Present*, edited by Duncan Bell, 157–75. New York: Palgrave Macmillan, 2006.

Munslow, Alun. *Deconstructing History*. London: Routledge, 1997.

Nathan, Daniel A. *Saying It's So: A Cultural History of the Black Sox Scandal*. Urbana, IL: University of Illinois Press, 2003.

Nevin, Tom. 'Olonga's Last Stand'. *African Business*, May 2003, 48–50.

Raftopoulos, Brian. 'The Zimbabwean Crisis and the Challenges for the Left'. *Journal of Southern African Studies* 32, no. 2 (2006): 203–19.

Sen, Satadru. 'History Without a Past: Memory and Forgetting in Indian Cricket'. In *Cricket and National Identity in the Postcolonial Era*, edited by Stephen Wagg, 94–109. London: Routledge, 2005.

Sengupta, Jayanta. 'Globalizing Patriotism? Some Lessons from the Cricket World Cup of 2003'. *The International Journal of the History of Sport* 21, no. 3/4 (2004): 585–612.

Tong, Andrew. 'Red Letter Day'. *Cricketer International*, March 2003, 4–5.

Uusihakala, Katja. 'Crisis in Zimbabwe'. *Finnish Journal of Ethnicity and Migration* 2, no. 1 (2007): 2–4.

Wagg, Stephen. '"To Be an Englishman": Nation, Ethnicity and English Cricket in the Global Age'. *Sport in Society* 10, no. 1 (2007): 11–32.

Ward, J. 'No-Win Situation'. *Cricketer International*, March 2003, 50.

Social change and popular culture: seminal developments at the interface of race, sport and society

Harry Edwards

Department of Sociology, University of California at Berkeley, USA

Outstanding achievement is enabled by the example of outstanding forerunners transmitted by traditions of community. This essay argues that the post-Second World War pattern of racial integration within the United States was one-way and selective, splitting the black community along class lines, giving the middle-class new access to the established institutions while leaving those left behind in deteriorating circumstances. These changes have been reflected in popular culture – including sports and feature films – and the escalating violence of many urban communities. The essay argues that this split has ruptured the cultural support for excellence in the black community. Reinforced by other changes within the US college and professional sport structures and exacerbated and accelerated by globalization, it has led to a spiralling decline in the number of black athletes in US sport.

According to Albert Einstein:

> During the last century and part of the one before, it was widely held that there was an irreconcilable conflict between knowledge and belief ... [But] the scientific method can teach us nothing else beyond how facts are related to and conditioned by each other ... Objective knowledge provides us with powerful instruments for achievement of certain ends, but the ultimate goal itself and the longing to reach it must come from another source ...

If one asks whence derives the authority of such fundamental ends, one can only answer: they exist in a healthy society as powerful traditions which act upon the conduct and aspirations and judgments of the individual; they are there, that is, as something living, without it being necessary to find justification for their existence. They come into being not through revelation, but through the medium of power personalities.[1]

In a similar vein, Eric Nisenson writes that great musician and jazzologist John Coltrane's 'greatest idol, Albert Einstein, changed the very idea of the universe ... The synchronicity [that Coltrane saw] between ... music and belief, the theories of modern physics, and his own discoveries through improvisation must have given [him] encouragement that he was on the right road ... in his great quest'.[2]

The essential thrust of these observations is that pursuit of the limits of performance is compelled neither by 'X-Factors' of individual potential or by a value inherent in the goal pursued. The *ultimate* goal and the longing to reach it must exist in a healthy society as powerful traditions which act upon the conduct and aspirations and judgments of individuals. They come into being not through revelation but the medium of powerful personalities. Vibrant, collectively held cultural traditions of high expectations and goals exemplified through the pursuits and achievement of individual personalities are more than just accompaniments *to* and evidence *of* an abiding commitment to excellence; *they are at its very foundations*. No matter the field or arena of endeavour, or how great and sincere the aspirations, without such features all effort inevitably erodes toward inconsistency, eccentricity and, ultimately, deficiency. High achievement environments – whether a team, an organization, a community, or a society – have always reflected cultural environments that generate and sustain living traditions made manifest through the medium of exemplary personalities (i.e. stars, heroes, high achievers). When the connection between healthy achievement and individual conduct, aspirations and judgments is weakened or severed, the individual, the community and the targeted realm of institutional achievement inevitably manifest the consequences.

The purpose of this essay is to illuminate how a confluence of evolved and emergent developments within the broader American societal context, within the traditional black community, and within sport and other realms of popular culture have precipitated a spiralling deterioration in the circumstances of the black athlete, and how this deterioration has been exacerbated and accelerated by globalization.

We begin with a clear delineation of the relationship between sport and society. This relationship is most succinctly defined in what I term the 'First Principle of the Sociology of Sport': *Sport inevitably recapitulates the character, structure and dynamics of human and institutional relationships within (and between) societies and the ideological values and sentiments that motivate and rationalize those relationships.* Today, as we approach the second decade of the twenty-first century, we are witnessing changes rooted most profoundly in relationships within American society (and globally between societies) that are so salient as to challenge American sports traditions. In consequence, sport in the twenty-first century increasingly exhibits significant departures from long-standing twentieth-century 'healthy' value dispositions and priorities. In the United States, no group has been more central to the change process or more significantly impacted by its consequences and implications than African-Americans. I have argued this previously to negligible response.[3] Today, the situation has deteriorated even more seriously. Before presenting an analysis of these broad-scale social dynamics, some contributing developments within the sports institution itself bear noting.

Changing relationships and dynamics within the American sports institution

From 1986 to 1999 I was Staff Consultant for Player Personnel Development and Relations for the San Francisco 49ers Professional Football Organization of the National Football League (NFL). Concurrently, from 1987 to 1995, I held a similar position with the Golden State Warriors of the National Basketball Association (NBA). In both capacities, my responsibilities included developing pre-draft social-psychological profiles on college athlete draft prospects, interviewing such pro prospects preliminary to the NFL and NBA drafts, and counselling those athletes actually drafted, acquired from the collegiate ranks as 'free agents', or signed as veteran free agents.

After several years, I began to discern what seemed to signal marked charges in both the attitudes and the athletic abilities of targeted collegiate football and basketball prospects. For example, between 1989 and 1992, an increasing number of both football and basketball pro prospects harboured significantly more positive estimations of their developed athletic capabilities and held more optimistic projections relative to their career potential than the pro scouts and coaches who had evaluated them as college players. Before the onset of the 1990s, prospects' profiles and interviews had clearly and consistently shown the opposite; that is, athletes' self- evaluations revealed that they were more guarded in projections of their own potential as compared to the projections of pro coaches and scouts. By 1993, it was clear that one factor significantly distinguishing less optimistic from more expectant collegiate pro prospects was, interestingly, *the frequency with which such players watched videotaped telecast of their own games.* In an increasing number of cases there emerged a connection between a player's valuation of his athletic abilities and pro potential and the turn-of-the-decade advent of the more economical, if not cheap, videocassette recorder – and therefore a player's access to this technology.

A generation of college football and basketball players exposed to videotaped telecasts of games wherein their performances were often 'hyped' (e.g., 'Wow! That was an NFL type move!' or 'He has NBA written all over him!', and other such hyperbolic declarations) by play-by-play and colour commentators left many players with unrealistic career expectations and levels of respect. So when asked during the course of interviews *'If this business was fair and the draft was an exact science rather than a fallible art, in what round would you be drafted based upon your evaluation of your abilities and your pro potential?'* the vast majority – over 80% – of the 637 elite college football and basketball prospects that I interviewed between 1992 and 1996 emphatically responded: *'The first round!'* Over 65% of those so answering privately taped their games. In the experts' judgment, however, successive player pools beginning as early as 1989, appeared to manifest a decreasing depth and scope of talent. This apparent trend could have well been exacerbated by other sports institutional developments.

An expansion of involvement by young athletes over the 1980s and into the 1990s in age, height, and or weight-graded football and basketball camps

Here, a 12-year-old who stood six-feet tall might be labelled and positioned as a centre in basketball because he was so much taller than his age-group peers, and so might be stifled in the early development of ball handling skills and his ability to play facing the basket. Similarly, a 10-year-old who weighed 170 pounds might be labelled and positioned as a lineman in football because he was so much heavier than his age-group peers, and so might be denied the opportunity of playing other positions. By comparison, in the informal and far less structured contexts of childhood play and pick-up 'sandlot' basketball and football games of past athlete generations, children usually had the option and opportunity to play a variety of positions and experience a variety of skills and challenges, thus avoiding rigid 'labelling' and premature limitations and closure upon their vision and aspirations as to what position might be most appropriate to their athletic capacities and potential. Since the 1980s, I have found fewer and fewer athletes who have played multiple positions in their sports since middle school.

Today, the online ranking of high school prospects by recruiting services has heightened the tendency to label young basketball and football players by projected position. In 2007, for example, one recruiting service had a 15-year-old high school freshman ranked as the '100th best offensive guard in the country'. That is a label that – if observations hold true – is likely to define the football career path of this young athlete – whether or not his greatest potential is at the guard position. Similarly in 2008, recruiting analysts and some recruiting services such as 'Hoop Scoop' were rating and ranking sixth grade basketball players and projecting player rank and position in the class of 2014. Here, the athlete's achievement aspirations, conduct and judgments are more likely to be guided by recruitment service projections and rankings than by 'healthy society traditions' contouring and motivating childhood sports activity.

Cutbacks in both football and basketball collegiate athletic scholarships (or grants-in-aid) and the expansion in the numbers of elite programmes appears to have diluted the athlete talent pools in basketball and football not only numerically but in terms of 'depth' or overall quality

The recruitment of athlete talent is an *art*, not a science. Even at the professional level where hundreds of thousands of dollars and the expertise of some of the most knowledgeable evaluators of football and basketball talent in the world are brought to bear in selecting among demonstrably elite collegiate candidates for the pro drafts, *mistakes in judging talent potential are commonplace*. A college coach who might see a potential high school recruit play only one or two games in person and who might study two or three reels of tape showcasing the yet evolving talents of such a player runs a correspondingly higher risk of misjudging the player's *collegiate* football or basketball potential. For these coaches, the few elite collegiate programmes competing for talent and the availability of a larger number of football or basketball scholarships provided a significant cushion against selection error. No less important, often the availability of 95 (as opposed to 85) football scholarships and 15 (as opposed to 14 or 13) basketball scholarships allowed the recruitment of promising but yet underdeveloped young athletes who (like a Bill Russell in his high school years, for instance) might show some promise but who require more time and competitive experience to realize their full collegiate athletic potential. Fewer scholarships and more numerous competing elite programmes have meant that such athletes are more likely to be passed over and lost to the talent pool while those who may have more limited 'top end' potential but who can contribute immediately are given grants instead, in the process diminishing the depth of collegiate talent.

The career-driven movement of both collegiate coaches and athletes has disrupted the stability, continuity and quality of talent development within athlete pools

As coaches have assumed more entrepreneurial as opposed to teacher/mentor dispositions under the impetus of unprecedented financial and career advancement incentives, they have changed jobs more readily, often in the process abandoning athletes they had recruited and leaving them to their fates (and often frustrations) under coaching staffs that did not recruit them and whose personalities, coaching styles and systems might not suit their talents. Of course, with increases in the financial and other rewards to be gained by institutions from collegiate football and basketball success, there has been a corresponding intensification of the pressures on coaches to *win or be fired*. A lack of success in this regard has been by far the most common reason for turnovers in coaching staff and yet another factor contributing to discontinuity and instability in the training and development of collegiate football and basketball talent. Movement among coaches also has frequently spawned movement among players – either voluntary or coerced – from one college to another. Likewise, more stringent academic requirements for collegiate athletic participation have added to the impetus for athlete movement. In the wake of such measures, increasing numbers of collegiate football and basketball prospects have had to attend two-year colleges prior to becoming eligible for matriculation and sports participation at elite four-year colleges and universities. Over my 25 years of profiling and interviewing collegiate pro prospects, it has not been at all uncommon to encounter players who have attended several two-year colleges attempting to secure enrolment and eligibility at a four-year institution.

At the professional level, movement among players due to free agency and by coaches under the pressure to win has created situations in both basketball and football that are less than optimally conducive to continuity in the development of players' talent potential once they reach the professional ranks – irrespective of their earlier developmental backgrounds

At every level, a player's talent develops and evolves in conjunction with his coaches' philosophies and game strategies and in complementarity with the development and contributions of his teammates (so-called 'team chemistry'). At the professional level, free agency all too often has become a major disruptive force, not only with regard to the above mentioned processes but in its impact upon younger players for whom accomplished veteran teammates have traditionally set standards and priorities of performance and professional deportment – which is to say, for whom veterans have traditionally functioned as 'powerful personalities' and exemplary models. In both professional basketball and football, I have discerned a gradual but nonetheless inexorable shift in player concerns toward issues of individual career and financial gain, to concerns over who is likely to be 'waived' (i.e. fired), to be traded, or to have their contracts 'restructured' under the 'salary cap' restrictions attendant to free agency, with a corresponding diminution or outright shift away from issues of team chemistry and loyalty, player pride in craft, and player respect for the game and its traditions. In short, for both players and franchises, football and basketball involvement has been increasingly focused upon the *business* of sport. The result has been a contribution to the erosion of both continuity and stability in the locker room and – consequently – in the players' athletic development. Compounding this type of disruption of traditional athlete development regimens has been the fact that high-round draftees and free-agent veterans often command far greater salaries and signing bonuses than many established veterans on teams acquiring the services of the former. In the locker room this situation essentially turns the traditional prestige order, rank and respect dynamics upside down. In a 'sports-business' locker-room culture and atmosphere, how does a lesser paid team veteran often with declining skills mentor a market-hyped highly paid, athletically promising younger player in the social-cultural nuances, in the traditions of personal and professional deportment, and in the obligations of membership in the 'fraternity of professional players'? Indeed, how does either a teacher-mentor coach or an entrepreneurial coach authoritatively and productively guide such young athletes? Relative to past standards of coaching authority and control, the answer in all too many cases is, only with great difficulty. Quite simply, today the elite athlete often controls the fate and future of the coach, not vice versa. Taken together, these institutional developments have added to the complexity of the troubled sojourn of the black athlete in American sport as we approach the second decade of the twenty-first century.

Racial integration and the bifurcation of African-American society: reflections on popular culture

As suggested in the First Principle, the much more basic and fundamental forces at work relative to the circumstances of the black male athlete emanate from social-cultural dynamics and relationships occurring in the broader society. The aim here is to illuminate the character, dynamics and impact of some seminal societal forces in this process. The main focus in this regard is the post-integration bifurcation of African-American society along class lines and the manifestation of this split and its consequences in the evolution of divergent value prescriptions, emergent cultural traditions and images, real life outcomes, and their reflection in popular culture – including sports. The situation we are witnessing today is rooted in the methods employed to achieve the racial integration of American sport and society. (And here, I hasten to stipulate that the problem has not been the *goal* of integration but the *methods* by which that goal was implemented.)

In 1946, Branch Rickey, owner of the Brooklyn Dodgers, established the template for racial integration in American sports and society. As would be the case with the military by way of President Harry Truman's 'executive order' that same year, and consistent with the ultimate outcomes of school integration over the decades following the 1954 US Supreme Court's decision mandating the desegregation of public schools, the results of Rickey's 'great experiment' with racial integration in Major League Baseball was that the process was *one-way* and *selective* rather than *two-way* and *inter-institutional*. That is, rather than the best Negro League teams (or at least two or three teams made up of the best Negro League players) joining the Major Leagues – ownership, managers, coaches, front office staffs, players and all – and, by design, ultimately participating in League player acquisition regimens involving both Negro and white players, competing in pennant races, post season competitions, etc. (as most Negro League owners, players, and sports writers advocated and envisioned), Major League owners, beginning with Branch Rickey's signing of Jackie Robinson, instead 'cherry picked' the Negro Leagues of their best player talent. As a direct consequence, by 1956 – within a decade – the Negro Leagues had all but totally collapsed. What was once a multi-million dollar sports entertainment enterprise, that produced players of the calibre of Jackie Robinson, Hank Aaron, Willie Mays, Ernie Banks, Roy Campanella, James (Cool Papa) Bell, and dozens of other great players, along with teams that regularly drew tens of thousands of fans to rented Major League stadiums for 'rivalry' and All-Star games, simply ceased to exist as viable sports enterprises.

While the broad scale integration of collegiate sport did not result in the collapse of the historically Negro colleges (given their priority mission of education), it did make it gradually more difficult for these schools to recruit 'blue chip' Negro athletes. With the onset of integration these athletes increasingly preferred to compete in athletically more prestigious mainstream college and university programmes where they could get greater national exposure and professional career opportunities. But as was the case with the Negro leagues, Negro collegiate athletic administrators, coaches and front office personnel were not brought into these programmes along with the Negro athlete. So not only was there a physical separation between the Negro athlete and his traditional athletic community, there was social-cultural isolation and alienation within the integrated collegiate environment. In most instances, there was a dearth of both Negro culture and people on these campuses beyond the presence of the athletes themselves. And typically, for them, there were no locally accessible 'powerful personalities' epitomizing and projecting the achievement traditions of the Negro community. In summary, for the Negro athlete the integrated college environment, notwithstanding the exposure and opportunities afforded, was at a fundamental level socially and culturally 'unhealthy' in the sense suggested by Einstein.

Simultaneous developments in other spheres sharpened the separation of traditional Negro communities along class lines, particularly America's urban centres. As was the case with athletes, those Negroes with the skills and capability simply out-migrated from the community. The motive forces here partly originated with Negro leadership of the Civil Rights Movement. The Civil Rights Movement of the 1950s and 1960s was middle-class in its leadership, methods and goals. And, commensurately, it was the Negro middle-class which benefitted most from the Civil Rights struggle. Here too, of course, change was *one-way* and *selective* – with Negroes moving into and onto the periphery of white society and institutions, businesses and social structures, and with little or no reciprocal movement by whites into Negro life circles. By the mid-1960s, the exodus of middle-class Negroes from their traditional communities had advanced to the point that there had begun to emerge a class-based separation and cultural disconnect within the Negro population. By the onset of the 1970s, the process had become permanent and for all practical purposes, irreversible.

The race-focused popular films of the decades following the Second World War illustrate this trajectory. In the 1950s and 1960s, the story-lines and characters played by the most prominent black actor of the era, Sidney Poitier, depict the aspirations of an under-class with talent and ennobling, integrationist values. Consider:

- *No Way Out* (1950): Negro doctor confronts white bigot.
- *Blackboard Jungle* (1954): Troubled Negro student has intelligence and leadership potential.
- *Edge of the City* (1957): Negro dock worker epitomizes working-class morality and integrity.
- *The Defiant Ones* (1958): Handcuffed together, Negro and white escaped convicts in the south confront their mutual predicament.
- *All the Young Men* (1960): A Korean War drama where Negro soldier is put in charge of a group of white troops under attack.
- *Raisin in the Sun* (1961): A Negro working-class family defies white bigotry and plans to move out into the suburbs.
- *Pressure Point* (1962): Negro prison psychiatrist tries to ferret out Nazi patient's problems.
- *Lillies of the Field* (1963): A Negro carpenter helps a group of hapless white nuns build a chapel.
- *A Patch of Blue* (1965): A blind white girl falls in love with an empathetic young Negro man who aspires to a professional career.

Like Poitier's characters, the athletic heroes of the era reflected the social-political aspirations as projected by the burgeoning Civil Rights Movement. Jesse Owens (track), Joe Louis (boxing), Jackie Robinson (baseball), Willie Mays (baseball), Ernie Banks (baseball), Tank Younger (football), Floyd Patterson (boxing), and Althea Gibson (tennis) were models of middle-class behaviour and personal discipline, who sought to bring respect to the Negro community and the 'Negro cause' of desegregation.

But gradually, increasingly, there was a new militancy, which Poitier's films soon reflected. In *In the Heat of the Night*, the Poitier character, Virgil Tibbs, slaps a white southern gentleman and patriarch who pointedly responds, 'There was a time when I would've had you shot for that', the clear implication being that time had passed. In what was increasingly defined as black society, the largely southern, church-based, middle-class, clergy-led established Civil Rights Movement was losing touch relative to new definitions of issues and interests. The Civil Rights Act of 1964 and the Voting Rights Act of 1965 were seen by many among these new urban activists – much the same as the Brown v. Board of Education Supreme Court edict had been – as products of a southern focus and strategy. In many places in the north, blacks could vote, blacks could serve on juries, and school segregation (as was depicted in the film *Blackboard Jungle*) was often as much by class as by race. Young black people in the urban north saw and experienced more subtle, but no less devastating forms of racism and discrimination that they increasingly deemed to be beyond the remedial capacities of change regimens and strategies devised to deal with the more blatant and direct race-based apartheid of the south. In response, by 1966 Huey P. Newton and Bob Seale had founded the Black Panther Party, Stokeley Carmichael, as chairman of the Student Non-violent Coordinating Committee (SNCC), had eschewed the organization's long-standing commitment to non-violent principles as the foundation of its strategy for achieving black freedom and equality in America, and had opted instead for 'Black Power – by any means necessary' as the guiding slogan. By the onset of the 1970s, black-oriented popular culture projected this new militancy, most particularly through more than a decade of productions dubbed 'blaxploitation' films – so labelled not by the Hollywood movie industry or the mainstream press, but by civil rights organizations such as the National Association for the Advancement of Colored People (NAACP), the Congress of Racial Equality (CORE), and some leaders associated with the post-Martin Luther King, Jr., Southern Christian Leadership Conference (SCLC). For these organizations, the new genre of black films was destructive of everything that the movement – and by implication, the likes of Sidney Poitier's earlier characters – had represented. But even Poitier came to more aggressive characters:

- *Guess Who's Coming to Dinner?* (1967): Generally regarded as a rather naked pro-integration apologia, on another level the film marked a break with the past where even the possibility of an inter-racial 'Romeo and Juliet' was denied. Here a Negro is invited to dinner at the home of the parents of his white fiancée – and both live to consider their options going forward!
- *To Sir With Love* (1967): West Indian engineer tries to teach rowdy London slum kids.
- *They Call Me Mister Tibbs* (1970): Here, Poitier reprises his character from *In The Heat of the Night* in an even more uncompromising guise. When asked what he is called up north, the Poitier character pointedly replies 'They call me Mister Tibbs!' in stark contrast to what Negro men by tradition were often called in the south – e.g., by their first names, or 'boy', or worse. 'Mister Tibbs' was a demand for respect.

But even as Poitier's characters changed, the profile of black identity and militancy in popular culture was on the rise:

- *The Dirty Dozen* (1967): An angry black condemned soldier, played by Jim Brown, not only departs from the morally upstanding, even superior, Negro soldier characters such as the one played by Poitier in *All the Young Men*, but he shows himself to be the equal in every respect of the other 11 disgraced military convicts chosen to make up a suicide mission commando unit.
- *100 Rifles* (1969): Black deputy, Jim Brown, in pursuit of gun runners, meets, falls for, and kisses rebel leader, Raquel Welch, on screen – a Hollywood first (in *Guess Who's Coming To Dinner*, Poitier never kisses his white fiancée on screen).
- *Shaft* (1971): Ultra-cool black private eye, Shaft (Richard Roundtree), is bad enough to challenge and insult whites, beat up gangsters, and walk through New York City traffic.
- *Sweet Sweetback's Baadasssss Song* (1971): Super stud black man, Melvin Van Peebles, runs from police in what is an angry, violent and highly controversial anti-white visual rant – so much so that the film was 'x-rated' when it was first released.
- *Black Gunn* (1972): Nightclub owner Jim Brown goes after the white mob after they kill his activist brother.

- *Slaughter* (1972): Black ex-Green Beret Jim Brown goes after a crime syndicate after they kill his parents.
- *Superfly* (1972): Tale of a Harlem drug dealer, played by Ron O'Neal, out to complete one last drug deal before he quits the business.
- *Hammer* (1972): Black boxer Fred Williamson takes on a white crime syndicate in this fast-paced action melodrama.
- *The Spook who Sat by the Door* (1973): Token black in the CIA, Ivan Dixon, uses his knowledge to organize bands of teenage urban guerrillas to bring 'whitey' to his knees.
- *Superfly TNT* (1973): Black ex-drug dealer Ron O'Neal tires of his idyllic life in Europe and decides to aid an official from an African country.
- *Shaft in Africa* (1973): Private eye Shaft, Richard Roundtree, projects his African roots and identity when he accedes to helping an African nation stop latter-day slave trading.
- *Take a Hard Ride* (1975): Jim Brown's and Fred Williamson's characters outwit, out-fight and outrun a host of violent adversaries while attempting to get a cache of money across the Mexican border.

Even black women broke out of their traditionally shallow, one-dimensional film role stereotypes of domestic, vice vixen, entertainer or poorly developed love interest to emerge as full-blown action figures – sensual and sexy enough to be attractive, physical and tough enough to single-handedly dispatch the bad guys. For example, in *Foxy Brown* (1974), Foxy Brown (Pam Grier) undertakes a violent vendetta against a drug ring that killed her lover.

Aside from the radical shift toward more angry and militant black images, these films from the heart of the blaxploitation era also exhibited another feature. While Jackie Robinson had been cast in a film playing himself (in *The Jackie Robinson Story*) typically black athletes did not follow in the footsteps of athletes turned film stars such as swimmers Buster Crabbe and Johnny Weismuller or football players Andy Devine, Dennis Weaver and John Wayne who parlayed their exposure and careers as athletes into film careers. (Conceivably, Paul Robeson might be considered an exception, but a case could be made that his stellar collegiate and professional football careers were merely early enabling sidebars to developing acting and singing careers).

As the character emphasis in black-oriented films shifted toward angry 'super stud' images, the black athlete, long a model of black masculinity, often was cast in various lead roles – with super stud character names to match. No more 'Virgil Tibbs' or 'Walter Younger, Jr.' (from *Raisin in the Sun*). Now 'Slaughter', 'Gunn' and 'Hammer' joined 'Shaft' and 'Superfly' in the pantheon of black movie heroes.

The black athletes most prominently associated with the era 1966–80 also epitomized the cultural shifts of the time. They represented a break with their institutional and ideological 'fathers and mothers'. Jim Brown (football), Bill Russell (basketball), Arthur Ashe (tennis), Curt Flood (baseball), Tommie Smith (track), Lee Evans (track), Spencer Haywood (basketball), Reggie Jackson (baseball), John Carlos (track), Muhammad Ali (boxing), and the 1965 American Football League black All-Star players were all outspoken 'activists' who saw a continuity between sports and society and, therefore, believed that there was an obligation that accrued to the black athlete to be engaged with the broader black struggle and to lead that struggle in the sports realm.

By the early 1980s, the Civil Rights Movement had faltered and substantially foundered. A burgeoning neo-conservative movement under the leadership and inspiration of Ronald Reagan was rapidly reversing 50 years of liberal gains, and not only was the gap between rich and poor growing, but the gap between the more integrated black middle class and the black poor and working poor in America's urban centres was expanding as well. The urban black masses were living under conditions of increasing political, economic and cultural isolation. Not unexpectedly, the reactionary 1980s spawned a resurgent rage against black urban conditions. And on many levels it also intensified the tensions and distinctions between the expanded black middle class and what was emerging as a potentially permanent social, cultural, economic and political black so-called 'under-class'. The extent to which the bifurcation of black America eventually hardened into separate, if not somewhat hostile, camps was expressed in the February 1988 issue of the broadcast industry publication *Black Radio Exclusive* where rap music pioneer 'Chuckie D' states as part of his critique of the black middle-class bourgeoisie and their culture: 'R&B teaches you to shuffle your feet, be laid back, don't be offensive, don't make no waves because, look at us, we're fittin' in as best we can. On the other hand rap music was seen as Black America's CNN, a popular culture form that could pull a race split by integration back together again – together, that is, around definitions, values and perspectives deemed "real", "authentic" and "truth-telling" from what came to be regarded as the "hip hop" viewpoint'. Ultimately, the black middle-class beneficiaries of the 1950s and 1960s civil rights struggle had little interest in being *that* 'hip hop real', and by the end of the 1980s, what had been a developing class-based split within black America was fast becoming an intergenerational gap as the children of the black middle-class (along with many young whites) became devotees of hip hop music and culture. The films that portrayed the evolving hip hop era made the blaxploitation movies of the latter Civil Rights and Black Power eras seem tame and tepid by comparison. And increasingly, particularly, as they emerged in the 1990s, it was the rap artists themselves, matched with established actors, who were cast in major roles. Like the rap videos of the 1980s, these films were efforts at portraying the hard realities of the communities that the black middle class left behind. Two films characteristic of the era's genre are:

- *Boyz N The Hood* (1991): Starring Ice Cube and Cuba Gooding, Jr., this film portrays a single father in south-central Los Angeles striving to raise his son and steer him away from aimlessness and an epidemic of violence in the neighbourhood. It is bloody, profane, and exudes a profound hopelessness among the community's young black men.
- *Menace II Society* (1993): An unflinching story of life in the Watts district of Los Angeles starring Too $hort and Samuel L. Jackson. A bloody tale, with lots of random violence, of young black men too caught up in the searing violence and instability of their community to escape.

As the decade of the 1990s gave way to the twenty-first century, consistent with popular top music videos over that span, films often reflected misogynistic sentiments. No more 'Coffy' or 'Foxy Brown', films which for all of their physicality did portray women as strong, frequently independent individuals with a prominent sense of self-worth. Entering the twenty-first century, the line between 'soft pornography' and films targeting mainstream black audiences began to blur with productions such as *Players Club*, *American Pimp*, *Pimps Up Hos Down*, and *Hustle and Flow*, which won an Oscar for the best film song of 2005.

The athletes who most epitomized the hip hop era were Dennis Rodman (basketball), Allen Iverson (basketball), Adam Jones (football), Michael Vick (football), Terrell Owens (football), Rickey Williams (football), Mike Tyson (boxing) and Carmello Anthony (basketball). What distinguished them was their 'street cred'; that is, they were regarded as 'real' and 'authentic' on the streets of the urban black community. To this extent the hip hop emphasis on 'keeping it real' redounded to sports. Athletes had become less models for youths in the community than youths in the community had become models for athletes. Consistent with this 'modelling reversal', athletes increasingly aspired to be rappers. The template was set by the 1984 San Francisco 49ers and the 1985 Chicago Bears football teams who did 'rap videos' in conjunction with their championship seasons. Since them, scores of professional athletes have cut rap records and albums. Sadly some athletes, like some of their rap idols, have ended up in prison or (as with Tupac Shakur, Biggie Smalls and Proof) have been killed while rolling with their 'posses', their 'crews', or 'homies', while keeping it real and 'representing' in the streets and clubs.

It is against this backdrop that we must turn to the diminishing scope and depth of black athlete talent. The deterioration of circumstances in America's urban centres, reflected so powerfully in popular culture, is having a decidedly negative impact upon the young men and women who are being recruited into sports today from elementary school through the high school ranks. Of particular concern is the levels of violence to which so many young people are exposed; their allegiance to gangs and gang culture that have arisen in response to, and as a principal factor perpetrating, violent environments; media and popular culture glorification and projection of 'ghetto-selective' language, values, imagery and life-style choices as appropriate and even obligatory if one is to have 'street cred'; and the emphasis upon sexual conquest and dominance over women as a prime marker of masculine prowess and stature.

One only has to survey the urban centres of America to gauge the magnitude of the problems associated with the above-cited behaviours. Focusing upon California as an example, consider the fact that nearly 40% – two-fifths – of African-American males ages 15–29 are under the control of the courts (i.e. either under investigation, under indictment, under arrest, incarcerated, on parole, or on probation). The homicide and gun assault rates within this group are at record levels and rising. Oakland, California, is a case in point. In 2005, there were 126 homicides with 381 wounded by gunfire. In 2006, those numbers rose to 148 homicides with 641 wounded by gunfire. Meanwhile, the statistics on both out-of-wedlock births and sexual assaults against women have been steadily climbing in California urban centres. The schools have not escaped the plagues of violence and social breakdown so prevalent in the broader urban communities of California. Today the second largest police force in the state – second only to the Highway Patrol – is to be found in the Los Angeles Unified School System. And even this has proven insufficient to even control – much less eliminate – gang and gang cultural activities in schools.

Considered from a national perspective the situation appears even grimmer. America incarcerates a greater number and proportion of its citizens than any other nation in the world, including China, which has four times the population. Of the 2.3 million people in America's jails and prisons, 43% are black – mostly men – though black people represent only 13% of the general population. Neither are national black homicide rates encouraging. To put this situation in proper perspective, over the first five years of the Iraq and Afghanistan wars, a total of fewer than 5,000 Americans of all races, ethnicities and genders died in combat (4,235 in Iraq and 628 in Afghanistan). According to statistics from the Centers for Disease Control in 2004, 5,475 black men died from gunfire alone in the United States.[4] (This does not, of course, include deaths by other violent means, e.g. stabbings, blunt force trauma, etc.). Extrapolated to the entire five-year war period, approximately 27,300 black men would have died on the streets of America (probably more given that the inner-city murder trends have been, on the whole, rising since 2004).

What this means is that a black man statistically would have had a better chance of surviving in the streets of Baghdad or Kabul than in the streets of many American inner-city communities.

It is little wonder that the black athlete talent pool is deteriorating. From the height of integration through the era of Black Power militancy, black athletes dominated the major sports. In boxing, for example, most of the heavyweight champions – e.g., Floyd Patterson, Sonny Liston, Muhammad Ali, Joe Frazier, George Foreman and Ken Norton – were black. By the 1980s, there were only three African-American heavyweight boxers of note: Larry Holmes, Evander Holyfield and Mike Tyson, and none of them achieved the mantle of respectability of their predecessors, even within black society. Today's black heavyweight contenders – James Toney, Chris Byrd or Shannon Briggs – would not even be recognized by most people. Similarly, the proportion of African-Americans in Major League Baseball dropped from 23% in 1973 to 14% by 1998. As we begin the 2009 baseball season, that percentage has fallen to 8.2% with no end to the decline in sight. In the NBA, black representation has declined from 82% in the 1980s to 78% today.

Exacerbating the situation in professional boxing, baseball and basketball is the phenomena of *globalization*. With global 'real time' broadcast capability made possible though satellite communications technology, sports are now marketed around the world. And where the fan appeal of a sport spans national boundaries and/or where there is the opportunity to cut athlete development costs, sport is more likely to be 'globalized' relative to its athlete pool. So today, 40% of the baseball players under Major League contract are foreign-born, as are 26% of the players who actually made Major League rosters. In the NBA, 102 – over a quarter of the players on team rosters – are foreign-born, while not insignificantly, three of the last four league's 'Most Valuable Player' awards have gone to foreign-born players.

Given the course and impact of the societal and sports institutional developments presented here, what is the future of African-American sports participation?

Activist, institutional and community collaboration: crafting a path forward

It is clear that there can be no simple, single or final resolution of the ever-evolving complex of challenges to be met. The issue, then, is more one of *strategic process options* than of immediate short-term answers. Sport is dynamic, so its challenges are inherently perpetual, and there can be no final answers or solutions. Commensurately, if we are going to strategically intervene to influence the course and substance of developments in sport, we must craft long-term, comprehensive strategies not short-term correctives. An example of the latter was the implementation of Proposition 48 in the early 1980s by the NCAA. The purpose of the rule was to compel student athletes to put more emphasis upon academic preparation as a condition of receiving grants-in-aid and of freshman collegiate sports participation. Proposition 48 was provoked largely by the disparate academic outcomes of black collegiate athletes as their numbers increased over the 1960s and 1970s in mainstream collegiate basketball and football. But because those who crafted Proposition 48 and subsequent collegiate athletics legislation failed to take into account the extent to which the problems involved were rooted in the evolving circumstances of post-integration black society, the relative outcomes of the black athletes have not appreciably improved (that is, freshman athletic eligibility rates and graduation rates for black basketball and football players still lag behind white athletes in those sports). Worse, if the course of societal developments is any guide, things will continue to deteriorate relative to black male athlete academic performance, particularly as a consequence of community and youth culture environments where pursuit of academic achievement and educational excellence is increasingly viewed as 'un-masculine', as not being 'real' or authentic. Here, it is not just the sports-related interests of African-Americans that are at stake or those of the colleges, professional franchises, or advance 'amateur' enterprises (such as the United State Olympic organizations). Of no less seminal significance is the issue of whether American Sports (particularly basketball, baseball and boxing) can depend increasingly upon offshore development of foreign athlete talent pools and sustain 'American' identities and development capabilities. Given the traditional role of sport as a social institution in reaffirming and reinforcing societal values and cultural 'blueprints' for success, in creating and showcasing 'powerful personalities', this is not trivial concern.

The appropriate path forward would appear to involve, first, recognition that everyone is on the same side. That is, no party to this situation – sports activists, athletes, sports authorities, the black community, or broader social institutional interests – stands to gain in the long run by a continued deterioration in black sports participation. The need to have the collaborative input and involvement of all parties in crafting a resolution process capable of the on-going generation of viable responses to critical problems, therefore, is self-evident. And one place to start would be to confront the challenge of re-channelling black youths' perspectives and values relative to those 'powerful personalities' that model their aspirations and goals. The fact that these youths too often are immersed in negative social-cultural environments need not limit their role model reach. And here I return to one of my initial points. Far beyond the realm of music, John Coltrane found the 'powerful personality' model and the motive values and perspectives that fuelled his creativity and pursuit of jazz excellence in the life, work and ideas of the great theoretical physicist, Albert Einstein. In the tack of teaching urban black youths to reach beyond the limits of their immediate environment and circumstances for role models, life strategies and goals, there is the hope of them learning more positive and constructive paths forward. In any event, in the era of Barack Obama that is a place where the process can start.

Notes

[1] Einstein, *Ideas and Opinions*, 41–2.
[2] Nisenson, *Ascension*, 114.
[3] Edwards, 'Educating Black Athletes'; Edwards, 'The Black Dumb Jock'; Edwards, 'The Collegiate Athletic Arms Race'; and Edwards, 'An End to the Golden Age'.
[4] Bill Marsh, 'An Accounting of Daily Gun Deaths'. *New York Times*, April 22, 2007.

References

Edwards, Harry. 'Educating Black Athletes'. *Atlantic Monthly* 252, no. 2 (August 1983): 31–8.
Edwards, Harry. 'The Black Dumb Jock: An American Sports Tragedy'. *College Board Review* 131 (Spring 1984): 8–13.
Edwards, Harry. 'The Collegiate Athletic Arms Race: Origins and Implications of the "Rule 48" Controversy'. *Journal of Sport and Social Issues* 8, no. 1 (1984): 4–22.
Edwards, Harry. 'An End to the Golden Age of Black Participation in Sports?' *Civil Rights Journal* 3, no. 1 (1998): 19–24.
Einstein, Albert. *Ideas and Opinions*. New York: Random House, 1954.
Nisenson, Eric. *Ascension: John Coltrane and His Quest*. New York: St Martin's Press, 1993.

Anti-apartheid boycotts and the affective economies of struggle: the case of Aotearoa New Zealand[1]

Malcolm MacLean

Department of Sport and Exercise, University of Gloucestershire, Gloucester, UK

One of the major manifestations of sport-centred activist political struggles in the latter half of the twentieth century centred on the demand for the sporting and broader cultural, social, economic and political isolation of South Africa during the apartheid era. The struggle saw apartheid-endorsed South African sports organizations expelled from international bodies beginning in the 1950s, with the South African National Olympic Committee being the only one ever to be expelled from the IOC. The sports boycott was one of the major successes of the international anti-apartheid campaign, yet the existing literature on boycotts is only marginally relevant to cultural (including sports) boycotts. Furthermore, the existing literature dealing with sports boycotts, with its focus on the multilateral politics of Olympic boycotts, is of minimal use in explaining mass activist campaigns such as the anti-apartheid movement. This essay centres on the campaign against the 1981 South African rugby tour of Aotearoa New Zealand to explore the multiple significances of sport in the target (South Africa) and sender (Aotearoa New Zealand) states, and the character of the mass movement to argue that the cultural significance of both sport and the politics of 'race' and colonialism are vital to an effective understanding of mass movement supported bilateral cultural boycotts.

During the southern winter of 1981 some of the most sustained anti-apartheid protests outside South Africa took place. A tour of Aotearoa New Zealand by South Africa's Springbok rugby team almost equally split public opinion in the host nation. Arranged against the institutions supporting the tour, a broad based anti-tour campaign demanded the total isolation of apartheid South Africa. During 56 days in the middle of 1981 and in an effort to prevent rugby matches being played, thousands of New Zealanders twice a week faced riot police who had logistical support from the military. They were baton charged, assaulted and imprisoned. They had telephone calls intercepted, police surveillance became routine, organizing meetings were infiltrated, and there was public discussion of the possibility of the declaration of, in effect, martial law. The movement was stronger in the cities than the towns and countryside, but had a potent provincial and rural presence; was young to middle aged in its activist fractions, but was actively supported by people of all ages; was centred on issues of 'race', but split the indigenous Maori community as much as, and in similar proportions to, any other ethnic group; the campaign was organized around principles of non-violent direct action, but its protests included establishment figures; and was designed to stop a series of rugby matches, but drew support from a number of high profile people in the rugby world including the captain until 1980 of the national rugby team, the All Blacks. There was nothing simple about this campaign.

Figure 1.   Produced by HART: the New Zealand Anti-Apartheid Movement (reproduced by permission).

The anti-tour campaign in 1981 not only secured, but kept mass public and activist support. During the course of the tour there was a slight increase in anti-tour feeling, although that may have been a result of the level of disruption, and the intensity of both the protests and the state's reaction. As significant as that reaction and response is, this essay focuses on the central political tactic of the campaign – the demand for the total political, economic, social and cultural isolation of South Africa's apartheid regime, and therefore of South Africa. The boycott, as a political tactic, is a deeply ingrained tool in campaigns centred on civil disobedience, resistance and demands for equity and liberation. The uses of the boycott tactic in civil rights and liberation politics – in nineteenth and twentieth century Ireland for instance, or more famously in the African-American bus boycott in Montgomery, Alabama in 1955 – centre on the struggles of the oppressed, and are of minimal use in analysing international solidarity campaigns, whereas the exploration of the boycott tactic in international relations literature centres on economic boycotts that are difficult to translate directly to sports and other cultural sectors. There is a body of literature in sports studies exploring boycotts – but it concentrates almost exclusively on the actions of states and national teams in multilateral sports events, such as Olympic and Commonwealth Games. There is little in this literature that explains the significance of the boycott as an organizing tool or tactic in a bilateral cultural relationship – such as an international visit by a sports team. Furthermore, there is little in this literature that accounts for the persistence of a mass protest solidarity movement in face of violent state

Figure 2.   Anti-tour march, Gisborne, 22 July 1981 (photo by Kapil Arn, reproduced by permission).

repression. Key parts of the explanation for this seemingly irrational action to continue to confront riot police to prevent a set of rugby matches lie in the structure and form of the protest movement itself, and in the ways that the boycott tactic, in the specific circumstances of Aotearoa New Zealand in the early 1980s, allowed protesters to assert a sense of communion as well as solidarity not only with oppressed South Africans, but a place in a global and local anti-racist movement.

The boycott tactic allowed New Zealanders campaigning against apartheid to assert an affinity with black South Africans. This affinity was enhanced by the circumstances of and relationships between anti-tour activists. The tour's circumstances, its everyday divisions and conflicts, meant that many of these protesters saw themselves as under siege from the rugby authorities, tour supporters and the state.[2] This sense of conflict combined with the use of the boycott tactic to heighten identification with South Africans opposing apartheid and to intensify the affective ties between anti-tour activists. The rugby boycott as a political tactic was the significant element in the establishment of the anti-tour campaign that combined identity and affinity politics in a moral community of activists, sympathisers and fellow travellers.

The movement to 1981

The campaign against the 1981 tour was not the first time New Zealanders had protested against sporting contact with South Africa. New Zealand and South Africa had been playing nationally representative 'Test' matches since 1921, with South Africa's Springboks visiting New Zealand in 1921, 1937, 1956 and 1965, while a planned tour in 1973 had been cancelled. In turn, New Zealand's All Blacks had toured South Africa in 1928, 1949, 1960, 1970 and 1976. Most opposition until the 1960s focussed on the requirement the South Africans imposed on touring teams that no Maori be selected, meaning that leading members of the All Black squads were left at home. By 1960, concern had intensified leading to activist opposition to the tour, and street protests in both 1959 and 1960. Opposition to the tours in 1949 and 1960 centred on the perceived sleight to Maoris by being excluded from visiting teams, and on the claim that the South Africans were exporting apartheid with the result that New Zealand's allegedly exemplary race relations were being undermined. In response to the 1959–60 protests, it seems that the New Zealand Rugby Football Union (NZRFU) put pressure on the South African Rugby Board (SARB) to ease their restrictions. In 1965 the lack lustre Springbok tour of Aotearoa New Zealand passed by with almost no comment, yet in 1970 the All Blacks toured with three Maori and one Samoan in the team. The NZRFU was confident that they had addressed tour opponents' concerns. The 1970 anti-tour protests were militant, disruptive, condemned the Maori and Samoan team members for accepting the appellation of 'honorary white', and called for the total isolation of South Africa. The terms of the debate had shifted markedly: there was now an internationally coordinated campaign for comprehensive sanctions against South Africa.

The 1970 responses by the NZRFU and SARB to previous anti-tour campaigns were several years out of date: they admitted Maori and Samoan players to a team that the activist campaigners now considered should not be touring. The concern was no longer the infection by apartheid of New Zealand's 'race' relations; the concern was now that apartheid needed to be isolated and overthrown. In the wake of the 1969 and 1970 campaigns in the UK over cricket contact, the 1971 turmoil in Australia over the Springbok rugby tour there, and the presence of the All Blacks in South Africa during the anti-apartheid protests in 1976 that led directly to the boycott of the Montreal Olympics, the international consensus had hardened. In the Commonwealth, only New Zealand and the UK did not unequivocally endorse state action to prevent sporting contact, but even they could not prevent the 1977 Commonwealth Heads of Government Meeting, in the Gleneagles Agreement, from accepting

> the urgent duty of each of the Governments vigorously to combat the evil of apartheid by withholding any form of support for, and by taking every practical step to discourage contact or competition by their nationals with, sporting organisations, teams or sportsmen from South Africa or from any other country where sports are organised on the basis of race, colour or ethnic origin.[3]

In Aotearoa New Zealand in 1981 this 'urgent duty' did not include withholding visas to the tourists, and did not prevent what was then the nation's biggest police operation or the mobilization of the armed forces to provide logistical support for that operation.

The 1981 anti-tour campaign in some ways represents the global apex of anti-apartheid solidarity protests around the cultural boycott. Although the tour itself was not announced until July 1980, it had been scheduled by the International Rugby Board for some time, and the various elements of the anti-apartheid movement in Aotearoa New Zealand had been planning for the campaign since at least the end of 1979. The principal anti-apartheid organization – HART: the New Zealand Anti-Apartheid Movement, formed by a merger of the Halt All Racist Tours group and the National Anti-Apartheid Council – made two key decisions in the early stages of the planning. The first was that the tactical objective was to stop the tour – either by preventing it from beginning, or halting it once it began by making it unmanageable. The second was that the HART name was a political problem, mainly because of the successful campaign by the state in the wake of the 1976 Montreal Olympic boycott in response to the All Black tour of South Africa to blame the New Zealand anti-apartheid movement. Anti-apartheid activists therefore set out to build broad-based local coalitions in which HART would participate, but would not lead. These groups developed quickly, and took on very different inflections based on the balance and shape of local political forces, the breadth and depth of local activist experience, and assessments by members of coalitions of local political cultures. These differences led to some significant tensions within the movement, especially as activists travelled to match venues where coalition cultures were more cautious – most publicly during the match in Palmerston North on 1 August.

The campaign may be understood as having three stages. The first and the longest was the 18-month organizing effort to prevent the tour from taking place. This stage was a multi-strand campaign combining domestic and international political pressure to give meaning to the Gleneagles Agreement commitments the New Zealand Government had made. The central domestic tactic combined a demand that the team be refused visas with mass anti-tour demonstrations as the tour dates drew near. These nationwide mobilizations attracted tens of thousands of marchers, and included a broad cross-section of the population. They were, for the most part, peaceful and broadly inclusive – the New Zealand Police reports 50,000 participants and one arrest during the 1 May national protests (the arrest was of a tour supporter in the southern city of Invercargill, for throwing eggs at the marchers), and 48,000 participants and three arrests during the 3 July mobilization.[4] The intransigence of the New Zealand government, however, meant that 10 days after this second mobilization the Springboks arrived. This intransigence was to a large extent the product of a correct assessment that allowing the tour to proceed would benefit the government in the election due in November, given that support for the tour was higher in marginal and rural seats where the government's slim majority and therefore hold on power was under threat.

The second and third stages of the campaign began once the Springboks arrived, and lasted for the next 56 days. The second stage was short, less than two weeks, and was marked by a significant escalation in violence on the part of the state during the second week, just as the balance of power had shifted quickly towards the protest movement during the first few days of the tour. Quite simply, the police seemed unprepared for the intensity of protest activity, despite the organization of the 'Escort Groups' – in effect, riot police in support of local police actions. The police were, throughout the tour, provided with logistic support by the armed forces (and had anticipated this, with the request to the Ministry of Defence on 22 September 1980[5]). The campaign escalated in two specific events, the first the pitch invasion by protesters preventing the second match of the tour on 25 July (Figure 3). Not only was the match prevented, but many of the group occupying the field and other protesters were assaulted by tour supporters, with the police contingent unable (or unwilling) to offer adequate protection, although to their credit they did attempt to prevent crowd action against the protesters inside the rugby stadium. The second event in the escalation took place over four days, beginning with a Wednesday (29 July) night baton charge on a march in Wellington's Molesworth Street, near the Parliament Buildings, that seemed to observers to have been an almost uncontrolled frenzy resulting in many injuries, and seems quite clearly to be an attempt by the state forces to reassert their control. This event ended on 1 August, when the match in Palmerston North took place inside a barbed wire fortified stadium with the 'Escort Groups' no longer held in support but in the front line, and the armed forces logistical support now extended from transport assistance to the installation of barbed wire and barricades.

The remainder of the tour, from 1 August until mid September, was contested on the fields and the streets under siege-like conditions. One further match was cancelled, in the South Island city of Timaru because the police argued that they could not secure the ground, protesters came close to a pitch invasion during the First Test in Christchurch, and

Figure 3.   Anti-tour demonstrators occupy Hamilton's rugby park, 25 July 1981 (photo by Steven Penny, reproduced by permission).

Wellington closed down for the Second Test. Local protest coalitions organized medical units to accompany protests (although many complained that despite their Red Cross marked vests they were treated as protesters), while protest marches were organized into contingents on the basis of the degree of confrontation marchers were willing to engage in. After the Molesworth Street baton charge, protective clothing including hard hats, shields and extra padding had become the norm rather than the exception. During the Second Test in Wellington, protesters and police faced off in MacAlister Park – across the road from the main rugby stadium where the match was being played – in a scene that resembled medieval armies, where protesters had helmets and shields, and the lines of police in helmets with face masks and metre long aluminium batons held like pikes. The tour reached its climax in Auckland on 12 September – the fourth anniversary of the murder by South African police of Black Consciousness leader Steven Biko – with running battles in the streets around Eden Park, the rugby stadium. In the meantime, local coalitions, aware that the intensifying protest was frustrating and alienating many supporters, sought to organize 'family days' promising no confrontations. Yet despite all of this, and the increasing number of arrests, anti-tour activists continued to take to the streets – whether they all thought they could stop the tour is unclear – but they did their best to disrupt it, and in doing so show their support for the calls from within South Africa for the complete isolation of apartheid.

The fundamental thing that made people with anti-apartheid views into anti-tour activists was not an abhorrence of apartheid, but advocacy of a sports boycott. In Aotearoa New Zealand during the late 1970s official debate about relations with South Africa was premised on a rejection of racism and of apartheid. The key difference in this debate was a tactical one of how to bring about change in South Africa: bridge-building or boycotts. These circumstances meant that advocacy of the sports boycott as a political tactic identified anti-tour activists and allowed them to identify with South Africa's oppressed majority. The campaign against apartheid in general and the Springbok tour in particular was a demand for the boycott, as well as a product of the particular cultural context in Aotearoa New Zealand.

Boycotts, sanctions and South Africa

The election in 1948 of the Nationalist Party to government in South Africa resulted in a rapid codification the country's racial order so that by 1954 the component pieces of apartheid as a legal system of law were all in place. Throughout the 1950s and 1960s internal and international political pressures saw South Africa increasingly isolated from international sport. To the newly emerging international forces, apartheid was a violation of the Universal Declaration of Human Rights (1948) and the Declaration on the Elimination of All Forms of Racial Discrimination (1965). One manifestation of this opposition may be seen in the 1972 United Nations General Assembly resolution 2922 describing apartheid as a total negation of the purposes and principles of the UN Charter, and more significantly describes apartheid as 'a crime against humanity'. The resulting 1973 International Convention on the Suppression and Punishment of the Crime of Apartheid pointed in article III to the 'international criminal responsibility' of those who 'directly abet, encourage or cooperate in the commission of the crime of apartheid'.[6] By the end of the 1960s the growing international activist consensus was not that contact with South Africa could avoid complicity in apartheid, but that political, economic, social and cultural (including sport) isolation of apartheid was essential if the perpetuation of the 'crime against humanity' was to be prevented: this meant full and comprehensive sanctions.

Analyses of sanctions, boycotts and embargoes tend to be limited by a focus on formal state actions and economic consequences. Drawing on this literature, Daoudi and Dajani define sanctions as 'actions initiated by one or more international actors (the "senders") against one or more others (the "targets") with either of two purposes: to punish the targets by depriving them of some value and/or make the 'targets' comply with certain norms the senders deem important'.[7] This discussion subsumes embargoes and boycotts within a general focus on sanctions. This is an unreasonable assumption in the case of sporting and other cultural boycotts because sanctions are seldom invoked as an isolated policy response.[8] The use of economic sanctions as a policy tool relies on the assumption of a simple and direct relationship between political power and economic strength, but is affected by a wide range of variables. These variables are as much about relations with other third-party states as those with the target state. Sanctions, boycotts or embargoes can achieve their intended outcome because they can maintain the perception that damage has been inflicted, can express a sense of morality and justice, can signify disapproval and displeasure, can satisfy the emotional needs of the sanctioner to be seen to be acting, can help maintain the sanctioner's positive image and reputation, can relieve domestic pressure on the sanctioner, especially if there is a broad popular movement, and can inflict symbolic vengeance on the target. Furthermore, if there is no short term solution or compromise there is on-going inconvenience, target states become examples, and the sanctioner's self-image and self-confidence can be restored.

The impacts of economic sanctions and of the sports and cultural embargo of apartheid suggest that the belief that sanctions have mainly symbolic value needs re-evaluation. This is especially so, as it was in South Africa, where a broad package of external pressures support forces in the target state. The effectiveness of sports boycotts and embargoes relies on several additional factors. Just as the impact of economic sanctions needs to be seen in the light of access to other sources of, or substitutes or close alternatives for, goods being denied, consideration needs to be given to access to additional or alternative sports events.[9] While Houlihan's argument that international sports bodies are monopolistic is correct, the full significance of the international structure of sport to analyses of boycotts may only be seen if bodies such as the International Rugby Board and the International Olympic Committee are understood as monopsonistic cartels, meaning that the specific product being denied cannot be acquired from elsewhere.[10] These international sports bodies are confederations that become the only purchaser, in part because they have devised and organized the 'market' in international sports competition. Furthermore, they are monopsonistic cartels of monopsonistic bodies: their market control as the single purchaser exists at both international and national level. Although an effective sports boycott of South Africa denied access to substitutes, the 1980s trend for 'rebel' tours of South Africa shows that access to close alternatives was available. Despite the claims that rebel tours provided second rate or near retirement players resulting in teams that were not of an international standard, to a sports-starved South Africa these teams seemed to be a suitable alternative. The South African government 'profoundly appreciated' rebel tours as 'an important blow not only in the sporting field but also in general against the concentrated efforts to isolate South Africa'.[11] Furthermore, throughout the 1960s and 1970s South Africa made concessions in the organization of sport to take account of some of the concerns of anti-contact campaigns, but without fundamental change to the apartheid sport system.

Analysis also requires an investigation of counter-leverages available to the target state, and the potential for domestic backlash. The interpretation of the impact of economic sanctions centres on the degree to which the target is a trade-dependent state. A common refrain is that the only effect of economic sanctions is that they diversify the target's economy.[12] All states wanting top class sports competitions are trade-dependent because they rely on international contact, and therefore access to a singular product: diversification seldom provides a suitable alternative that meets the political, competitive and cultural needs catered to by international representative sport. Analyses of economic sanctions must address the target's access to foreign exchange reserves and the key components of the target's foreign trade dependence. In sports terms, this points to the need to ensure that the tactic has the greatest possible impact through a clear identification of the target's sporting values and the cultural significance of particular codes. It is therefore not surprising that the isolation of South African weightlifting came nearly 30 years before the isolation of South African rugby union, and that rugby union was the last sport to be isolated from top-level international contact, and for only four years (1985–89).

The practice of sports and economic isolation challenges the assertion that it is ineffective. This claim is often based on a desire for immediate results, or out of a quest for a simple cause-and-effect analysis. Sanctions do not work quickly; they are attritional and are only effective as a part of a wider range of measures. There are a number of points of interpretation where common conclusions do not exist. Most specifically, the experience of economic sanctions shows that hinting at them is sometimes more effective than imposing them. This cannot be said of sports or other cultural boycotts. There is only minimal risk in cultural boycotts for friction to develop between the sanctioner and its allies because the latter are adversely affected. Many sports fixtures involving nationally representative teams, with the partial exception of a small number of multinational events, are bilateral and controlled by autonomous international governing bodies although managed through international (monopsonistic) federations. These are affected only in the context of a meaningful multinational agreement such as the 1982 Commonwealth Code of Conduct concerning third party (that is, non-Commonwealth Games sports) contact with South Africa adopted by the Commonwealth Games Federation.[13] Neither are sports sanctions likely to undermine the credibility of the sanctioner leading to them being seen as an unreliable supplier, in large part because international sport is monopsonistic.

There are two general points where common ground exists. First, the sanctioner needs to be fully aware of the potential costs. While in analyses of economic sanctions these are relatively straight forward and may be accurately calculated, in sporting and cultural boycotts there is a far greater number of factors to consider, ranging from the domestic political response to the effect on the cultural standing of particular activities or sports.[14] Second, the target's responses may lead to new sources of supply being discovered, the stimulation of conservation to reduce demand, or development of substitutes – in the South African sports case, these responses include the celebration of domestic competition, the 'rebel' tours, and the strenuous efforts on the part of the South African government and key elements of its civil society to circumvent the boycott.[15]

Neither do conclusions derived from consideration of Olympic boycotts neatly fit the isolation of South African sport. The anti-apartheid boycott was different from Olympic boycotts, particularly Moscow in 1980 and Los Angeles in 1984, in two senses: it was based on strong popular protest movements with clear objectives, and it was a single issue with a single institutional focus. By dealing with individual sports and a single organizing body as well as having a focus on governments through domestic political pressures, the campaign developed a form different from the Olympic boycotts. It could be presented as a response to a call from within South Africa and as directly linked to South Africa's conditions. However, the idealist sentiment asserting a supra-political status of sport was still powerful and able to be utilized by governments in South Africa and elsewhere to oppose the protest movements. This indicates that the issues on which to focus in considering the isolation of apartheid sport are the political structures of the protest movement as opposed to those of single sporting bodies/governments, the existence of a popular protest movement leading the call for a boycott, and the use of the apolitical sports argument and the anti-apartheid movement's ability to counter that through, in this case, the significance of rugby and the politicization of South African sport.

Aotearoa New Zealand's affective economies of sports boycotts

The analysis that follows is shaped by my involvement in the campaign. It was almost impossible to grow up in Aotearoa New Zealand during the 1970s and not in some way have engaged with the debate about sporting contact with South Africa. Rugby union was extremely important to the men in my family, and to my mother who stayed actively involved in competitive sport into her 50s. Like many other New Zealand boys, I had got up in the early morning hours with my father to listen to radio broadcasts of All Black matches during tours to different time zones, and during 1970 had joined him in the 30 km drive to my brother house's to watch the matches on television. In my case, however, the involvement had a more personal component: I had lived for one of my teenage years in rural Natal (South Africa) in 1977, arriving not long after the final suppression of the popular rising that began in Soweto in June 1976. This experience had changed my disquiet about sports contact with South Africa to support for the anti-apartheid movement's demands. By 1980 I had become active in HART, attending its National Council meetings on behalf of the Manawatu (Palmerston North) branch on occasion, and was my university's representative on the New Zealand University Students' Association's anti-tour national organizing group. During the lead up to, and throughout, the tour, we were sure our telephone was being monitored; my flatmate – a military policeman in the Territorial Army – was informed by his superiors that he was a designated security risk; and I was regularly followed home by police cars, at walking or cycling pace. It seemed as if the police state I had lived in four years beforehand was not too far away. Consider this historical ethnography.

The focus on the sports boycott as an international policy tool is only part of the story. Understanding of the anti-apartheid movement and the anti-tour campaign requires consideration of the boycott as an organizational tool and base. The most significant contact between New Zealand and South Africa was sporting, specifically rugby union.[16] The socio-cultural significance of rugby union to white South Africa gave the movement a sense of striking a blow at the cultural heart of apartheid's projection of itself into the world community.[17] To impose a total sporting embargo on South Africa was seen by anti-apartheid campaigners as striking a blow for liberty in South Africa by culturally weakening the apartheid system. This analysis has been rehearsed by most, if not all, sympathetic interpretations of New Zealand's campaign against apartheid. What is generally missing from all these interpretations is an analysis of the effect and significance of the sports boycott on the protest movement. Along with this sense of striking a cultural and emotional blow, the boycott tactic provided a means for an affective response to the condemnation of apartheid by allowing the assertion of the existence of an emotional and moral community. The structure of the protest movement provided many different ways to be involved and form alliances and allegiances as part of this community. These two factors – the many ways to assert campaign involvement and the effectiveness of the boycott tactic as a means to assert moral communion – gave the campaign a vague and general, rather than an elaborate and specific, organizational schemata that was fundamental to its broad-based support.

This affective and emotional component of political protest and the associated cultural activities is seldom recognized in the analyses of social movements, yet movement participants often speak of the emotion, the elation and the transcendent moments and character of mass action protests. For instance, the analysis of social movements by McAdam, McCarthy and Zald, although an attempt to bridge the theoretical and intellectual gaps between European and North American analyses, remains focused on value-rational and resource mobilization issues.[18] These analyses prioritize structural questions such as access to public sector agendas or constructing meaning through media use. A significant shift in the literature may be seen in analyses focussed on individual motivations within the social movements, as well as to the cultural collectivities that are those movements.[19] Developing this, Soule has argued that the situational factors that encourage individuals to take political action may also be seen to impel collective actions.[20]

The focus on value-rationality and resource mobilization directs attention away from the equally important issue of the bonds and relationships developed by and between members of those new social movements (NSMs). These questions centre on the ways in which the emotional relationships between parties to the anti-apartheid struggle (campaigners in Aotearoa New Zealand, elsewhere in the world, and black South Africans) construct and are constructed by the interplay of political connections. Affective relationships are explored in Herman Schmalenbach's early twentieth-century work on non-institutional, expressive and elective communities, which he calls Bünde.[21] The analysis of Bünde organization is not restricted to formal issues of group structure and dynamics, but includes factors associated with identity, identification, belonging and solidarity that can be expressed through group character. This usefulness is enhanced by Schmalenbach's invocation of Bünde as a third force or form of grouping opposed to community (inspired by tradition) and society (inspired by rationality), and driven and inspired by instinctiveness and sentimentality. In this sense, a Bünd is derived from, and produces, shared affective relations.

Any social movement where mass mobilization is a primary or significant campaign tactic cannot be understood as an undifferentiated mass. Motivations for participation in activist events are diverse, and although a sense of communion may be shared with all others in the movement, for practical purposes the communion is with an immediate, often contiguous, group of people. These immediate groups need not have existed before the event, and indeed may only exist for the event and on the day: the practical reality of mass protest is that there are faces, places, settings or groups that an individual may see only at the regular protest meeting place. They may be recognized and acknowledged but not seen anywhere else, or if they are seen they may well not be recognized because they are out of place or out of costume. The movement should therefore be seen as an assortment and alliance of smaller groups.

Bünde, as a third force, move beyond both the tradition-rationality dichotomy underpinning Weberian influenced analyses and the utopian-scientific dichotomy in crudely mechanistic Marxist interpretation. Neither of these dichotomies comfortably incorporates affectivity as a basis for social relations. For many in Aotearoa New Zealand in 1981 it was not a rational choice to gather in the city's main street early on a Saturday afternoon, dressed in protective clothing, link arms with neighbours and march off to confront riot police – simply because 30 men were chasing an oval ball around a park somewhere else in the country. This analysis based in emotion, mood and affect also recognizes that for many, the experience of protest and social movement practice is out of step with usual activities: it may even be a liminal experience where the usual rules of rational social relations are to be set aside in favour of heightened and passionate interactions with strangers.[22] Unlike liminal phases in rites of passage, these experiences were intermittent and recurrent as well as interspersed with the daily norms of work and domestic life. Whereas rites of passage end with a restoration of the established order, in this case there was little sense at the time that reintegration could occur or would be the nature of the social relations into which protesters might be reintegrated. Whatever the post-tour social order would be, many hoped at the time it would not and could not be the same as the pre-tour order.[23] Turner's notion of communitas is therefore a useful mechanism through which to understand the emotional experiences of protest day.

The nature of the mass protest experience is that, in the giant movement of bodies, individuals may be, and often are, separated from their usual social circle. The practical effect of that separation, depending on the nature of the demonstration and the intensity of confrontation, is that those new individuals with whom the protester is standing, walking or sitting may be temporarily incorporated into a new protective circle. The feeling of safety and trust may not be the same, but it may be tentatively restored. In situations where the confrontation became intense and where protesters risked both physical and psychological harm, the norm was for people to watch out for those around them, even if they were (outside of the demonstration) strangers. At the most intense times, the communion for the day was between those who happened to be standing next to each other. In those moments trust was given and taken, almost implicitly, and might have been little more than linking arms. This faith in one's fellow protester was part of the affective relationship; it was implicit and assumed because of where in the protest group the individuals were. Bünde, as emotional communities, allow for this kind of incorporation of strangers because the event was riddled with signs that helped participants assume identity, identification, belonging and solidarity.

Conceiving the anti-tour campaign as Bünde allows for four significant conclusions. First, it allows for the campaign to be seen as a coalition of smaller groups, not only in terms of the broad organizing groups nationwide, but also in terms of the regular mass action demonstrations. Second, as emotional communities accentuating affective relations, they do not presume a rational organizational basis or that members act in a way that might be considered 'rational' by prevailing epistemological or ontological codes. Third, the approach allows for recurrent and repetitive liminal experiences interspersed by periods of apparent normality but with uncertainty (mitigated by hope) about the terms of reincorporation. Finally, Bünde are flexible enough to allow for contingent and circumstantial membership among individuals. Bünde is a concept that allows for a specific way that people involved in the anti-tour campaign connected with each other, with politics and with the underlying social order. Bünde have an elective membership that participates on the basis of a set of strongly held values and totemic symbols, a shared sense of belonging, and with a tendency to charismatic group leadership. Bünde are most potent in the context of a perceived breakdown of organic ties of community and increasing social instrumentalism meaning that they can be seen as a basis for re-communalization with elective membership, rather than membership derived from class, gender, ethnicity or other structural characteristic. A time of hegemonic dissolution is therefore ideally suited to the formation of Bünde.

These characteristics point to the limitations as well as the strengths of this model as a means to understand issue-based campaign groups. In the case of the anti-tour campaign, HART had developed a national strategy of stretching police and state resources in an effort to make the tour unmanageable, and in doing so force its cancellation. HART had also decided that it was not the best organization to front the campaign so it involved itself in local anti-tour coalitions such as, in Palmerston North, MAST (Manawatu Against the Springbok Tour), which drew on a broad collection of groups and individuals, had a strong church base, and was fronted by the local Catholic Bishop. Although HART had a national strategy, each local group developed its own approach – but this remained organized around a common set of 'values and totemic symbols' such as social justice, opposition to contact with South Africa, revilement of apartheid and condemnation of the New Zealand Government's perceived complicity in apartheid.

The model's tendency to charismatic leadership is less convincing. There was a broad grouping of nationally identified leaders among whom there were significant differences. These differences at times became open hostility between the positions adopted by those, in some individual cases charismatic, leaders: fractions or tendencies within the campaign may therefore be seen as having charismatic leadership. Charismatic leadership of the movement as a whole might be seen in the moral authority and leadership derived from the South African/Azanian liberation movements – but distance and the mythic embellishments of many of those individuals (most notably Mandela and Biko) make them more totemic than charismatic leaders.

A Bünd requires some form of centrality, and as an organizational form uses a charismatic mode of governance to which members submit. This is not submission to a charismatic (individual) leader but commitment to a group and the values espoused by that group. The diffuse and diverse anti-tour campaign groups may be seen as this type of organizational form: supporters and members could commit to the group and its values in many different ways. Coalitions recognized this and several, mainly those in the largest centres, organized demonstrators into squads prepared to go to different lengths during the action planned for the day, or on occasion 'family days'. The 'organization' lacked a formal national centre (although HART and various sectors – students, trade unionists and others – did organize national strategies and tactics) meaning that the central organization for most was provided by the local anti-tour coalition group.

The key element of Bünde for this analysis is that they differ from *gemeinschaft*[24] in being elective – consciously chosen – rather than having an unconscious taken-for-granted community membership. This difference is significant in that Schmalenbach argues, against Weber, that feeling is not derived from either unconscious or irrational motivations.[25] It is a consciousness that derives not from the simply rational or irrational, but from the affectual. This points to the in-between-ness of the organizational form where the choice to join a Bünd-type group makes the decision of communion closer to *gesellschaft*[26] and conduct of Bünde become closer to *gemeinschaft*. As a result, the affective associations of Bünde are reliant on regular and proximate relations with others. In the perceived state of siege that was the time of the tour, these regular and proximate relations (based on regular meetings and protests, often several times a week) further intensified those affective associations.

In analysing the anti-tour campaign as a collection of Bünde, it is useful to pay closer attention to the similarity between Bünde and Turner's notion of communitas. During the liminal phase of a rite of passage communitas is an affectual and experiential condition of togetherness that may become autotelic: that is, they become goals in themselves. Even those that do not become fully autotelic may include some autotelic aspects, and there is likely to be conflation of awareness of the group and the individual leading to a loss of ego. Related to this is an increasingly narrow awareness of fewer stimuli as well as an increasingly subjective sense of control accompanied by coherent demands for action.[27] The anti-tour objective became, for many people, their *raison d'être* during those 56 days that the Springboks were in the country: the tour dominated discussions in the national media and tended to shape interactions with all around. There are stories of ended friendships, family rifts and tension beyond all comprehension in most if not all work places.[28] These moments of heightened emotional engagement are synonymous with Bünde's expressive organization and form of governance.

Despite the usefulness of the notion of Bünde to developing an understanding of the anti-tour campaign as a confederation of affective groups, it does not in itself adequately explain the emotional aspects of the campaign or the subtlety and complexity of the emotional ties it built. They have explanatory power if Bünde are seen as part of a broader altruistic NSM, and the anti-tour campaign in all its diversity can be seen as politically altruistic, understood as

> a form of behaviour based on acts performed by a group and/or on behalf of a group, and not aimed to meet individual interests; it is directed at a political goal of social change or the redefinition of power relations; and individuals involved in this type of social change do not stand to benefit directly from the success deriving from the accomplishment of those goals.[29]

This sense of political altruism (with *directly* as the operative word) allowed the anti-tour movement to become powerful and to incorporate many: the participants could 'act collectively with a clear political aim, and their actions [were] pursued to the benefit of other people'.[30] The focus was clear. Apartheid presented a morally unambiguous issue to New Zealanders – those who actively or openly supported apartheid in official or public debates were few and usually linked to the extreme right, as opposed to those who accepted it as the least worst option (or as an alternative to 'tribalism'). Furthermore, in terms of the politics of 'race' it was distant enough both geographically and in terms of dominant understandings of New Zealand's colonial politics to stimulate indignation. Finally, the importance of rugby to white South Africa provided a focal point and leverage. Crucially, it was the question of distance and indignation that made the movement altruistic in its generality but not necessarily in its constituent parts – for some participants who keenly felt their colonized status there is little doubt that the struggles were one and the same. Distance and indignation as the fundamental bases of the altruism of the campaign along with New Zealand's powerful myths of nationhood, especially the myth of exemplary race relations, are the principal reasons why the debate within the movement in 1982 over a proposed shift in focus to 'domestic racism' was so intense and disruptive.

The centrality of the boycott

The key tenet of all those involved in the anti-tour campaign was the veracity and integrity of the boycott tactic. It was the campaign's *only* embracing site of agreement amid difference over the nature and form of its various identity politics. It transcended differences over the relationships between apartheid and racism in Aotearoa New Zealand, over organization of the anti-tour campaigning groups, over the socio-cultural significance of rugby, over the tactics of direct action versus mass passive protest, and many other distinctions. As such, adherence to the boycott tactic provided an embracing basis on which to build a sense of connection with others opposing apartheid sport leading to a strong sense of oppositional alliance and oppositional politics. It gave a basis for anti-tour action and as such was the philosophical justification of the Bünde as morally elect. This leads to the question of the meaning of the boycott, and the affective affinities it elicited.

The demand for the total isolation of South Africa produced four sets of political identification or affinity. First, there were affinities with black South Africans; second with an international anti-apartheid movement; third, with Aotearoa New Zealand's indigenous and other colonized subaltern although the focus on rugby union extended this to create a related set of gendered associations; and finally with a broader anti-racist political outlook. In the first instance, the boycott demand was raised by all the liberation movements – groups that were seen as the legitimate voice of black South Africans. The only notable black leaders not advocating the boycott strategy were most closely associated with the 'homelands' policy at the core of apartheid praxis during and after the 1970s – and as such they were seen to have little if any legitimacy. In acting in support of a comprehensive boycott, New Zealand's anti-apartheid activists asserted affinity with black South Africans through accepting the demands of their legitimate representatives. This may be seen as a significant moral blow against the apartheid regime and its allies, who in New Zealand included most of the conservative political leadership.

In the second instance, affinity with, and membership of, an international anti-apartheid movement was an assertion of a particular form of moral power that transcends national barriers. For instance, New Zealand anti-tour activists were aware of the protests against the Springbok's three games in the USA during the return leg of their journey from New Zealand to South Africa. Whereas the significance in South Africa of those games was minimal in comparison to the New Zealand games, the fact of the protests in both countries and the intensity of the New Zealand protests, allowed an affinity with anti-apartheid activists in the USA. In addition, that New York anti-apartheid activists picketed the New Zealand mission to the United Nations every time a tour match was played in New Zealand showed that the solidarity flowed both ways.[31] Furthermore, anti-apartheid activists were well informed about the international history and nature of the movement and, given the number of times they were discussed informally at HART meetings, seemed well aware of the British campaigns in 1969 and 1970, and the Australian anti-Springbok protests of 1971. Activists seemed very aware of not only international solidarity between Aotearoa New Zealand and South Africa, but also third party links. It was clear from formal and informal discussions at HART National Council and General Meetings that the organization was strongly internationalist in outlook, and placed great emphasis on the United Nations Centre Against Apartheid and the links that it facilitated.[32]

The identification with Aotearoa New Zealand's subaltern is the most complex element of the moral economy of the anti-tour campaign. This complexity meant that no single anti-tour campaigner could claim a simple and non-problematic relationship with all of Aotearoa New Zealand's subaltern. The most unproblematic were Maori able to claim an affinity and identification with black South Africans through strategic essentialism on the basis of a common colonized status – but even that is layered by relations of class, gender and sexuality.[33] It may be argued that Pakeha (New Zealanders of European descent) campaigners gained most from the campaign's affinity assertions. Pakeha activists were able to claim a relationship with black South Africans as well as Maori, through support of their campaigns for justice. They were not able to claim identifications based on 'race' or on the basis of a mutually recognized status as colonized, as indigenous, as *tangata whenua* ('people of the land'). Amongst many Maori anti-tour activists this common colonized status was forcefully asserted, although some recognized the weaknesses of strategic essentialism as the sole strategy in a colony of settlement. Witness, for instance, Ripeka Evans' strategic universalist statement that work within the anti-tour campaign was an important way to reach out to potentially sympathetic Pakeha, identified as the 'whites who would care about our brothers and sisters in Azania [and who] would be the ones who would have the most potential to care about our struggles'.[34] The complexity of these relationships is linked to the fluidity of identity meaning that the social configuration of political action is determined by the specific characteristics of the issue. This suggests that the affectivities and moral economy of the anti-tour campaign exist only in that context and for that issue. This specificity then links to a set of issues arising out of the fourth set of identifications.

Finally, the association that asserted adherence to a broader anti-racist outlook was a significant element of anti-tour positions. The significance of anti-apartheid politics in this broader anti-racist outlook seemed borne out when it was revealed that members of the American National Socialist (Nazi) Party would assign 100 of its members to guard the Springboks during their match in Chicago in September 1981.[35] A common charge levelled at anti-tour campaigners was that the focus on South Africa was improper and unfair. Favourite 'straw-countries' included Russia (it was almost never referred to as the USSR), and the rest of black Africa. Anti-tour campaigners were also regularly accused of making 'race' an issue in rugby – to which they usually responded that it was the South African government and not the anti-apartheid movement that was making 'race' an issue. For anti-tour campaigners, linkages with other anti-racist activists from Maori communities, Australian Aboriginal, and other first nations was an important assertion of affinity and identification.

The terms of that identification with first nations reveal a significant weakness resulting from the strength of the anti-tour campaign. The general schemata (the many means of campaign involvement, and the boycott tactic as the basis of moral communion) underpinning the anti-tour movement meant that there was no agreed understanding of the specific colonial characteristics of apartheid and its difference from other colonial settings. This deficiency became significant in the post-tour debates about what was termed 'domestic racism' as emotions ran high over the demand to shift the campaign's focus to

Aotearoa New Zealand's continuing history of the colonization of Maori. The tensions and intensities of the debate were primarily produced by the schism between many anti-tour activists' strong affective identification with both indigenous peoples and fellow anti-racist activists, the pervasive grip of New Zealand's all-one-people-best-race-relations-in-the-world national iconic myth, and a tactical sense that the anti-apartheid movement was an important part of a broader anti-imperialist movement that should not be diverted. These tensions were produced by the relatively low level of conceptual analysis in both the anti-tour campaign and the anti-apartheid movement: this was a central element of its ability to keep its broad support base. There is a clear similarity between the anti-apartheid movement in Aotearoa New Zealand and the German anti-racism movement analysed by Koopmans, both of which relied not on one overarching frame of reference, but on several and many selective frames linking existing social networks and actors with some level of integration to provide a collective and common focus. The success of the movements relied on vague and general frames or schemata rather than one that was elaborate and specific.[36] The very strength of the movement lay in its ability to clearly identify an enemy – apartheid – and a cause – its destruction. For the anti-tour campaign the attribution of cause and blame to both the New Zealand government and, to a lesser extent, the NZRFU was a basic element in the success of the movement. As Richards has argued, the success of HART, and with it anti-apartheid politics in Aotearoa New Zealand, lay in 'focus, pragmatism, determination and relevance. We concentrated on one issue, and did not allow ourselves to become distracted.'[37] These characteristics of success made those post-tour debates the difficulty they were.

This tactical and strategic clarity and focus was not and could not be matched by rigid and detailed political analysis of South Africa or apartheid if the movement was to retain broad support and unity. The New Zealand anti-apartheid movement had never reached an agreement on the particular form of South Africa's colonial relationships and generally organized loosely around the terms of the Freedom Charter. This apparent adherence to the African National Congress' position should not be overstated: HART was the only major international anti-apartheid support organization that refused to take a position on either side of the ANC-Africanist split. HART did not formally support any one of South Africa's liberation movements (ANC, Pan-Africanist Congress of Azania, Black Consciousness Movement of Azania, or any of the other groups). As a consequence, apartheid was seen by many as a peculiarly South African form of prejudice allied to state power. This reluctance to analyse South African colonialism was a significant factor in the intensity of the strategic debates in 1982 just as it was in the ability of the movement in 1981 to retain broad support. This broad anti-racist identification combined with the affinities with, and myth-challenging demands of, Aotearoa New Zealand's subaltern prevented a shift in focus from apartheid to locally focussed anti-racist or anti-colonial activism. The unity of the anti-tour movement had limited cachet beyond that specific issue: a new moral economy was needed.

That the New Zealand anti-apartheid movement supported the demands of black South Africans meant that the boycott tactic was never publicly questioned. Its acceptance was fundamental to anti-apartheid and anti-tour politics; the nature of the official and public debate in Aotearoa New Zealand meant that to be anti-tour on anti-apartheid grounds by necessity required the acceptance of the legitimacy of the boycott strategy. In accordance with the liberation movements' political programmes, ostracism of the apartheid government was the key objective. This affinity-based tactic gave anti-tour campaigners the right to claim morality as theirs in that they stood for justice and freedom from oppression. There was an emotional and affective satisfaction in supporting the demands of the oppressed to totally isolate apartheid while striking a blow at the confidence of the apartheid regime. Ironically, the protesters' occupation of Hamilton's Rugby Park on 25 July, preventing the playing of the second game of the tour, appears to have had more of an effect in South Africa than any other aspect of the campaign against the tour. Here black and white South Africans saw the range of New Zealanders that stood against them. White South Africans speak of shock and a disturbing realization that their opponents were not the wild subversives and *skollies* (hoodlums) that they had been told were protesting, but a broad cross-section of New Zealanders. Springbok tourist Rob Louw later wrote that as a reserve for the cancelled Hamilton match he

> could see the different faces among the demonstrators. At one stage I noticed a communist banner and a religious banner side by side. Amongst the demonstrators were anarchist trouble makers who knew and cared very little about South Africa. There were also highly principled people who believed that it was right to stop the tour at any cost. Together they made a highly formidable force.[38]

Louw's assessment, written during the apartheid era, stands at odds with the received views in white South Africa of the protests as led, initiated and peopled by *skollies*, and unsettles prevailing white South African views. In South Africa, the sight of New Zealanders protesting en masse against a Springbok rugby tour was perhaps even more unsettling than it was in Aotearoa New Zealand.

The New Zealand anti-tour campaign was not successful in its primary objective, which was to stop the tour and thereby have a direct effect on South African confidence and the security of apartheid. The campaign did not immediately deprive apartheid of one of its major cultural allies: New Zealand rugby. The anti-apartheid movement does appear to have been successful in the secondary objectives of demands for sanctions or boycotts, which is to show that the sender has seized the moral high ground. It was also successful in the tertiary objectives of boycott and sanction demands, the deflection of domestic and international criticism and in the assertion of both domestic and international leadership. The political credibility accruing to the people of Aotearoa New Zealand as a consequence of the campaign in 1981 was significant. In 1995, Nelson Mandela commented on the significance of the 1981 anti-tour campaign and the credibility and status that New Zealand's anti-apartheid movement secured as a consequence.[39]

Conclusion

A crucial strength of the anti-tour campaign was that the issues it was confronting and the way that it addressed them had many resonances with the New Zealand cultural order. Between them, Bünde and boycotts blended diverse and often contradictory affinities and identities into a single campaign with a single focus defined by the acceptance of the boycott of South Africa. This focus was able to build a powerful campaign based on political affinity with black South Africa by drawing on the concerns accentuated by identity politics in Aotearoa New Zealand, but the nature of those identities meant that the alliances were likely only ever to be tactical and temporary. The essential mechanism building this link was the significance of rugby to South Africa that made the boycott tactic useful and relevant in Aotearoa New Zealand. Rugby contact with New Zealand was South Africa's single most valued international sporting relationship. This symbolic significance meant that the New Zealand protest movement's focus on the sports boycott could strike a great cultural blow at white South African confidence. This significance also produced a particularly rich vein of symbolic, emotional and affective responses from within the protest movement that elevated the movement's view of its own place in the moral economy of protest and demands for freedom and justice in South Africa, and at home. The significance of the decision by the New Zealand anti-apartheid movement was that it had recognized that in both South African and New Zealand terms, rugby was much more than a game.

Notes

[1] I am grateful to Jim McKay and Murray Phillips for comments on earlier versions of this essay, to the participants in the Crossing Boundaries: Boycotts, Sport and Political Goals panel at the 'To Remember is To Resist' conference in Toronto, May 2008, and especially to Roy McCree for his commentary in that session. They bear no responsibilities for any remaining shortcomings.

[2] See Chapple, *1981: The Tour*; Morris, *With All Our Strength*; and Walker and Beach, *56 Days*.

[3] The Gleneagles Agreement on Sporting Contacts with South Africa, 1977, Commonwealth Heads of Government Meeting, Gleneagles, Scotland, June 1977, http://www.thecommonwealth.org/files/211690/FileName/GleneaglesAgreement.pdf.

[4] New Zealand Police, *Operation Rugby*, Appendix W. For an analysis of one violent response to the 3 July protests, see MacLean, 'Competing Fandoms'.

[5] New Zealand Police, *Operation Rugby*, 25.

[6] 1973 International Convention on the Suppression and Punishment of the Crime of Apartheid, United Nations General Assembly 30 November 1973.

[7] Daoudi and Dajani, *Economic Sanctions*, 7.

[8] Barber. 'Economic Sanctions'.

[9] Barber and Spicer, 'Sanctions Against South Africa'; Hayes, *Economic Effects*; and Jenkins, *Effects of Sanctions*.

[10] Houlihan, *Sport and International Politics*.

[11] Gerrit Viljoen, South African Minister of Sport, 1983, cited in Booth, *The Race Game*, 145.

[12] Hayes, *Economic Effects of Sanctions*.

[13] This Code of Conduct sought to give teeth to the 1977 Gleneagles Agreement, and was the direct consequence of the New Zealand Government's refusal to intervene in the 1981 tour. The text may be found in Templeton, *Human Rights*, 299–301.

[14] Although as Jenkins, *Effects of Sanctions* shows, this is not always so.

[15] Ramsamy, *Apartheid*, especially 61–83.

[16] Richards, *Dancing on Our Bones*; and Black and Nauright, *Rugby*.

[17] Grundlingh, Odendaal and Spies, *Beyond the Tryline*; and Black and Nauright, *Rugby*.

[18] McAdam, McCarthy and Zald, *Comparative Perspectives*.

[19] Stryker, Owens and White, *Self, Identity*; and Guigni and Passy, *Political Altruism?*

[20] Soule, 'Situational Effects'.

[21] Hetherington, *Expressions of Identity*, 83–100. Note on spelling: Bünd is singular, Bünde are plural.

[22] Turner, *The Ritual Process*, 80–119.

[23] The political significance of hope is explored in Zournazi, *Hope*.

[24] Derived from the work of Ferdinand Tönnies, *gemeinschaft*, often understood as community, is a form of association between individuals shaped by traditional social rules, greater responsibility to the collective than the individual or self, and that carries with it a sense of involuntary membership.

[25] Schmalenbach 'Communion'.

[26] Derived from the work of Ferdinand Tönnies, *gesellschaft*, often understood as society, is a form of association between individuals shaped by modern, rational, impersonal relations, greater responsibility to the self than the collective, and a sense of an active selection of membership.

[27] Turner, 'Frame, Flow and Reflection'; Turner, *The Ritual Process*, especially 94–130.

[28] King and Phillips, 'A Social Analysis', especially 12–14.

[29] Passy, 'Political Altruism', 6,

[30] Ibid., 7.

[31] *The Dominion* (Wellington), August 16, 1981.

[32] Richards makes recurring references to international work throughout *Dancing on Our Bones* as important from the outset for HART, see 41–2. See also Walker and Beech, 56 Days, 80–1.

[33] Strategic universalism is 'a political design and standpoint which recognises human differences but elects to try to find bases for coalition in organising for remedies to problems seen to impact on people across human differences'. It is not oppositional to tactical essentialism where there may be a need to organize around a central antagonism, such as 'race' or ethnicity. The anti-tour campaign relied on both strategic universalism and tactical essentialism in building itself, as will be discussed below in an assessment of the boycott tactic. Alleyne, *Radicals Against Race*, 176–7.

[34] Evans, 'The Maori Strategy', 16.

[35] *The Dominion* (Wellington), September 10, 1981.

[36] Koopmans, 'Better Off Doing Good'.

[37] Richards, *Dancing On Our Bones*, 245.

[38] Louw with Cameron-Dow, *For the Love of Rugby*, 90.

[39] *New Zealand Herald*, November 14, 1995.

References

Alleyne, Brian W. *Radicals Against Race: Black Activism and Cultural Politics*. Oxford: Berg, 2002.

Barber, James. 'Economic Sanctions as a Policy Instrument'. *International Affairs* 55 (1979): 367–84.

Barber, James, and Michael Spicer. 'Sanctions Against South Africa – Options for the West'. *International Affairs* 55 (1979): 385–401.

Black, David, and John Nauright. *Rugby and the South African Nation*. Manchester: Manchester University Press, 1998.

Booth, Douglas. *The Race Game: Sport and Politics in South Africa*. London: Frank Cass, 1998.

Chapple, Geoff. *1981: The Tour*. Wellington: A.H. & A.W. Reed, 1984.

Daoudi, M.S., and M.S. Dajani. *Economic Sanctions: Ideals and Experience*. London: Routledge & Kegan Paul, 1983.

Evans, Rebecca. 'The Maori Strategy'. *Broadsheet* (October 1982): 16.

Grundlingh, Albert, André Odendaal, and Burridge Spies. *Beyond the Tryline: Rugby and South African Society*. Johannesburg: Ravan Press, 1995.

Guigni, Marco and Florence Passy, eds. *Political Altruism? Solidarity Movements in International Perspective*. Lanham, MD: Rowan and Littlefield, 2001.

Hayes, J.P. *Economic Effects of Sanctions of Southern Africa*. Aldershot: Gower; London: Trade Policy Institute, 1987.

Hetherington, Kevin. *Expressions of Identity: Space, Performance, Politics*. London: Sage, 1998.

Houlihan, Barrie. *Sport and International Politics*. Hemel Hempstead: Harvester Wheatsheaf, 1994.

Jenkins, Carolyn. *The Effects of Sanctions on Formal Sector Employment in South Africa*. Brighton: Institute of Development Studies, University of Sussex, 1993.

King, Peter, and Jock Phillips. 'A Social Analysis of the Springbok Tour Protesters'. In *Counting the Cost: The 1981 Springbok Tour in Wellington*, edited by David Mackay, Malcolm McKinnon, Peter McPhee, and Jock Phillips, 3–14. Wellington: Victoria University History Department, Occasional Paper No.1, 1982.

Koopmans, Ruud. 'Better Off Doing Good: Why Antiracism Must Mean Different Things to Different Groups'. In *Political Altruism? Solidarity Movements in International Perspective*, edited by Marco Guigni and Florence Passy, 111–31. Lanham, MD: Rowan and Littlefield, 2001.

Louw, Rob, and with John Cameron-Dow. *For the Love of Rugby*. Melville: Hans Strydom Publishers, 1987.

MacLean, Malcolm. 'Competing Fandoms and Local Responses to Apartheid Sport: Spatialized Clashes in the Affective Economies of Aotearoa/New Zealand during the 1981 Springbok Rugby Tour'. In *Sport and Postcolonialism*, edited by John Bale and Mike Cronin, 57–72. Oxford: Berg, 2003.

McAdam, Doug, John D. McCarthy and Mayer N. Zald, eds. *Comparative Perspectives on Social Movements: Political Opportunities, Mobilising Structures, and Cultural Framings*. Cambridge: Cambridge University Press, 1996.

Morris, Juliet. *With All Our Strength: An Account of the Anti-Tour Movement in Christchurch, 1981*. Christchurch: Black Cat, 1982.

New Zealand Police. *Operation Rugby, 19 July–13 September 1981*. Wellington: New Zealand Police, February 1982.

Passy, Florence. 'Political Altruism and the Solidarity Movement: An Introduction'. In *Political Altruism? Solidarity Movements in International Perspective*, edited by Marco Guigni and Florence Passy, 3–25. Lanham: Rowan and Littlefield, 2001.

Ramsamy, Sam. *Apartheid: The Real Hurdle. Sport in South Africa and the International Boycott*. London: International Defence and Aid Fund for Southern Africa, 1982.

Richards, Trevor. *Dancing on Our Bones: New Zealand, South Africa and Racism*. Wellington: Bridget Williams Books, 1999.

Schmalenbach, Herman. 'Communion – a Sociological Category'. In *On Society and Experience*, ed and trans. Günther Lüschen and Gregory Stone, 64–125. Chicago, IL: University of Chicago Press, 1977.

Soule, Sarah A. 'Situational Effects on Political Altruism: The Student Divestment Movement in the United States'. In *Political Altruism? Solidarity Movements in International Perspective*, edited by Marco Guigni and Florence Passy, 161–76. Lanham, MD: Rowan and Littlefield, 2001.

Stryker, Sheldon, Timothy J. Owens and Robert W. White, eds. *Self, Identity and Social Movements*. Minneapolis, MN: Minnesota University Press, 2000.

Templeton, Malcolm. *Human Rights and Sporting Contacts; New Zealand Attitudes to Race Relations in South Africa, 1921–1994*. Auckland: Auckland University Press, 1998.

Turner, Victor. *The Ritual Process: Structure and Anti-structure*. Harmondsworth: Penguin, 1974.

Turner, Victor. 'Frame, Flow and Reflection: Ritual Drama as Public Liminality'. In *Performance in Postmodern Culture*, edited by M. Benamou and C. Caramello, 35–55. Madison, WI: University of Wisconsin-Milwaukee/Coda Press, 1977.

Walker, Geoff and Peter Beach, eds. *56 Days: A History of the Anti-Tour Movement in Wellington*. Wellington: COST, n.d.

Zournazi, Mary. *Hope: New Philosophies for Change*. London: Lawrence and Wishart, 2002.

It's not just sport: Delhi and the Olympic torch relay[1]

Boria Majumdar[a] and Nalin Mehta[b]

[a]Lancashire Business School, University of Central Lancashire, UK; [b]Department of Politics, La Trobe University, Victoria, Australia

This essay studies the 2008 Tibetan protests in Delhi over the Olympic torch relay as a case study to understand the political and social symbolism attached to the rituals of the Olympic relay. It analyses the impact of the political tightrope walked by the Government of India as it sought to balance its diplomatic priorities, in pursuing the recent thaw in Sino-Indian relations, with the imperatives of a democratic public culture. India has been host to the Dalai Lama since the 1950s and the Beijing Olympics provided the trigger for a renewed focus on the Tibetan question. The Delhi leg of the Olympic flame relay emerged as an important cog in the global chain of pro-Tibetan protests that the Games ignited. This essay studies the local manifestations of the Delhi protests, the organization and mechanism of the agitation, the counter-measures adopted by the state, the national and international implications of the protests and its broader meaning for the institution of the flame relay itself.

This looks more like a warzone and not something to do with sports or the Olympics. The Olympic movement is supposed to be about the people.

NDTV reporter covering Delhi Flame Relay[2]

We could have provided you with a more 'spectacular' protest today if the security arrangements were a little more relaxed than 17,000 police personnel, including commandos, on their toes. China has once again proved that with its military power it can even turn the central heart of the capital of a free and democratic country like India into a military zone, throw the city's roads into gridlock. Even if for a few hours.

Tenzin Tsundue, Tibetan activist and writer[3]

Seven levels of security checkpoints, 21,000 security personnel, the heart of India's capital almost at a standstill, an attempt to storm the Le Meridian – a hotel turned into a fortress and the site where the Olympic torch was kept since its arrival from Islamabad at 1.10 a.m. on the night of 16 April – and finally a series of peaceful, synchronized democratic protests by Tibetans and human rights groups from 8.00 a.m. in the morning across the country. The Indian leg of the Olympic torch relay was in all senses extraordinary. For the record, international legs of the Olympic torch relay have often been mired in controversy. While some say that the 2008 edition of the international torch relay has witnessed unprecedented turmoil the world over, Olympic history demonstrates otherwise. While the situation in Islamabad and Delhi was unusual, in that the relays weren't open to the public and only invitees were allowed to attend, this too was not without precedent.

The only other time that sections of the torch relay have been completely closed to the public was during the flame-lighting ceremony at ancient Olympia for the 1984 Los Angeles Games. Then, armed Greek troops had closed off the sanctuary, refusing entry to either the Greek public or hundreds of demonstrators who had vowed not to let the Americans have the flame. They were protesting the Los Angeles Olympic Organizing Committee's decision to sell the rights to be a torchbearer, a decision that many Greeks saw as an insult to Greek national sovereignty. The traditional public relay and key ceremonies in Greece, as John Macaloon points out, were cancelled. The Olympic priestess lit the flame in spite of death threats. The Americans took the flame out by helicopter to Athens airport and left immediately for the safe haven of their own shores.[4]

Such protests lay at the very core of what is widely understood as 'Olympism'. As the popular saying goes in Olympic academic circles, 'Take sports out of the Olympics and you still have the movement to fall back on'. While this is certainly an exaggeration, it is time to accept that the Olympics or the torch relay was never only about sportspeople. The relay is not restricted to countries that win the most number of medals or those that have the best sports facilities for its athletes. Rather, it is meant as a mechanism to include mass support in the poorest of countries, men and women who will hardly ever make it to an Olympic sports contest. That is why, traditionally, attendance at the Olympic torch relay is free. While Olympic sports competitions are prohibitively expensive, enthusiasts don't need tickets to attend the relay. For countries that can't dream of hosting the games in view of the escalating costs, the torch relay remains the second best alternative. It is this aspect of Olympism and the Olympic movement that makes the world's biggest sports spectacle relevant and real for us in India. The flame, unlike the torch, can never be commercialized and is arguably one of the most powerful modern peace symbols. The meanings attached to it belong neither to the IOC nor to local organizing committees. Rather, it has emerged as an enduring symbol of global harmony and mobilization, a fact evident on the streets of Delhi on 17 April 2008.

Before every summer games for the last 25 years, the Olympics have provided a forum for issues of international concern, the dispossessed and the marginalized using the glare of public spotlight to focus world attention on their causes. While Seoul highlighted the Korea crisis, Barcelona brought to light ethnic differences within Spanish society. Atlanta drew world attention to the race issue in the US and Sydney highlighted the Aboriginal crisis Down Under. When Cathy Freeman lit the flame at the Sydney Games in 2000 much more than a sporting ritual was performed. It had immense symbolism for the tensions at the heart of modern Australian society, more so when she later wrapped herself in the Aboriginal flag in full view of the world's cameras.

Similarly, when the Tibetans organized a parallel relay in Delhi on 17 April 2008, the Tibet crisis became the cynosure of international attention. In a country which has hosted the Dalai Lama since the 1950s, and which has remained embroiled in a border dispute with China for over five decades, the Olympic flame relay provided the trigger to focus attention on the Tibetan question as never before. This first part of this essay analyses the political response of the Indian state as it sought to balance its diplomatic priorities in pursuing the recent thaw in Sino-Indian relations with the imperatives of a vibrant and democratic public culture. The Delhi protests were an important component of the global chain of pro-Tibetan protests that the Games ignited, and the second part of this article uses ethnographic techniques to unpack the local manifestations of the Delhi protests, the organization and mechanism of the agitation, and the national and international implications of the protests. The form of the agitation was such that it necessitates, at least in part, a first-person account to bring out its full flavour and complexity. Historians had to become ethnographers and our journey into the heart of the agitation further extends our research into the Olympic movement in the sub-continent, while offering some important pointers towards the social meanings of the Olympic flame relay itself.

Delhi's diplomatic dilemma

Prior to the Indian leg of the torch relay, there was considerable debate on whether New Delhi would allow Tibetan protesters to carry on with their demonstrations. With the Left Front West Bengal and Kerala governments adopting a hardline approach towards such protests, the issue had assumed added significance. The Left Front government in West Bengal went so far as to ban Tibetan protests ahead of the torch's arrival in India.[5] At one level, this was simply a case of the Left's repeated support for positions taken by the Chinese Communist Party. With the Left also a crucial partner, at the time, in the Congress-led coalition government in Delhi, such an approach by a powerful partner in the alliance reduced the manoeuvring space for the Central government. But, at another level, the prospect of widely publicized Tibetan protests also created apprehensions in New Delhi about their diplomatic impact on ongoing boundary disputes with China. At the same time, the world's largest democracy could not be seen to be muffling dissent, even if this dissent was opposed by those who are advocating a closer strategic engagement with China.

Caught in a bind, the Congress, therefore, hedged its bets. On the one hand, the Congress government in Arunachal Pradesh followed its Left counterparts in West Bengal to ban Tibetan protests in Tawang, a key border district that is central to the boundary dispute with China and one which was invaded by Chinese troops in the 1962 Sino-Indian war. The Tawang Superintendent of Police imposed the punitive Section 144 of the Indian Penal code on his district to prevent rallies of any kind and then pointedly told reporters that this had been done on directions from the Central government. The Tawang ban came just four days after police personnel had been forced to fire tear gas shells at a 2,000-strong gathering of protesters in Tawang, home to a fifteenth-century monastery, the oldest and the most revered outside Tibet. The firing led to strong protests by lamas at the monastery and, reacting to news of a ban on further demonstrations, a local lama was quoted as saying, 'If this is true, it is a whiplash in general to the people of the Himalayan region and elsewhere'.[6]

The reportage of the unrest among thousands of Tibetan exiles, many of whom had been born and brought up in India after their parents migrated in the 1950s, was now emerging as a serious concern for internal security officials in New Delhi. This had assumed added urgency after some Tibetan protesters managed to break the heavy security cordon outside the Chinese embassy in New Delhi's diplomatic enclave of Chanakyapuri and scaled its walls to register their concerns. Two concerns played on their minds: It was one thing to ban protests in a remote outpost of India, quite another to ban protests *per se*, in the national capital, which would play host to the Olympic torch. Secondly, the government was acutely aware of the strategic conclusions that Beijing would draw from New Delhi's handling of the Tibetan protests.[7] So they decided on a two-pronged approach. The protests would go on elsewhere in India – in any case it would have been impossible to police a wider ban – but the protesters would not be allowed anywhere near the Olympic torch itself. Everyone, therefore, could save face.

Allowing the protests in Delhi and elsewhere also provided a subtle mechanism for protesting against the million square metres of Chinese occupation in the disputed Aksai Chin region[8] and China's reported illegal intrusions into Arunachal Pradesh and Sikkim.[9] It was New Delhi's way of remonstrating against the Chinese decision to call the Indian Ambassador, Nirupama Rao, at 2.00 a.m. in the morning in Beijing, threatening her with dire consequences over India's failure to check alleged Tibetan attacks on the Chinese embassy in New Delhi. It was a delicate balancing act: allow the Tibetans their fundamental right to protest in full public view but guard against a diplomatic incident by ensuring that the torch relay itself, guarded by Chinese commandoes, is not disrupted. This please-all strategy was not, however, one that endeared itself to those that advocated a hardline Indian response to China on the border talks. From their point of view any concession to Chinese opinion was a sign of weakness. *The Indian Express* summed up the views of New Delhi's foreign policy hawks a day after the unprecedented security arrangements for the torch relay:

> A day after the might of the Indian Republic was applied to ensure the safe passage of the Olympic torch through New Delhi, it is time for sober reflection. This over-reaction was incongruous with India's democratic credentials, and it has also put on India a striking handicap in bilateral relations … Of late, China has been moving the goalposts on border issues that had been taken to be settled … the repercussions will be felt in foreign policy. In these weeks, China has seen the ease with which it could have the Indian vice president's long scheduled meeting with the Dalai Lama cancelled – or compel India's envoy in Beijing to show up at the foreign office in the middle of the night. Tenor in foreign policy creates its own momentum. India will have to reckon with it.[10]

The diplomatic impact of New Delhi's double-edged response to the flame relay is open to question but one thing is certain; the price tag was the excessive security and the huge inconvenience caused to Delhi's residents on the day of the ritual, which left a bitter taste with many.

Policing the Tibetans

The police force is a state subject in India's federal structure of governance. Each of the 28 states has its own police force administered by the Home Ministries of individual elected state governments. Delhi, though, is different. Even though it is a full-fledged state with its own state government, by virtue of being the national capital its police force is administered directly by the Union Home Ministry, which is also responsible for all internal security duties across the country. Once the decision was taken to quarantine the Olympic torch from the Tibetan protestors the Ministry swung into action. It announced an unprecedented security clampdown for the torch relay, of the kind that Delhi witnesses once every year on Republic Day when the central parts of the city are sealed off completely to all traffic to facilitate the annual military parade to celebrate the Indian Republic. The Chinese Ambassador to India personally met the city police chief Y.S. Dadwal at the police headquarters, a total of 21,000 security personnel were specially deployed across the city, central paramilitary forces and commandoes were requisitioned, and the rally route was curtailed from the planned 9 km to 2.7 km. As a senior ministry official said, 'It will be like Republic Day. NSG commandoes are likely to take control of all the high-rises along the venue and keep a watch from the rooftops. The venue will be sealed from all sides.' Cameras, except for those with accredited journalists, were not to be allowed anywhere near the event and entry for spectators would only be by select invitation. In addition, several quick reaction teams were also formed to thwart self-immolation bids by protestors and nine companies of paramilitary forces were deployed around the Chinese embassy. *The Times of India* summed up the massive security build-up in a telling full-page banner headline: 'It's a fortress out there'.[11]

Despite this huge presence, on 15 April, a day before the torch arrived in Delhi, Tibetan protestors demonstrated their organizational skills by lighting a replica of the Olympic torch at an under-construction Metro station just a kilometre away from the Rashtrapati Bhawan (President's House) in central Delhi. They called it the

'Tibetan Independence Torch Relay'. In the heart of Delhi's most secure zone, a short walk away from Parliament and the Central Secretariat they came in quietly in auto-rickshaws, hiding their banners and flags under their clothes before suddenly unfurling them before thousands of armed policemen deployed for just such an eventuality. They wanted to walk towards India Gate – memorial to Indian war-dead – to hold a protest vigil but as the policemen tried to snuff out the Tibetan flame, the flames caught the clothes of a woman protestor. They were quickly put out and the protestors led away in police trucks but it had been a powerful demonstration of what could happen when the Olympic flame actually came to town.

Jittery now at the prospects, on the same day the Union Home Ministry convened a high level meeting to review the security arrangements. This was monitored at the highest levels of the government. National Security advisor M.K. Narayanan, whose duties include keeping track of the national nuclear arsenal, personally took stock of the security measures for the relay. At the meeting were Indian Olympic Association (IOA) officials, representatives from the Intelligence bureau, the Delhi Police and the Union Minister of State for Home, Shakeel Ahmad who told reporters, 'It is our responsibility [to ensure safe passage for the torch]'.[12]

One measure of how seriously the government was taking the relay was the fact that even the Delhi Metro was asked to close services to all stations in the vicinity of the torch for the day. The Olympic torch had now turned into an issue of national importance, diplomatic gamesmanship and civic inconvenience. As such, between 14–18 April it became the lead story on the front-page of virtually every national newspaper. All the Delhi-based national newspapers also had special pages devoted entirely to advise citizens on the torch relay route and how to avoid the resultant traffic congestions.[13] Even the UN advised all its staff in India to avoid any movement in the relay route due to safety reasons and to reschedule or postpone planned meetings in the area.[14]

A mini-Tibet in Delhi: following the agitators

It was an incredible experience. Following the Tibetan protesters from Gandhi's resting place at Rajghat to Jantar Mantar[15] in the scorching Delhi heat, trying to make sense of most of their slogans, was to go back into an older, idealistic world where agitations and public dissent of this kind still had meaning. It was to be reminded of the simple idealism of agitational politics, of the most basic principles of civil action, where the participants were aware that they were marginal but found power and agency in simply making themselves heard.

For us, the experience of the relay had begun on the night of 16 April when we watched Tenzing Tsundue, a noted activist and leader of the Free Tibet movement, on the 24-hour satellite news network *Times Now*.[16] Soon after the show, Tsundue, we were later informed, was dropped off at an unknown location with the police desperate to detain him. The *Times Now* driver, Amjad, who ferried him to his hideout and who was with us the following day, took us to the secret location at the stroke of dawn. It was cloak and dagger stuff – a trip that led us to a hideout where 200 or more Tibetans were busy planning an assault on the flame. A group of senior Tibetan leaders were in attendance and were keen to ensure that 17 April 2008 turned into a day of international impact for their cause. Knowing full well that the police would outnumber them, they were planning guerrilla attacks on the flame on its way out of the Meridian on Janpath Road and on its way to India Gate. That such meticulous planning resulted in little tangible gain in the end is a different matter altogether. The police clampdown on central Delhi put paid to all such plans but to be here was to see the cold determination of these protestors – the steely look in their eyes, the idealism in their venture, and the vociferous arguments over tactics. While these Tibetans were determined to make a mark and weren't averse to violence, others who had already made Jantar Mantar their home were single-minded in their determination in trying to keep things peaceful. For them non-violent protest was the way to capture world attention and hence the life-sized cut-outs of Mahatma Gandhi that were juxtaposed with those of the Dalai Lama at the forefront of most protest rallies.

For these and thousands of other Tibetans who had arrived in Delhi the night before, things got underway in the small hours of the morning of 17 April with an assembly at Rajghat. This was a giant venture that needed planning and coordination on a national scale – from the strategic to the mundane. When we reached Rajghat at 7.30 a.m., we saw groups of men and women bracing themselves for the day's events by writing out posters or painting placards. Some were busy packing pouches of water and food, while others, who had travelled thousands of miles to be part of the movement, were busy catching up on a quick hour's sleep. Young Tibetan girls and boys, mostly students in leading Delhi colleges, wrapped themselves in 'Free Tibet' flags and were busy distributing 'Free Tibet' T-shirts to anyone who wanted to join in. Members of the Tibetan Parliament-in Exile, key organizers of the rally, were busy putting final touches to preparations for the protest march. 'We wanted the Dalai Lama to be visible alongside Mahatma Gandhi for both are messiahs for global peace',[17] was their reasoned answer to our query on why most posters had the Tibetan leader sharing stage with the man who the Indian state calls the father of the nation.

Just as the clock struck 10.00 a.m., there arrived at Rajghat a slew of Hindu, Muslim and Sikh religious preachers for joint prayers in solidarity with Tibetans at Gandhi's Samadhi. It was surreal, a motley mix of preachers from varied religious backgrounds coming together to pray for a cause of real global significance. It was good event management to be sure but none but the most cold-hearted cynic could afford not to be moved by the solemnity of it all and fail to observe the fact that the global appeal of

Figure 1.   Scene from the torch relay in Delhi on 18 April 2008.

Figure 2.   While walking with the Tibetans in Delhi on 18 April 2008.

contemporary sport had made it possible. With the prayers over, the Tibetans lit their own parallel flame. This was different in shape to the Olympic torch and was more in the nature of a *diya* (traditional earthen lamp) that was subsequently placed inside a round frame. They had been told that only a 'non-official' torch of this kind would pass official muster. As chants of '*Karuna ki jyoti amar rahe*' (May the torch of tenderness live forever) and '*Shanti ki jyoti amar rahe*' (May the torch of peace live forever), shattered the silence, assembled leaders from all major religious groupings joined in carrying the flame out of Rajghat. This was the point at which the huge police contingent, men and women who did everything possible to cooperate until now, began to visibly look a tad jittery until the rally leaders assured them that the march would be kept peaceful. So powerful was the group dynamic that some security men too were caught up in the emotionalism of the moment, a couple of those standing nearest to the protestors with tears in their eyes.

Once out of Rajghat, the rally began its 4 km march to Jantar Mantar, the site that the Tibetans had made home for the day. Thousands of Tibetans from Varanasi, Mcleodgunj, Bangalore and Dharamshala had already assembled at Jantar Mantar the night before, carrying with them bare minimum supplies. The location was not unsurprising. Jantar Mantar after all is the permanent protestors' corner in Delhi. For years it has been the site where dispossessed and the marginalized of India come to present their woes before the national media, hoping for higher visibility with the powers that be. And so the Tibetans came, jostling for space in this parliament of the oppressed, alongside stalls set up by the Bhopal gas tragedy victims, the Vishwa Dalit Parishad (World Council of Dalits), the Foundation for Common Man: Justice for Natihari, and even the Group 4-Securicor Mazdoor Union asking for better wages.

But this was a day primarily for the Tibetans. As hundreds of specially deployed policemen watched from the sidelines and scores of reporters took notes, the entire panoply of anti-Chinese dissent was on display in a tent city that had sprung up virtually overnight on one of the side lines leading up to Jantar Mantar. At its entry point, someone had prominently placed a huge poster on the windshield of a parked car: 'Just raped in Tibet'. It summed up the mood and to enter the tent city was to enter a virtual marketplace of oppression. The centre-piece was a day-long funeral service to those who died at the hands of the Chinese conducted by specially imported monks. As their chants and gongs filled the air, the observer could see a whole range of stalls – representatives of the banned Falun Gong, posters showcasing the pictures of those dead and missing and pictures of torture and death at the hands of Chinese troops. The posters were telling: 'Shame on you China', 'Where are you UNO', and even one depicting the Chinese President as an incarnation of Dracula. Policemen and intelligence sleuths in plainclothes mingled with the protestors although none tried to intervene.

This was where the bulk of the protest groups took residence for most of the afternoon, once the 4 km distance from Rajghat had been covered, for a day-long ritual of songs, chants and slogans. With hundreds of local students joining hands, Jantar Mantar was turned into a mini-Tibet, the adjoining alleyways and streets leading up to the now virtually deserted Janpath Road, Connaught Place now choc-a-block with activists sporting 'Free Tibet' T-shirts and head bands. Their one-point demand: China must open its doors to envoys of the Dalai Lama. Their slogans shouted out in Hindi, mixed their animosity with China to chants of friendship with India: '*gali-gali mei shor hai, Hu Jintao hatyara hai*' (every street rings, Hu Jintao is a killer), '*azadi sab ko pyara hai*' (freedom is beloved by all), 'North Pole South Pole, *Bharat hamara saath do*' (India, support us).

How spontaneous was this agitation and what had gone into its planning? Our interviews with nearly 100 of the protestors provide a clear picture. One of the agitators had been arrested two weeks earlier for breaking into the Chinese embassy. His story summed up the story of this gathering. Born of Tibetan refugee parents in Mysore, Karnataka, he was a farmer who had been camping in Delhi for 45 days. He was a member of the Tibetan Youth Congress but he said that initially 'it all happened suddenly' once the Tibetans realized that they could use the Olympic torch to showcase their cause. He had come down to Delhi because 'it was the national capital' and it was important to magnify protests here.[18] The Tibetan protestors saw this is an unparalleled opportunity to put pressure on the Chinese government, using the oxygen of publicity, because for the national and international media, their story now had immediacy. This was also the argument given by Dhondup Dorji, Vice President of the Tibetan Youth Congress. Appearing on a special half-hour live programme called 'Torch of Protest' on 'Times Now', he argued that this was the first time that the electronic media had given support to their cause. 'Normally we have support from the print media only', he opined.[19] He had a point. On the same programme, television viewers saw two young Tibetan college students from Mumbai breaking from their prepared speeches to suddenly ask Dorji about how he will motivate the Tibetan youth after this event. The young questioners had been rustled to the live satellite link by the channel's reporters to show their national coverage of the protests but this was a spontaneous question, one that reflected the internal dilemmas of the Tibetan movement on how to sustain momentum. Sitting in the Delhi studio, Dorji answered on the live satellite link: 'Tibetan youth have a moral responsibility to keep up the struggle. We must dedicate our lives to Tibet.'[20] It was an extraordinary moment; it was like listening to an inner-party discussion forum. The Tibetan Youth Congress on that day had a national platform to reach out to its own cadres on national television and to disseminate internal messages that would normally have passed through the usual hierarchies of leadership. This was direct communication and it came at a time when protests had also simultaneously broken out in Bangalore, Mumbai, McLeodganj and Dharamsala.

By early afternoon, when the Tibetans had once again resumed their peaceful march after a gap of almost three hours, the scene of action had shifted to the stretch between Raisina Hill and India Gate, the venue for the official Olympic torch relay. This was when the cost of the protest to the ordinary Delhi commuter came home to us most forcefully. The five-minute drive from Jantar Mantar to India Gate turned into a 90-minute walk with the police having closed all access roads to vehicular traffic. As we pleaded with the first police access point on Copernicus Road, we could hear the desperate pleas of a middle-aged man whose mother-in-law had suffered an accident near Safdarjang but who was stuck on this side of town with the police clampdown. 'What do I do?' he pleaded, 'How do I get there? Will you let me through?' The policemen were sympathetic but there orders were clear. These roads were off-limits. 'Try another route', was the advice to the distraught man. As for us, we were by now late for the function, after having taking numerous diversions to reach the venue and, despite possessing all the necessary invites and IOA advisories, the policemen on duty had the same answer: 'Sorry, the road is now closed'. So we put on our best humble faces, protested about us being academics writing on the torch relay, one of us invited to be a torchbearer and finally dropped a thousand names before the wall of resistance reluctantly melted. We could still hear the man with the injured mother-in-law arguing his case with another group of police guards as we entered but there seemed little hope. We were entering on foot. With his car, he had no chance. A policeman was explaining a long circuitous alternative route to him as we crossed the barricade.

Even on foot, only a handful of select invitees were allowed inside and lined up across the entire relay route stretching for 2.7 km and manned by more than 3,000 security personnel. With the sponsors' cheering groups performing their customary song and dance numbers with not a soul in sight, it seemed a superficial act in comparison to the intensity of the protests of the morning. Declared Randhir Singh, Secretary General of the IOA:

> We have done everything possible to ensure the torch relay goes through peacefully. We did not intend it to be a closed one but there isn't much we could do. We would have loved the public to come and be part of this historic occasion in keeping with established Olympic tradition. But the situation is such that one blemish might lead to violence. Our national pride and international standing was at stake.[21]

And so it was. At exactly 4.40 pm Kunjarani Devi, India's legendary female weightlifter, kickstarted the carefully orchestrated flame relay. Seventy sportsmen and celebrities including one of us were involved and as the official run began, the tension in the air was palpable. The IOA and the government were determined to get through the day's events as soon as possible. Within 50 minutes the flame had travelled the distance from Raisina Hill to India Gate, escorted by Chinese commandoes. Finally, when Leander Paes and Mahesh Bhupathi lit the cauldron, Suresh Kalmadi, President of the IOA, looked justly relieved. As one NDTV reporter on the spot summed up, however, in a live report: 'Who saw it [the torch], certainly not the people of Delhi'.[22]

When the torch was worshipped

The high-intensity spectacle around the torch in 2008 was a far cry from 1964 when the Olympic torch first appeared in Delhi en route to the Tokyo Olympics. On that occasion, its journey has been as smooth as its organizers had envisioned:

> Shoppers in Connaught Place and Janpath stopped whatever they were doing and rushed to cheer the relay, managed by smart Japanese in dark suits and neat white gloves. The flame rested for the night at New Delhi's Town Hall before being given a ceremonial send-off the following day on its flight to Tokyo. No security problems those days, no fears of protests and demonstrations.[23]

Though the Olympic flame itself first appeared in Delhi in 1964, the first Indian exposure to the idea of the sporting flame can be traced back further to 1960. Hidden amid the IOC archives at Lausanne is the intriguing story of an attempt to create an Indian equivalent of the torch relay, in the town of Jwalamukhi. Just as an Olympic torch is carried from Olympia to each venue of the Olympics every four years, Indian sport administrators emulated this practice for the XIX National Games of 1960 from the Jogmaya Temple in the holy town of Jwalamukhi near Hoshiarpur in Punjab. With officials trying to create a national sporting culture, the Greek ceremony got an Indian twist with high priests chanting Sanskrit *shlokas* (chants) and lighting the relay flame from the temple's sacrificial fire. This was a deliberate strategy by the organizers to build local interest. Such was the popular interest in the 1960 event that the IOA's chronicler noted: 'As the torch emerged from the temple, there was a tremendous ovation from the crowd of 10,000 that had collected outside the temple'.[24]

About 1,500 torch-bearers carried the flame for the 350 km from Jwalamukhi to Delhi over ten days and it is significant that as many as a 'million people' turned up to see them en route. The Jogmaya connection seems to have given the Indian equivalent of the Olympic flame a kind of religious sanctity that fuelled the fervour. At Jullunder, for instance, the Town Hall, where the torch was kept for the night, became a 'virtual *mandir*' (temple) and thousands filed past the flame and 'made their offering'. At Ludhiana, on 18 February, as many 50,000 lined up on both sides of the Grand Trunk Road as the torch-bearers made their way into the city. Such was the rush that policemen and soldiers 'found it difficult to control the rush of people who wanted to pay their homage to the flame'.[25] When the torch reached Patiala, the IOA's effusive chronicler noted:

> almost the entire population of Patiala came out to give an unprecedented reception to the torch on February 20. The main bazaars wore a festive appearance unknown in the recorded history of that city ... at various corners in the city people distributed sweets. Milk, fruits and flowers were offered to the runners. Thousands of men and women filed past the torch at Yadavindra Stadium where it was kept for the night.[26]

Similarly at Ambala city and Cantonment, 'all arrangements to control the crowds broke down' as the thousands gathered far exceeded the expectations of the organizers. From Panipat to Delhi, the Grand Trunk was lined up with thousands as they came to get their glimpse of this holy torch that was to start the National Games.[27] Part of the fervour was certainly stoked by the sanctity attached to the Jogmaya Temple of Jwalamukhi but no one doubted the sporting nature of the event. The ancient rituals of Olympia had been Indianized and the breathtaking popular response was a measure of the support that the National Games and Olympic sport had at the time, at least in north India. The 1960 Jogmaya relay was also a fascinating example of how similar rituals around the lighting of a flame in two quite different ancient cultures could provide such deep resonance with the modern Olympic movement today.

The success of the 1960 Jogmaya relay set the grounds in India for the highly successful Olympic flame relay of 1964. The obvious retrospective question to ask is why did Tibetan protesters not take a cue and use the 1964 event as a vehicle for publicizing their cause in India, as they did in Delhi 44 years later? In 1964, after all, the Tibetan refugees were still recent immigrants to India and India had just suffered a humiliating military defeat at the hands of the People's Army. Even though, publicly, at least, China was still firmly in the Communist camp in the Cold War, the Soviet Union had refused to support its military foray into India. If anything, Indian public opinion would arguably have been ripe to support anything that could diplomatically embarrass the Chinese.

The difference between 1964 and 2008 can possibly be attributed to the nature of globalization and the impact of communication technologies. The global pro-Tibet people's protests in 2008, of which Delhi formed only a part, were as much a product of politics as they were of new communication technologies, being fuelled by the oxygen of the internet and the power of global satellite television imagery. The potential of such imagery and the possibilities it offered were further enhanced by the deep new inter-linkages between the China of 2008 and the rest of the world. In contrast, in 1964, China was relatively closed off from the pushes and pulls of international public opinion. The military clashes with the Soviets on the Ussuri River were still five years away and Kissinger's path-breaking trip to Beijing even further in the future. China remained firmly isolated from the international stage and Tibetan protests in New Delhi would have received little traction internationally. By 2008, though, the world had changed, and so had China. As such, the high-velocity protests in 2008 were as much a reflection of the changed international power balance as the new weight of international opinion against the Chinese leadership in the year of the Beijing Games was a testament to the organizing capacities of Tibetan groups.

As the troubled flame left Indian shores for Bangkok and then onto Canberra, Osaka and Seoul, a stock taking of the tumultuous events surrounding the flame in Delhi helped drive home the truth that the Olympic movement is not simply a sports movement. It is a complex vehicle that, by virtue of its global and public nature, provides a high-profile playing field for the competitive interplay of various kinds of competing interests, agendas and diplomatic manoeuvring. This is a claim that needs some explaining. The IOC officially champions sport as a medium for inter-cultural communication and peaceful democratic exchange; and it has been argued by many that the Tibetan protests were an illustration of the fact that the meaning of Olympism has now expanded from promoting the unity of sport and culture alone – as espoused by de Coubertin in the twentieth century – to embrace human rights as well. The unfolding of the Delhi protests, however point to a much more complex reading.

The imperatives of international politics and security concerns meant that Delhi was turned into an armed camp, the relay was shortened, and the dialogue between competing groups was reduced to shouting over barricades. It could legitimately be argued that 'peaceful inter-cultural communication and exchange' could not happen under such circumstances. Further, if one listened closely to the Tibetan protesters, they argued that the very fact of the Games being held in Beijing constituted a backwards step for the human rights movement and a global act of solidarity with the Chinese regime. In their eyes, the Games symbolized support for repression, not human rights. Simultaneously, the IOC itself was deeply embarrassed by the relay of worldwide protests that engulfed the Olympic torch even as it talked the talk on human rights. As Richard Pound put it:

> The nature of an international torch relay is an example of how the IOC should be assessing risk profiles in certain of its activities before the event and not in response to a crisis. I have a personal aversion to an international torch relay, on the basis of the costs, logistics, high risk and low rewards. The first three elements are self-evident, while the fourth, the low rewards, can be summed up by asking the question of what benefit is derived from a half-day event several months prior to the Games in a single city? Someone should have been paying greater and sooner attention to the likelihood of disruption of the relay, given the long-standing protests relating to certain of China's domestic and foreign policies. While, in the end, the protesters damaged their own cause, there was initial and conflicting attention focused on the IOC and even the sustainability of the Games themselves. While the Games are to some degree extra-political, the IOC needs to have a more active appreciation of the signals that are sent and the possibility of the Games being hijacked for political purposes.[28]

Could such a movement be legitimately called a true torchbearer for promoting human rights? Or, was it an accidental vehicle, forced against its will by the ingenuity, the intensity and the spontaneity of Tibetan protesters worldwide to be the harbinger of their cause?

On balance, it seems that the moral promise of the Olympic movement is such that it can not publicly be seen to repudiate human rights causes. Even if it compromises the marketing and political alliances that the IOC makes, it cannot, even despite itself, allow itself to be seen to be supporting what are considered to be unjust causes. This explains the acute discomfiture of the IOC when it was confronted by the Tibetan challenge. It could not publicly denounce their cause and at the same time it was placed in the unenviable task of keeping Beijing in good humour. Yet, as Steven McCarthy, founder and Chairman and CEO of Além International Management Inc., the leading transnational provider of operational services for the Olympic flame relay suggests:

> The Olympics torch relay affords an opportunity to individuals or groups to pronounce and promote a political or social statement because the relay commands a lot of global media coverage. In other words, people don't attack the Flame or what it stands for, they consider using it as a low cost vehicle to get their messages out.[29]

Stung by the worldwide negative publicity, IOC President Jacques Rogge repeatedly dismissed calls for a boycott of the Beijing Games saying that it would mean 'penalizing innocent athletes and … stopping the organization from something that definitely is worthwhile organizing'.[30] Even though the IOC insisted that it would speak to the Chinese government on human rights issues and that 'every use of violence is a step backwards',[31] it firmly stood by the idea of the Games. There was simply too much at stake for the IOC: money, organization, sport, politics. The IOC after all is a profit-making venture since the mid-1980s, sustaining itself on the successful marketing of the Olympic Games. This is why its response seemed to reflect a certain ambivalence, a tightrope performance to

Figure 3.   Sport as a Social Movement—a perfect examplifer.

balance the avowed idealism of de Coubertin's vision with the hard-headed practicalities of *realpolitik*. At the same time, the accessibility and the publicity around the international relay was such that it became an ideal site for legitimate protest against the denial of human rights by those involved with the Olympic movement. In a sense, the relay, in real terms, became what it was always intended to be: a people's movement. It was organized by officials, no doubt, but it was no more in their control than a speeding car whose breaks had failed. The flame relay became a flashpoint for the human rights movement and the Tibetan cause, *despite* the IOC. Herein lies the real success of the Olympic movement as a moral cause and one that will always be a tempting site to be used by the dispossessed of the world to their benefit.

Delhi and its aftermath

When questioned on the impact of the 2008 international torch relay, Jim Yardley of the *New York Times*, reporting from Beijing, had this to say:

> I do think China miscalculated the depth of passionate protest not just about Tibet but also other issues. It is rare that China oversees an international event outside its own borders, particularly one that is politically charged. This shows that even as China is accusing the West of failing to understand China, China also still has a lot to learn about the West.[32]

The Tibetan protests around the Olympic torch in India highlighted the potential for a high-visibility event like the Olympics to be used as a vehicle for political mobilization.

But China is not the only country to be wary of such mobilization. With Delhi all set to host the Commonwealth Games in 2010, IOA President Suresh Kalmadi justified the tight security in the capital on 17 April arguing that, 'We're hosting the Commonwealth Games in 2010, what if some nations want to boycott it citing our rights violation record in Kashmir?' Kalmadi had hit upon the raw nerves that the protests had ignited in world capitals, especially those with unpleasant histories to be fearful of. It can be suggested that India might soon find itself confronted with unpleasant questions over issues of human rights violation in Kashmir ahead of the forthcoming 2010 Commonwealth Games. As Rohit Mahajan writes in *Outlook*:

> Kalmadi wasn't speaking up for the world's downtrodden. He was merely cautioning those fanning the flames of trouble for the torch's truncated run in Delhi. His message: keep it quiet, for India has skeletons of its own in its cupboard. All of our rights groups, at home and abroad, agree – India's record on human rights is deplorable.[33]

Also, with the Commonwealth Games village built by demolishing slums on the Yamuna riverbed and with the displaced slum dwellers not properly catered for, Delhi 2010 is a sure site for protests from civil rights groups and NGOs. While some are of the opinion that such protests will hinder Games preparations, a counter view is that only because of the Commonwealth Games will the poor and the displaced get a chance to be heard. To go a step further, more than the medals won or records broken, such actions using the sporting stage make major international sports events like the Olympics what they are: events that do much to promote inter-cultural communication and understanding.

A key outcome of the spotlight on Beijing and the pressure of the global protests was that ahead of the Games, China agreed to hold negotiations with envoys of the Dalai Lama. In trying to put this radical turn around in context, Yardley states, 'Under increasing pressure from Europe and elsewhere, the Chinese government announced Friday (25 April) that it would meet with envoys of the Dalai Lama, an unexpected shift that comes as Tibetan unrest has threatened to cast a pall over the Olympic Games in August'.[34] This development, made possible wholly by the global symbolism of the Olympic flame, once again helped underscore the potential of this global peace movement, often unknowingly passed off as a simple sports competition. Since then, of course, the talks have made little progress with both sides attacking each other for being intransigent. Whatever the outcome of the talks in the future, the trigger was the political mobilization around the Olympic flame relay, with the Indian government in Delhi playing no small part, and this remains an enduring legacy of this institution.

Notes

[1] An earlier version of this essay was previously published in Nalin Mehta and Boria Majumdar, *Olympics: The India Story* (New Delhi: Harper Collins, 2008). We are thankful to Bruce Kidd and Russell Field for their insightful comments that helped us to sharpen many aspects of it.

[2] Suprita Das reporting on Delhi leg of Olympic flame relay on NDTV 24x7. Television broadcast, April 17, 2008.

[3] Tenzin Tsundue, 'Helping Hand, Some Muscle: Torch Made India Gate Forbidden City'. *The Indian Express*, April 18, 2008.

[4] Macaloon, *Flame Relays*.

[5] Pradeep Thakur, 'Tibetan Protests Banned in Arunachal'. *The Times of India*, April 16, 2008.

[6] Ibid.

[7] The protest ban in Arunachal and the heavy security was scathingly critiqued as a sign of Indian weakness before Beijing by many media publications. See, for example, 'Torching the Lines: India's Lack of Self-Esteem in Duplicating China's Over-reaction Carries Huge Costs'. *The Indian Express*, April 18, 2008.

[8] Aksai Chin is a region located at the juncture of China, Pakistan and India. One of the main causes of the Sino-Indian War of 1962 was India's discovery of a road China had built through the region, which India considers its territory. It has been under Chinese control ever since.

[9] Both Arunachal Pradesh and Sikkim are under Indian control but claimed by China. The Indian and the Chinese Armies observe a line of actual control on the disputed borders but through 2007–08 the Indian press has reported more than a hundred intrusions by the Chinese Army. Many of these intrusions are a result of poor demarcation of the line in the mountainous terrain. The Indian Army Chief, Gen. Deepak Kapoor, cited this as the reason when questioned about the reported intrusions in March 2008 and refuted talks of any illegal offensive actions by the Chinese Army. 'Times Now' report, broadcast March 2008.

[10] 'Torching the Lines'.

[11] Rahul Tripathi, 'It's a Fortress Out There'. *The Times of India*, April 16, 2008.

[12] 'Foolproof Security for the Torch Relay'. *The Hindu* (New Delhi), April 16, 2008.

[13] See, for example, the saturation full-page coverage in *The Hindustan Times*, April 16, 2008. Its entire metro page was devoted to this issue.

[14] This advice was issued by UN Security officers on 11 April 2008.

[15] Jantar Mantar is a seventeenth-century observatory situated near Connaught Place in New Delhi.

[16] 'Times Now' is India's most popular 24-hour English news channel. It is owned by Bennett and Coleman company which also runs *The Times of India*.

[17] Personal interview at Rajghat, 17 April 2008.

[18] Interview with Tibetan protestor, New Delhi, 18 April 2008.

[19] Dhondup Dorji, Vice President of the Tibetan Youth Congress on 'Torch of Protest'. 'Times Now' special, broadcast on 17 April 2008.

[20] Ibid.

[21] Interview with Randhir Singh, 17 April 2008.

[22] Anusuya Mathur, report on NDTV 24xt, broadcast on 17 April 2008.

[23] K. Datta, 'Keep Politics Away from Sports: Protests, Boycotts Only Affect the Athletes'. *The Times of India*, April 16, 2008.

[24] Butalia, 'Jwalamukhi', 35.

[25] Ibid., 36–7.

[26] Ibid., 38.

[27] Ibid.
[28] Pound, 'The Future of the Olympic Movement', 2–3.
[29] Quoted in MacAloon, *Flame Relays*.
[30] Jacque Rogge, quoted in 'IOC: Don't Boycott Olympics Over Tibet'. Associated Press, March 15, 2008. http://www.breitbart.com/article.php?id=D8VE054O1&show_article = 1.
[31] IOC Vice President Thomas Bach, quoted in ibid.
[32] Interview with Jim Yardley, 27 April 2008.
[33] Rohit Mahajan, 'Ah The Human Race'. *Outlook*, April 28, 2008.
[34] Jim Yardley, 'China Says It Is Ready to Meet Dalai Lama Envoys'. *New York Times*, April 26, 2008.

References

Butalia, J. 'Jwalamukhi: The Olympia of India'. *Indian Olympic Association Official Bulletin* 2 (January–March 1960): 35.

MacAloon, John. *Flame Relays and the Struggle for the Olympic Movement*. London: Routledge, forthcoming.

Pound, Richard. 'The Future of the Olympic Movement: Promised Land or Train Wreck'. In *Pathways: Critiques and Discourse in Olympic Research*, edited by Robert K. Barney, Michael Heine, Kevin Wamsley, and Gordon MacDonald, 1–19. London, ON: Centre for Olympic Studies, University of Western Ontario, 2008.

Between small everyday practices and glorious symbolic acts: sport-based resistance against the communist regime in Czechoslovakia

Dino Numerato

Department of Institutional Analysis and Public Management, Bocconi University, Milan, Italy

This essay presents a socio-historical interpretation of sport-based resistance against the communist regime in Czechoslovakia. It argues that the sphere of sport was never absolutely subordinated to the prevailing political order and it maintains that sport provided a space for expressions of resistance. Such resistance is not just evident in cases of large demonstrations during which Czech and Slovak sport celebrities reinforced public protests with grand symbolic and mass-mediated gestures. The same level of importance to opposition against the dominant power can be attributed to small everyday practices. Hence, while considering glorious acts of resistance and protest with a large-scale impact, the study simultaneously explores subtle and everyday subversive strategies that have appeared in public participation in sport. The study is based on a secondary analysis of documents and on semi-structured interviews with a number of representatives from the Czech sport movement.

Introduction

How were you accepted by his family [family of her husband], *as a signatory of the manifest Two Thousand Words?* (interviewer)

When I met first his father, he asked me whether I read *Rudé právo.* I told him that I do not. And he has never spoken to me ever again.[1]

There are few examples that so saliently express the everyday dimension of sport-based resistance to the communist regime in former Czechoslovakia as the abovementioned quotation by Věra Čáslavská, a successful Czech gymnast from the 1960s. To better explain its significance to those who might not be familiar with the reality of Czechoslovak public life: *Two Thousand Words* is a document that was drawn up during the period of the Prague Spring, initiated by a group of academics and intellectuals, written by the Czech writer Ludvík Vaculík and published in June 1968. The manifesto expressed discontent with Soviet pressure and with reforms based on communist ideology, calling for democratization and liberalization. It was signed by hundreds of personalities from Czechoslovak public life (among whom were such sport representatives as the ski jumper Jiří Raška, the runner Emil Zátopek[2] and his wife, the javelin thrower Dana Zátopková), as well as by 100,000 Czechoslovak citizens. *Rudé právo,* which literally means 'The red right', was the major communist daily newspaper in the country.

In light of these facts, it is clear that Věra Čáslavská was one of the opponents of the communist regime. The quoted statement not only shows her political stance, but also demonstrates some of its consequences for her personal life and sport career. These consequences doubled as a reaction to Čáslavská's publicly visible gestures of protest at the 1968 Olympic Games in Mexico, where she twice used the victory podium (once after winning the gold medal in the floor exercise routine and once after winning the silver medal in the balance beam competition) to express her political stance – although her gesture remained slightly overpowered by the 'Black Power' salute of two African-American 200m sprinters, Tommie Smith and John Carlos. She has described her symbolic gesture during the floor exercise final medal ceremony in the following way:

> When they started the first chords of the Russian national anthem ... I ostentatiously turned my head down from the Russian flag. I had a calling to put my hand up and to make a V, for Victory, but I remembered how the African-Americans raised their fists and they were disqualified ... Therefore, I just made the tenuous, suppressed V ... on the arms closed to the body lower and I held it in a disciplined way until the end of the Soviet anthem. Some people spotted it and the American journalists wrote that it had been 'silent protest'.[3]

To illuminate the context of this protest, it is worth noting that it happened three months after the Soviet invasion of Czechoslovakia in August of 1968. Following this incident, Věra Čáslavská risked being arrested for having signed the aforementioned *Two Thousand Words* manifesto and decided to hide in a small village in Northern Moravia. Whereas her Soviet rivals were already in Mexico to acclimate themselves, she continued her training for the upcoming Olympic Games using pine-tree limbs instead of a beam, practicing her floor exercises on a mossy green and loading coal with a shovel to keep her muscles strong. She joined the Czechoslovak Olympic Team only after obtaining the special permission of the Czechoslovak government. Her performance at the Olympic Games fascinated the sporting public: she won four gold and two silver medals. After the Olympic Games, she decided to end her career. Notwithstanding her success, her life remained affected by the communist regime, since she refused to withdraw her signature from the manifesto. As a result, she could not officially participate in sports, nor could she fully take advantage of her success. She was prohibited from collaborating with the American and Japanese production of a film focused on her biography, from participating in advertisements, from being invited to sport events as a guest, and even from coaching abroad. She kept coaching only in secret: 'I could not show up myself, I only could coach small children. When a visitor came, I had immediately to go to the dressing-room.'[4]

The slightly unusual introduction of this essay, dedicated to the detailed description of Věra Čáslavská's case, captures some facets of resistance against the communist regime in former Czechoslovakia. In particular, this example outlines the significance of *glorious symbolic protest acts* and their *resonance in the everyday lives* of sporting heroes. Further into the essay, the emphasis on *everyday bases of resistance*, represented here only partly by Věra Čáslavská's personal life, is expanded upon in consideration of the ordinary practices of common representatives of Czechoslovak sports movements. Therefore, in addition to the category of *glorious symbolic acts*, the notion of *small everyday practices* is introduced as a significant form of sports-based resistance.

These two forms of resistance may be characterized in the following way: First, the notion of *glorious symbolic acts* refers to large-scale symbolic protests that are exemplified by sport celebrities' mass-mediated protests (and needless to say, they were mediated in two different ways: the Western and the Communist), which are symbolically grounded and have the potential to reach a large percentage of the population. These strategic acts of resistance are manifest, extraordinary, deliberately designed and aimed to delegitimize communist power.

Second, the notion of *small everyday practices* refers to the common and publicly unknown behaviours of prevalently ordinary sports volunteers. Frequently, these practices do not represent overt and conscious acts of political protest but rather are unintended tactics that are used to cope with oppressive political power. Considering the all-embracing nature of a dominant political order and its interconnectedness with the sphere of everyday life, including leisure, the realm of sport represents a space in which hegemonic power can be contested. These forms of a rather latent resistance might be silent, invisible and ordinary. This study aims to illustrate this resistance using several examples, and simultaneously, to identify its different facets.

The notion of *small everyday practices*, in addition to being supported by secondary documents and stories from sports volunteers, is inspired by a theoretical intuition and, in particular, by De Certeau's writings on the subversive acts of production and consumption[5] and their development in Edelman's work on the resistance potential of spectator sports under Soviet socialism.[6] In a more general way, the attention given to everyday resources reflects the recent developments in sociologically and anthropologically driven research on resistance.[7]

The socio-historical analysis of sport-based resistance is primarily based on secondary evidence from newspaper articles; interpretations written by direct actors such as journalists, athletes or politicians; official documents such as Communist Party declarations or resolutions; meeting minutes of the Communist Party of Czechoslovakia; and on those secondary resources with a historical provenience, such as books and academic papers. Furthermore, in order to describe the everyday nature of resistance, the research capitalizes on some qualitative interviews with representatives of three sport movements (soccer, sailing and handball) in the Czech Republic and their memories of the communist regime in former Czechoslovakia.[8]

In the sections that immediately follow, the essay briefly summarizes contemporary conceptualizations of resistance through sport. In subsequent sections based on empirical evidence, sport-based resistance is presented as a product of large symbolic acts, after which the everyday nature of resistance in sport during Communism is captured. The conclusion summarizes the different means of sport-based resistance against the communist regime.

Sport-based resistance

In a brief overview of the relatively short tradition of sport-based resistance, Rinehart[9] defines three modes of opposition towards the dominant culture or ideology. He distinguishes between colonial, cultural and political types of resistance, while simultaneously contending that these modes are not mutually exclusive. The history of the protests reflected in academic studies may actually be read through the lens of this categorization.

From this perspective, we can first recognize the importance of sport-based resistance in colonial or post-colonial circumstances. In this vein, Ok shows how football, although being tolerated by Japan, in the curricula of physical education in Korean schools as a Western competitive 'war game' created a platform for Korean resistance to Japanese colonialism. Ok highlights the role of supporting songs that were 'partisan, and obliquely patriotic'.[10] In a similar way, Majumdar demonstrates how cricket was appropriated in India and in rural areas as a tool of resistance against British imperialism.[11] A significant body of literature describes the political developments in South Africa and particularly the role of the South African Council on Sport, founded in 1973, which strongly contributed to the more general fight against the apartheid system.[12]

Second, sport-based resistance is oriented against hegemonic features of culture, as it has mainly been implied by the recent studies on resistance. In this sense, sport becomes a platform for resistance against globalization,[13] gender stereotypes,[14] and class-based[15] and race-based[16] constraints. Furthermore, several subcultures such as those of climbers, surfers, rugby players[17] or bicycle road racers[18] have been conceived of as deliberately contesting dominant cultural patterns. A recent study has even shown how the practice of cricket liberated from its traditional context – the cricket pitch – and played in city streets and squares can challenge established perceptions and uses of urban space.[19]

Third, the last – and, for this study, the most relevant – dimension of sport-based resistance is political. The long history of Olympic boycotts represents a great example in this respect.[20] Most often, the role of resistance has been strong in the totalitarian and authoritarian regimes. It seems that the forbidden *colles castelleres* (human towers) or trekking excursions represented an important source of Catalonian resistance against Franco's fascist regime.[21] In the same geographic area, the support of FC Barcelona became an act of resistance against the Fascist nationalists in Spain. Similarly, the support of Spartak Moscow was sometimes an act of political resistance against other clubs linked to the official establishment, such as CSKA, Dinamo, Torpedo or Lokomotiv Moscow.[22] Another example of protests that attracted international attention arose from the aggressive water polo match between Hungary and the Soviet Union at the 1956 Melbourne Olympics. The match, labelled in Hungarian as a 'Blood Bath', was played in a very aggressive manner and Hungary defeated the Soviet Union 4–0; this all took place against the background of the Hungarian Revolution in 1956. Some of the Hungarian athletes decided to wear a black ribbon across the Hungarian flag as a symbol of protest against the Soviet invasion.[23]

Notwithstanding these contributions, we can still notice the lack of attention paid to the role of sport-based resistance in the communist reality of Central and Eastern Europe. The aforementioned work by Edelman and his systematic explorations of resistance against Soviet socialism represent an exception. As Edelman noted: '[t]he consumers of Soviet spectator sports did not uncritically accept the political-ideological messages the state and Party sought to ascribe to sports. Rather, as one element of popular culture, sports proved to be an arena of ongoing contention.'[24] The irreducible spontaneity of sport, the relatively uncensored descriptions of sporting events in the media, the barely controllable actions of crowds of sports spectators and the links with black and grey markets that sport entails, are all features of sport that created many occasions when the socialist political order was subverted.[25]

A similar role was attributed to sport in some general studies of resistance in communist Czechoslovakia. Sport was understood as an alternative public space for the articulation of opinions outside the official one-dimensional public sphere.[26] To a certain degree, the resistance potential of sport was often underestimated by political proponents of the communist regime. The Department of Complex Modelling, Sportpropag, was officially founded within the ČSTV[27] in 1970 to conduct apolitical research on sport and physical education, using social scientific methodologies. However, in practice the research did not remain strictly apolitical. Under the guise of researching an apparently neutral topic such as sport, the Department attracted critical scholars who challenged the ideology of communism. In fact, Sportpropag was abolished in 1983 after its members published a critical monograph that was ideologically unacceptable.[28]

As mentioned, this essay captures both the large-scale and the mass-mediated type of protest linked with important sporting events and sport celebrities, as well as the resistance of unknown and ordinary sport practitioners.

The aim of the study is to understand resistance in its different modalities and contexts, instead of searching for a categorical definition. From this point of view, sport-based resistance can be collective or individual, more or less intentional,[29] recognized or not.[30] Also, its impact may vary, as argued by Budd.[31] According to him, resistance may lead either to a mere critique of a system with no contribution to systematic social or political change, or it may carry the potential to reshape and overthrow the dominant social structure.

The next sections will capture two different types of resistance against the communist regime in Czechoslovakia. Whereas the next part will focus on the Ice Hockey Protests as an example of an extraordinary and manifest protest, the section that follows will present more subtle and ordinary roots of sport-based resistance against the communist ideology, exploring the everyday resources for resistance.

A glorious symbolic act[32]

No sporting event during the era of communist Czechoslovakia was as strongly linked to glorious symbolic protests as the happenings around the two victories of the Czechoslovak ice hockey team against the Soviet Union during the 1969 World Championship in Stockholm. The Czechoslovak team won 2–0 (21 March 1969) and 4–3 (28 March 1969) and these two ice hockey games were more than mere sport matches in which two competing teams struggled for victory. The peculiar atmosphere of the games was a result of the fact that they happened seven months after the Soviet[33] invasion of Prague (21 August 1968), which was followed by the 'temporary'[34] stationing of Soviet armed forces in Czechoslovakia, an act which was labelled in communist newspeak as 'fraternal assistance'.

The games took place in the period of political instability characterized on the one hand by Soviet efforts to strengthen its influence and control in Czechoslovakia, and on the other hand, by Czechoslovak efforts to resist the normalization pressures initiated after the invasion in August 1968. The sphere of sport represented one of the arenas where political struggle took place. In a sense, the games against the Soviet Union's team were interpreted as an opportunity for revenge for the occupation, and the ice hockey rink became an important arena of the political battle. Historians analysing the event[35] refer to it as the 'Ice Hockey Protests'. The symbolic importance of the sporting events on the ice spread to Czechoslovak households, city centres, newspapers and political corridors; the celebration that ensued when the second game was won even turned into mass protests.

The ice hockey games were linked to a moment in Czechoslovak history, called 'fraternal assistance', which was in fact an occupation that provoked the final rupture of the last so-called period of the Prague Spring, a period which has been characterized in Czechoslovak history by reinforced intellectual and civil life and a set of actions that expressed resistance to Soviet domination. The media played a specific role in reinforcing resistance, publishing reports laden with hidden meanings, irony and metaphors. In particular, sport pages with less developed mechanisms of censorship and political control offered a great opportunity for this kind of subversive writing.[36]

The first game was already full of emotions and strong motivation for a Czechoslovak victory, whose players were pushed ahead by an audience displaying banners that referred to the Soviet occupation in August 1968. Among others, slogans such as 'Not even with tanks, today!' or 'August was yours, today is ours' fuelled the game's atmosphere of conflict which ended in the intense eruption of the crowds as they shouted the name of the reformist Czechoslovak politician: 'Dubček, Dubček!' The Czechoslovak team won the first game 2–0 on 21 March 1969, and the final result was not the only expression of revenge and national satisfaction. Immediately after the winning team's national anthem finished, the players from the Czechoslovakian team returned directly to their dressing rooms without shaking hands with their rivals.[37] The team captain, Jozef Golonka, commented on the symbolical character of that day of the month, the 21st, which represents both the day when the first game was played and the day when the Soviet invasion started: 'This is our 21st. The Russians had theirs in August.'[38]

The animosity that was already expressed during the first game was to be doubled after the second match that took place one week later, on 28 March 1969, when the Czechoslovak players repeated their success. The tension before the match and the particular atmosphere of revenge and national feeling invaded both public and private spaces. Even if the official media tried to keep the comments before the match limited purely to sport, the infiltration of political topics into public discourse was unavoidable. Hundreds of thousands of people followed the match at home in front of their TVs and the audience share in Czechoslovakia stood at 93%.[39]

Particular symbolic gestures happened on the ice. Five of the Czechoslovakian players covered the red star on their jerseys, part of the national sign symbolizing the communist ideology, with black tape. This courageous gesture was well-hidden in the live television broadcast.[40] Another clear gesture was made by Jozef Golonka, who held his hockey stick as a rifle and pointed it at the Soviet players.[41]

When the referee's final whistle concluded the dramatic battle, in which the Czechoslovak team had beat the Big Red Machine[42] 4–3, the stadium exploded – and so did streets and squares in the whole of Czechoslovakia. Even if it was just a partial victory in an ongoing tournament which, in the end, did not result in an overall victory,[43] it did not change anything about the intensity of enthusiasm shared by Czechoslovak fans. The political importance of the victory had a stronger value than a mere sport success.

Celebrations in the streets accompanied by anti-Soviet slogans after the first match[44] seemed negligible in comparison with the range and intensity of the celebrations that spontaneously appeared after the second game. The town centres, normally calm and empty at that hour, were unrecognizable. Half an hour after the end of the match, at 10.30 p.m., more than 150,000[45] came to Wenceslas' Square in Prague to celebrate the victory and to share in the satisfaction of beating the political enemy, if only on the ice. The celebrations were not limited only to Prague. There were massive celebrations during which more than half a million people in different towns took to the streets and squares. The town centres were spontaneously filled by crowds of celebrating fans expressing their satisfaction at this successful act of revenge.[46]

Many of these celebrations soon turned into protests against the Soviet occupation. These acts of resistance were not limited only to verbal attacks against the Soviet Union; in some cases, they led to the physical demolition of Soviet objects, namely military headquarters, cars and memorials. In different places, slogans such as, 'This is for August!, Brežněv is a hooligan!', 'Czechoslovakia 4 – Occupation forces 3!'[47] were seen on the walls and heard. Czechoslovakia witnessed the biggest demonstration since the Soviet invasion in August 1968.

The symbolism of the protests remained connected with the destruction of Soviet airline Aeroflot's office in Wenceslas' Square in Prague. Demonstrators smashed the windows with cobblestones, invaded the offices, and threw out the furniture and set it on fire. According to some historical interpretations, the demolition of the Aeroflot office was deliberately encouraged by the State Security under Soviet control,[48] whose primary aim was to provoke evidence of political instability in Czechoslovakia and thus to destroy the persistent efforts at resistance against the so-called normalisation process.

Immediately after the protest in Prague, the government of Czechoslovakia called an extraordinary assembly at which its members criticized the behaviour of the public. They also expressed this in a special resolution.[49] According to reactions arriving from Moscow, the Czechoslovak government's standpoint had not been strong enough. The Russian daily *Pravda* published an editorial on 31 March 1969 which critiqued the Czechoslovak government's declaration from 28 March 1969. According to this editorial article, the protests were the result of a counterrevolution which was organized and managed from abroad and happened with the direct participation or passive observation of some of the functionaries of the Communist Party of Czechoslovakia.[50]

The protests were used as an excuse for stronger intervention by the Soviet Union and as a motive for breaking up Czechoslovak resistance and eliminating the reformist efforts of Alexander Dubček, the First Secretary of the Communist Party of Czechoslovakia. A delegation led by Marshall Andrei Grechko from the Soviet Politburo was sent to Prague, and Dubček was forced to resign on 17 April 1969 and the position of First Secretary was assigned to the ideologically acceptable and loyal politician Gustav Husák.[51] The oscillation of Czechoslovak politics caused by two ice hockey games reached its end and socio-political life remained trapped under the pressures of normalization.

The ice-hockey protests represent a typical example of resistance which might be called *a glorious manifest protest*. As has been emphasized, these symbolic acts were not unique sources of sport resistance against the communist regime. In support of this idea, the next section explores, in detail, various layers of the resistance that stem from everyday practices.

Small everyday practices

Returning to the example of Věra Čáslavská, she again found herself in conflict with the official Czechoslovak political authorities due to the fact that she got married just one day after her victory, in Mexico, in a cathedral: a place that was absolutely unacceptable for the strongly secular communist ideology. Such a step suggests the notion of the *resonance of the glorious symbolic protests in the personal life* of sport celebrities. Similarly oppressive situations were met by 10 of the ice-hockey world champions from 1949. Before leaving for the world championship in 1950, they were arrested and accused of seditious activities against the communist regime.[52] This aspect of the politicization of sport approaches the first layer of everyday resistance which can be defined as *personal resistance*.

A similar form of resistance can be seen in the decision to opt for political emigration. Tennis players Jaroslav Drobný and Vladimír Černík, figure skaters Ája Vrzáňová and Jiřina Nekolová, and swimmers Jiří Kovář and Jiří Linhart were among the first wave of emigrations after February 1948, when the Communist Party took control of the government of Czechoslovakia. The history of emigration is long and the many other examples of émigrés include tennis players Martina Navrátilová and Ivan Lendl[53] and such ice hockey players as the Šťastný brothers.

Considering the interrelatedness all of these acts with the personal lives of the sports celebrities and their public invisibility in the former Czechoslovakia in the years after they emigrated, these steps approach everyday resistance practices. In addition to considering *personal resistance*, this essay identifies other layers of everyday resistance that can be defined as follows: *organizational, legal, material* and *cultural*.

Second, the notion of *organizational resistance* is linked to the political potential of sports volunteering and, in particular, to the activities of the members of those sports associations that were banned or radically transformed according to the rules of the communist regime. This form of resistance can be identified among the members of the traditional sports associations founded on the ideas of democracy and Catholicism, such as Sokol and Orel, respectively. Various acts of resistance were observed after 1948, when the communist regime was initiated, and after 1968, when it was reinforced. Roubal reflected upon the resistance potential of the Sokol Slet, a mass gymnastic display, in 1948 in Czechoslovakia. He wrote that 'the 1948 Slet was the last massive protest against recently established communist rule, resulting in mass persecution and the banning of the movement'.[54] These persecutions also forced some of the Sokol members to leave their country in two different waves of emigration after 1948[55] and 1968.[56] Political engagement became one of the principal activities employed by Sokol unions in exile. They contributed to disseminating democratic values in opposition to the oppressive communist regime.[57] There exists evidence about Sokol unions and clubs operating in exile and economically supporting the activities of anti-communist dissenters within Czechoslovakia.[58]

The example of Sokol demonstrates the fact that resistance not only includes extraordinary large-scale events and sport celebrities, but also ordinary sport activity and common athletes. From this point of view, engaging in some of the sports forbidden or limited by the communist regime can *per se* be understood in some contexts as an act of resistance. This organizational layer of everyday resistance does not just include selected multisports associations but also encompasses sports-specific associations. This, in particular, concerns sports that were labelled as 'bourgeois' such as sailing, tennis or golf.[59] According to the memories of various sailors, as they presented them during interviews with representatives of the Czech sailing association, the strategic building of apolitical social networks with local functionaries of the Communist Party served as an important tactic to ensure tolerance for sailing, which was less tolerated by the official ideology.

This organizational resistance also presents a creative means of coping with complicated formalized and ideologically driven procedures. In this vein, offshore sailors from the country, which is situated far from the seaside, contributed to 'etching the regime'.[60] They had to render their hobby official in order to enjoy the possibility of travelling to Western countries. In other words, they had to rationalize and bureaucratize their activities to display agreement with the regime. In the book published by the Czech Sailing Association in celebration of the one hundred year anniversary of sailing in the Czech Republic, this tactic was described in the following way:

> To render it [offshore sailing] recognisable, it had to produce results that were subsumed under 'a unified sports classification' of the former ČSTV. Therefore we had to found an organisation which would somehow legalize the foolishness and, at the same time, set up clear criteria for competition.[61]

The apparent adherence to official rules, albeit done without adopting their ideological background, suggests another, third form of small everyday practices: that of *legal resistance*. A more symptomatic example of *legal resistance*, and one that is linked narrowly to the (fourth) notion of *material resistance*, can be identified in the sailors' quest for high-quality equipment and facilities from Western countries. Some sailors challenged the communist regime by violating the law in order in order to attain Western equipment and facilities. The sailors shared ideas on how to avoid payment regulations on import duty, how to smuggle gasoline and how to obtain Western currency, which was officially accessible only with great difficulty.[62] These subtle tactics had the more or less intentional objective of political resistance, which also contributed to undermining the communist regime.

Unavailability of sports equipment and training facilities also reinforced other means of rather invisible resistance. Representatives of the football clubs remember how they helped themselves and their clubs by producing training equipment from the state-owned factory material produced during official working hours. Similar comments might be heard from representatives of Czech sailing movements, as it is well documented by the following quotation of a sailor: 'Being hard up taught us... The factories [where they worked] were well-furnished with material and you could sometimes steal something... It was all about looking for a way to find it, how to make it.'

The material resistance was not necessarily linked to travel abroad. Stories from physical education classes of the youngest volunteers discuss purchasing Converse-like, completely white shoes imported from China. It was quite common to decorate them with a felt pen; for example, by drawing three stripes to make them resemble the Adidas brand – a brand missing in the state-owned communist shops but known from the television broadcasts of sport matches of the socialist heroes against their Western rivals.

This symbolic 'Westernisation' of sports products suggests, finally, the notion of *cultural resistance*. This category refers to the production of signs and the circulation and consumption of cultural products, as well as the attribution of particular meanings to sporting events. The very limited possibility of travelling to Western countries was slightly increased among athletes, and in particular among high-level practitioners, with the impending downfall of the communist regime approaching. Their journeys abroad, therefore, permitted a circulation of cultural products such as books or audio discs with popular music scarcely available in communist countries. Moreover, these few athletes who travelled abroad had the unique opportunity to interact with so-called Western life and Western culture and, therefore, they could have gained a different perspective on life in communist Czechoslovakia.

Another facet of cultural resistance (and, in a sense, also of organizational resistance) was represented by a specific approach towards participation in official sports governance meetings. Notwithstanding the ideological appearance of these meetings imprinted into the language used, the style of the discussion, and the overt respect displayed for hierarchical divisions among sports officials, some sports volunteers retrospectively attributed to their participation itself a kind of passive resistance. They considered their participation in the sport governance activities as a legitimate excuse for their absence, or even escape, from compulsory political meetings. Even though the official ideology labelled civic volunteering in sport as 'a socialism building activity', its impact was often damaging to the political system. This might also include some politically subtle jokes that sometimes appeared during the official meetings dealing with sport governance and irony regarding the ideological manner in which the decisions were made. In some cases the element of cultural resistance was even more apparent, as in the circumstances surrounding a Czech golf challenge trophy named after Tomáš Garrigue Masaryk, the first president of Czechoslovakia, whose democratic ideas were incongruous with communist ideology. Despite this fact, the trophy with his name on it was courageously awarded to the golf champion of Czechoslovakia even in 1949, when the first symptoms of communist pressures appeared.[63]

Conclusion

The case of Věra Čáslavská, the Ice Hockey Protests of 1969, and the stories remembered by common sport practitioners do not provide an exhaustive enumeration of the expressions of resistance that became manifest during the communist regime. Under the shadow of communism, other examples undoubtedly appeared which could potentially enrich such a characterization.

Making the distinction between glorious symbolic acts and small everyday practices captures the plurality of forms of resistance against the communist regime in Czechoslovakia and allow sport-based resistance to be explored in all its complexity. Although these two forms of resistance are contrasting in their nature, they represent complementary expressions of resistance and both could assist in weakening the communist ideology.

In the first case, descriptive analytical attention was directed towards the logic of symbolic events and the interconnectedness between specific sporting events, stands, politics, public spaces and the media. In the second case, a rather interpretative analysis was focused on five different facets of everyday resistance, defined as personal, organizational, legal, material and cultural.

Whereas the protest-oriented nature of the glorious symbolic acts is apparent, the resistant nature of small everyday practices needs to be cautiously interpreted. The examples presented here cannot be generalized. Their resistance potential must be addressed contextually, respecting the meaning attributed, often retrospectively, to everyday practices by sports actors. Consequently, one can discuss the impact of the enumerated types of resistance in ways that might differ greatly and that 'going Western' does not necessarily possess the same power to resist as an open criticism of the system made during a general assembly meeting.

Therefore, existing counter-evidence must be taken into consideration. Perhaps there were members of Sokol exile clubs who explicitly refused to mix sports with politics. By the same token, stealing or smuggling could occur as a manifestation of resourcefulness in a time of need, rather than as a politically driven tactic. What unifies the enumerated examples of everyday resistance is the fact that resistant potential was attributed to the actions by the sports volunteers themselves.

Summarizing, the various modes of resistance differ in their frequency, intensity, visibility and impact, but all of them have their important place in the complex and robust architecture of sport-based resistance. More or less collective, coordinated and intended acts that were born in the sport environment played a small role in the collapse of the communist regime. Obviously, sport-based resistance has to be understood in congruence with other forms of resistance expressed in the realms of politics and international relations, economics, research and education, culture or religion.

Acknowledgements

The research was funded by the European Commission 6th Framework Marie Curie Excellence Grant MEXT-25008 'Sport and Social Capital in the European Union' awarded to Dr Margaret Groeneveld and Bocconi University. I would like to thank Russell Field and Bruce Kidd for their insightful comments and critical remarks on the first draft of this essay.

Notes

[1] Vačkář, 'Nezkrácená verze rozhovoru s Čáslavskou'.
[2] Emil Zátopek was politically active after the Soviet invasion of Czechoslovakia in August of 1968 when he asked for the exclusion of the Soviet athletes from the upcoming Olympic Games in Mexico City. Giuntini, *Pugni chiusi*, 70.
[3] Vačkář, 'Nezkrácená verze rozhovoru s Čáslavskou'.
[4] Ibid.
[5] De Certeau, *Practice of Everyday Life*.

[6] Edelman, *Serious Fun*.

[7] Hollander and Einwohner, 'Conceptualizing Resistance'; Marada, *Kultura protestu*; Reed-Danahay, 'Talking about Resistance'; Scott, *Weapons of the Weak*; Shaw, 'Conceptualizing Resistance'; Sivaramakrishnan, 'Some Intellectual Genealogies'.

[8] The selection of three sport disciplines was primarily driven by the aims of a larger project 'Sport and Social Capital in the European Union'. This project was realized as a multi-sited ethnographic study and was focused on sport governance and its social impact in four specific countries of the European Union (Denmark, France, Italy and the Czech Republic).

[9] Rinehart, 'Fists Flew'.

[10] Ok, 'The Political Significance'.

[11] Majumdar, 'Cultural Resistance'.

[12] Keech, 'Contest, Conflict and Resistance'.

[13] Duke, 'Local Tradition'; Horne, 'The Politics of Sport'; Thomson and Soós, 'Research Note Youth Sport'.

[14] Broad, 'The Gendered Unapologetic'; Elling, de Knop and Knoppers, 'Gay/Lesbian Sport Clubs'; Iannotta and Kane, 'Sexual Stories'.

[15] Jamison, 'The Sandgate Handicap Riot'.

[16] Pęlak, 'Negotiating Gender/Race/Class Constraints'.

[17] Donnelly, 'Resistance Through Sports'.

[18] Williams, 'Sport, Hegemony'.

[19] Gilchrist and Ravenscroft, 'The (Sub)politics of Sport'.

[20] Lennartz, 'Olympic Boycotts'.

[21] Conversi, 'Immigration and Statelessness'.

[22] Edelman, 'A Small Way of Saying "No"'.

[23] Rinehart, 'Fists Flew'.

[24] Edelman, *Serious Fun*, 24.

[25] Ibid., 16.

[26] Marada, *Kultura protestu*; Thorne, 'Ideologies and Realities'.

[27] ČSTV – Czechoslovak Association of Physical Education, the only officially recognized state-driven umbrella association.

[28] Round Table, 'Kulatý Stůl', 738.

[29] Shaw, 'Conceptualizing Resistance'.

[30] Hollander and Einwohner, 'Conceptualizing Resistance'.

[31] Budd, 'Capitalism, Sport and Resistance'.

[32] This section is based on the paper 'Sport as Resistance: "Ice Hockey Protests" in Czechoslovakia in 1969s' presented at the XIth International CESH-Congress in Vienna in 2006 and published in the proceedings of the event. See Numerato, 'Sport as Resistance',

[33] In fact, the invasion was effected under the Russian captainship, but the army was comprised of soldiers from five countries belonging to the Warsaw Pact: the German Democratic Republic, Poland, Hungary and Bulgaria. Balík et al., 'Politický systém českých zemí 1848–1989', 140.

[34] The term 'temporary' is used here in the same way that it was used in expressions of key political actors.

[35] Felcman, 'Počátky ostré etapy normalizace', 52; Williams, *The Prague Spring*; Agnew, *The Czechs*, 269.

[36] The tension of the games and their political significance was already anticipated before they started. In fact, some Czech journalists, particularly those from dailies such as the *Reportér*, *Svobodné slovo*, *Mladá fronta*, *Zemědělské noviny* and *Práce* were later accused in the official statement of the Communist Party of Czechoslovakia of provoking tension and negative emotion in connection with the game. *Rudé právo*, 'Ještě k hokejovému zápasu ČSSR-SSSR', 13.

[37] Pacina, 'Hokejová pomsta za okupaci', 32.

[38] L. Brostrom, 'Cold as Ice: The Triumph in 1969: Seven Months after Russia Invaded, Tension Filled Stockholm Arena'. *The Prague Post*, April 22, 2004)

[39] Národní muzeum exhibition, '. . . a přijely tanky. 1968', Prague, 2008.

[40] M. Jenšík and T. Večeřa, 'Jak na Rusy? Rozhodit je'. *Mladá fronta Dnes*, February 15, 2008, Sport, 32.

[41] Pelletier, 'Czechoslovakian Victory'; Jokisipilä, 'Cold War on Ice'.

[42] This was the nickname of the Soviet Union's team referring to its domination in international games, which had lasted for years.

[43] Notwithstanding the victory against the Soviet Union, the Czechoslovak team came away from Stockholm with the bronze medal, since it lost twice against Sweden and even if it reached the same number of points as did both Sweden and the Soviet Union, the better score determined that the World Cup was awarded to the Soviet team and the silver medal to the Swedish players. IIHF, 'Nothing Equals the Rivalry of the Spring of 69', 2.

[44] According to some estimates, there were about 2,000 people gathered at Prague's Wenceslas Square. Casper, 'The Ice Hockey Crisis of 1969'.

[45] Národní muzeum, '... a přijely tanky. 1968'.

[46] Agnew, *The Czechs*, 269; *Rudé právo*, 'Ministerstvo vnitra ČSR k událostem z 28. a 29. března', 1–2.

[47] Casper, 'The Ice Hockey Crisis of 1969'.

[48] The pile of cobblestones had been brought in front of the Aeroflot office only the night before the match happened. See Pacina, 'Hokejová pomsta za okupaci'; Casper, 'The Ice Hockey Crisis of 1969'.

[49] *Rudé právo*, 'Vláda ČSR k událostem v noci ze dna 28. na 29. března 1969', 1–2.

[50] *Rudé právo*, 'Ještě k hokejovému zápasu ČSSR-SSSR', 13.

[51] Agnew, 'The Czechs'.

[52] These activities, among others, included attempts at emigration or public criticism of communism. Macků, *Utajené stránky hokejové historie*, 2.

[53] Děkanovský, *Sport, média a mýty*, 156.

[54] Roubal, 'Politics of Gymnastics', 6.

[55] Uhlíř and Waic, *Sokol proti totalitě 1938–1952*.

[56] Vašíčková, 'Sokolské hnutí'.

[57] Ibid.

[58] Bäumeltová, 'Jednota Sokol Bern'.

[59] ČSJ, *100 let jachtingu 1893–1993*, 41; Sedlák, 'Historie golfu v Českých zemích'.

[60] ČSJ, *100 let jachtingu 1893–1993*, 41.

[61] Ibid.

[62] Numerato, 'Revisiting Weber's Concept'.

[63] The trophy has not actually been awarded since 1950, most probably in order to prevent accusations of political provocation. Sedlák, Historie golfu v Českých zemích'.

References

Agnew, H.L. *The Czechs and the Lands of the Bohemian Crown*. Stanford, CA: Hoover Institution Press, 2004.

Balík, S., V. Hloušek, J. Holzer, and J. Šedo. 'Politický systém českých zemí 1848–1989'. Brno: Mezinárodní politologický ústav Masarykovy univerzity, 2003.

Bäumeltová. 'Jednota Sokol Bern'. Sokolská župa švýcarská. 2003. http://www.sokol.ch/jednota-sokol-bern.

Broad, K.L. 'The Gendered Unapologetic: Queer Resistance in Women's Sport'. *Sociology of Sport Journal* 18, no. 2 (2001): 181–204.

Budd, A. 'Capitalism, Sport and Resistance: Reflections'. *Culture, Sport, Society* 4, no. 1 (2001): 1–18.

Casper, P. 'The Ice Hockey Crisis of 1969'. *The Prague Post*, 2004. http://www.praguepost.com/P03/2004/Art/0422/sprts2.php.

Conversi, D. 'Immigration and Statelessness: Political Participation of Immigrants and their Descendants in Catalan and Basque Mobilizations (1959–1978)'. Paper presented at the ECPR Joint Session, Torino, Italy, March 22–27 2002.

ČSJ. *100 let jachtingu 1893–1993*. Praha: ČSJ, 1993.

De Certeau, M. *The Practice of Everyday Life*. Berkeley, CA: University of California Press, 1984.

Děkanovský, J. *Sport, média a mýty*. Vimperk: Dokořán, 2008.

Donnelly, P. 'Resistance Through Sports'. In *Sports et Societes Contemporaines: Proceedings of the VIIIe Symposium de L'ICSS*, Paris, France, July 6–10, 1983.

Duke, V. 'Local Tradition versus Globalisation: Resistance to the McDonaldisation and Disneyisation of Professional Football in England'. *Football Studies* 5, no. 1 (2002): 5–23.

Edelman, R. *Serious Fun: Soviet Spectator Sports*. New York: Oxford University Press, 1993.

Edelman, R. 'A Small Way of Saying "No": Moscow Working Men, Spartak Soccer, and the Communist Party, 1900–1945'. *American Historical Review* 107, no. 5 (2002): 1441–74.

Elling, A., P. de Knop, and A. Knoppers. 'Gay/Lesbian Sport Clubs and Events: Places of Homo-Social Bonding and Cultural Resistance?'. *International Review for the Sociology of Sport* 38, no. 4 (2003): 441–56.

Felcman, O. 'Počátky ostré etapy normalizace'. In *Československo roku 1968 2.díl: Počátky normalizace*, edited by M. Bárta, O. Felcman, J. Belda, and M. Mencl, 51–81. Praha: Ústav mezinárodních vztahů, 1993.

Gilchrist, P., and N. Ravenscroft. 'The (Sub)politics of Sport: Space Hijacking and Culture Jamming'. Paper presented at the 2nd Annual Conference of the PSA Sport and Politics Group. Liverpool, UK, February 15, 2008.

Giuntini, S. *Pugni chiusi e cerchi olimpici*. Roma: Odradek, 2008.

Hollander, J.A., and R.L. Einwohner. 'Conceptualizing Resistance'. *Sociological Forum* 19, no. 1 (2004): 533–54.

Horne, J. 'The Politics of Sport and Leisure in Japan: Global Power and Local Resistance'. *International Review for the Sociology of Sport* 33, no. 2 (1998): 171–82.

Iannotta, J.G., and M.J. Kane. 'Sexual Stories as Resistance Narratives in Women's Sports: Reconceptualizing Identity Performance'. *Sociology of Sport Journal* 19, no. 4 (2002): 347–69.

IIHF. 'Nothing Equals the Rivalry of the Spring of 69'. News Release: IIHF World Championship Special, 2002.

Jamison, B. 'The Sandgate Handicap Riot: Sport, Popular Culture and Working Class Protest'. *Sporting Traditions* 12, no. 2 (1996): 17–48.

Jokisipilä, M. 'Cold War on Ice: Cold War on Ice International Ice Hockey as an Arena of Ideological Confrontation Between East and West'. Paper presented at the Conference Sport between East and West. University of Zürich, Switzerland, October 8–10, 2005.

Keech, M. 'Contest, Conflict and Resistance in South Africa's Sport Policies'. In *Power Games: A Critical Sociology of Sport*, edited by J. Sugden and A. Tomlinson, 161–80. London: Routledge, 2004.

Lennartz, K. 'Olympic Boycotts'. Paper presented at the ISSA and ISHPES Joint World Congress 2007 'Sport in a Global World'. Copenhagen, Denmark, July 31–August 5, 2007.

Macků, J. *Utajené stránky hokejové historie 2: Kauza Zábrodský, Na oltáři komunismu*. Praha: Typo JP, 2004.

Majumdar, B. 'Cultural Resistance and Sport: Politics, Leisure and Colonialism – Lagaan – Invoking Lost History'. *Culture, Sport, Society* 5, no. 2 (2002): 29–44.

Marada, R. *Kultura protestu a politizace každodennosti*. Brno: CDK, 2003.

Numerato, D. 'Sport as Resistance: "Ice Hockey Protests" in Czechoslovakia in 1969'. In *Sport and the Construction of Identities: Proceedings of the XIth International CESH-Congress*, Vienna, September 17–20, 2006, edited by B. Kratzmüller, M. Marschik, R. Müllner, H.D. Szemethy, and E. Trink, 704–12. Wien: Verlag Turia + Kant, 2007.

Numerato, D. 'Revisiting Weber's Concept of Disenchantment: An Examination of the Re-enchantment with Sailing in the Post-communist Czech Republic'. *Sociology* 43, no. 3 (2009): 439–56.

Ok, G. 'The Political Significance of Sport: An Asian Case Study – Sport, Japanese Colonial Policy and Korean National Resistance, 1910–1945'. *The International Journal of the History of Sport* 22, no. 4 (2005): 649–70.

Pacina, V. 'Hokejová pomsta za okupaci'. *MF Dnes*, March 25, 2004, Magazín.

Pelak, C.F. 'Negotiating Gender/Race/Class Constraints in the New South Africa: A Case Study of Women's Soccer'. *International Review for the Sociology of Sport* 40, no. 1 (2005): 53–70.

Pelletier, J. 'Czechoslovakian Victory Tops Summit Series for Emotion'. www.hockeyfights.com (2004). http://www.hockeyfights.com/articles/191.

Reed-Danahay, D. 'Talking about Resistance: Ethnography and Theory in Rural France'. *Anthropological Quarterly* 6, no. 4 (1993): 221–9.

Rinehart, R.E. 'Fists Flew and Blood Flowed: Symbolic Resistance and International Response in Hungarian Water Polo at the Melbourne Olympics'. *Journal of Sport History* 23, no. 2 (1996): 120–39.

Roubal, P. 'Politics of Gymnastics: Mass Gymnastic Displays under Communism in Central and Eastern Europe'. *Body & Society* 9, no. 2 (2003): 1–25.

Round Table. 'Kulatý Stůl. Česká sociologie v letech 1965–1989'. *Sociologický časopis* 5 (2004): 695–744.

Rudé právo. 'Vláda ČSR k událostem v noci ze dna 28. na 29. března 1969'. (March 31, 1969): 1–2.

Rudé právo. 'Ještě k hokejovému zápasu ČSSR-SSSR: Z úvodníku sovětského listu Pravda'. (April 1, 1969): 7.

Rudé právo, 'Ministerstvo vnitra ČSR k událostem z 28. a 29. března'. (April 1, 1969): 1–2.

Scott, J.C. *Weapons of the Weak.* New Haven: Yale University Press, 1985.

Sedlák, P. 'Historie golfu v Českých zemích (a na Slovensku)'. www.golf.cz (2001). http://old.golf.cz/historiemain.htm.

Shaw, S.M. 'Conceptualizing Resistance: Women's Leisure as Political Practice'. *Journal of Leisure Research* 33, no. 2 (2001): 186–201.

Sivaramakrishnan, K. 'Some Intellectual Genealogies for the Concept of Everyday Resistance'. *American Anthropologist* 107, no. 3 (2005): 346–55.

Thomson, R.W., and I. Soós. 'Research Note Youth Sport in New Zealand and Hungary Globalisation versus Local Resistance'. *International Sports Studies* 22, no. 2 (2000): 74–82.

Thorne, V. 'Ideologies and Realities of the Masses in Communist Czechoslovakia'. PhD diss., University of Pittsburgh, 2005.

Uhlíř, J., and M. Waic. *Sokol proti totalitě 1938–1952.* Praha: FTVS UK, 2001.

Vačkář, M. 'Nezkrácená verze rozhovoru s Čáslavskou'. www.idnes.cz (2007). http://sport.idnes.cz/nezkracena-verze-rozhovoru-s-caslavskou-fpv-/sporty.asp?c=A070503_130207_sporty_ber.

Vašíčková, Š. 'Sokolské hnutí v životě československé emigrace po II. světové válce na příkladu Austrálie a Jihoafrické republiky'. PhD diss. summary, Fakulta tělesné výchovy a sportu, Univerzita Karlova, Praha, 2007.

Williams, K. *The Prague Spring and its Aftermath: Czechoslovak Politics, 1968–1970.* Cambridge: Cambridge University Press, 1997.

Williams, T. 'Sport, Hegemony and Subcultural Reproduction: The Process of Accommodation in Bicycle Road Racing'. *International Review for the Sociology of Sport* 24, no. 4 (1989): 315–33.

The ambiguities of development: implications for 'development through sport'

David R. Black

Departments of Political Science and International Development Studies, Dalhousie University, Halifax, Canada

This essay brings the perspective of the academic sceptic to bear on Development Through Sport (DTS) – an area of rapid growth and burgeoning enthusiasm in the theory and practice of international development and organized sport respectively. It highlights some of the challenges and dangers of engaging in the development 'enterprise' for this comparatively new and hopeful field. While acknowledging the valuable contributions that may be made to development through sport, it identifies some core ambiguities in the idea and experience of development, and therefore some cautionary implications for those who come to development through this prism. Indeed, one of the key advantages of DTS advocates and actors is that they are latecomers to the development enterprise, with the opportunity to learn from the dangers and missteps that have befallen more 'mainstream' development practitioners through its post-Second World War history. Three key themes are explored: the ambiguous meanings and experiences of development; some of the core challenges they give rise to, particularly in the post-Structural Adjustment era of the late 1990s and beyond; and some key issues and possibilities for the DTS community in this context.

One of the more intriguing trends in the recent theory and practice of international development and of organized sport respectively is the rapid growth of initiatives that seek to advance development (both social and economic) through sport. There are many indicators of this: the proliferation of Non-Governmental Organizations working to promote development through sport; the increasing involvement of official (governmental) development agencies (such as Norway's NORAD, the UK's DFID, and Canada's CIDA) in supporting sport-based development initiatives; the increasing involvement of multilateral organizations, notably the United Nations and the Commonwealth, in this area; and the growing enthusiasm of youth – athletes, students and student-athletes – for research and volunteer opportunities in the development-sport nexus.[1] This trend, often characterized as the 'Sport for Development and Peace' (SDP) movement, has been described by scholar and activist Bruce Kidd as 'a timely, progressive impulse, and one of the most encouraging initiatives in sport in the last few years'.[2] Indeed, there is much to admire about the enthusiasm, idealism and 'can-do' zeal of many of those caught up in it. Their preoccupation with development *practice* – with the imperative of 'making a difference' in the lives of poor, marginalized and often conflict-affected communities globally – is also both admirable and inevitable. As John Loxley has noted, development as a field of study indissolubly links theoretical reflection on issues of justice, equity and social change with the imperative of *action*.[3] There is therefore much to be gained through interchange between development scholars and SDP practitioners.

It is also fair to say, however, that in its contemporary manifestation, the SDP emphasis on practice has come, for the most part, at the expense of critical and theoretically-informed reflection.[4] The aim of this essay is therefore to bring the perspective of the academic sceptic to bear on the consideration of development and Development Through Sport (DTS),[5] and to highlight some of the challenges and dangers of engaging in the development 'enterprise' for this new[6] and hopeful field. I am not going to suggest that there are not valuable contributions to be made to development through sport; rather I will highlight some core ambiguities in the idea and experience of development, and therefore some cautionary implications for those who come to development through this prism. Indeed, one of the key advantages of DTS advocates and actors is that they are latecomers to the 'development enterprise', with the opportunity to learn from some of the dangers and missteps that have befallen more 'mainstream' development practitioners through the chequered post-Second World War history of this enterprise.

In short then, I will touch on three key points:

(1) the ambiguous *meanings* and experiences of development;
(2) some of the core challenges they give rise to, particularly in the 'post-Structural Adjustment' era of the late 1990s and beyond; and
(3) some key issues and possibilities for the DTS community in this context.

The ambiguous meanings of development

There has long been a substantial cottage industry devoted to defining development. What this underscores is the inherently contentious and contested character of this ubiquitous concept. For purposes of this discussion I will use Jan Nederveen Pieterse's definition of development as 'the organized intervention in collective affairs according to a standard of improvement'.[7] Though relatively broad and vague, this definition has some key implications. First, it implies that development is *interventive* and *intentional*. There are obviously a vast number of forms that such interventions can take and an equally wide range of actors that can intervene, but this definition conceives of development as fundamentally purposive. It is noteworthy that even this is contested, as there is an alternative sense of development as 'immanent' process, often cyclical in nature, which is distinct from and may even be disrupted and corrupted by well-meant, purposive or 'intentional' development efforts.[8] Moreover, there are widely disparate conceptions of what constitutes *improvement*. These range from grand and universalistic theories, often associated with the world's most influential development agencies, including the World Bank and the International Monetary Fund (collectively the International Financial Institutions, or IFIs), to highly localized and contextualized conceptions growing out of specific cultural communities and localities. Frequently, the results are 'hybridized', as 'universalistic' or 'top-down' ideas get adopted, re-interpreted and/or exploited through distinct national and local prisms.

Given this complex and contested landscape, my general starting point is that virtually all serious development scholars are deeply ambivalent about the very *idea* of development in its institutionalized forms. We know that there have been substantial achievements through development interventions, in health, education, the generation of economic and other opportunities for individuals and communities, and the amelioration of human suffering. We also know that developmental achievements are notoriously difficult to sustain, and that developmental knowledge is very difficult to apply across diverse social and cultural settings, as well as in different time periods. *In extremis*, we know that developmental interventions *can be* severely damaging to the communities they are engaged with, whether by omission or commission. Perhaps the most disturbing contemporary example is Rwanda which, as Peter Uvin argues, was widely portrayed as a developmental 'success story' virtually right up to the genocide of 1994, and in which development policies and projects both failed to anticipate the possibility for genocidal violence, and contributed to the conditions from which it emerged.[9] However, scholars in rich and 'highly developed' countries such as Canada need think no further than the tragic legacies of interventive development in our own First Nations communities to appreciate its risks and dangers. Those who engage in development, whether as scholars or practitioners, therefore take on a major responsibility. It is very challenging, though also potentially very rewarding, to 'keep faith with' one's development 'partners'. It is also necessary to approach the challenge with a good deal of humility, openness, and ongoing self-reflection. Goodwill and idealism are not enough; as Kidd notes, '…the single-minded purpose and confidence that sport instils in champions, a commendable attribute when transferred to many other settings', may be ill-suited to the uncertain landscape of development.[10]

What, then, are some of the key alternative conceptions of development that have influenced its practice? The following thumbnail sketches are highly superficial, but capture key dimensions of this idea and tensions within it.[11]

First, development can be both large-scale and 'top-down' in conception and implementation, and small-scale or 'bottom up'. There is a long, more or less cyclical, history of development 'mega-projects' – often symbolically charged infrastructure projects (think hydro-electric dams, airports or indeed national stadiums) – on the one hand, and small-scale 'community' or 'grassroots development' initiatives on the other. Sport is increasingly implicated in both these forms of development. For example, much of the work of organizations such as the Mathare Youth Sports Association (MYSA), Right to Play, and Athletes for Africa/Gulu Walk consists of small-scale, community-level interventions in rural and marginalized urban communities or refugee/Internally Displaced Persons (IDP) camps. Yet much of it also depends on the support of large official development agencies and/or the profile and resources generated by transnational linkages and celebrity 'athlete ambassadors'. On the other hand, major games bids are a key focus of development policy in a growing number of 'semi-peripheral' developing countries seeking enhanced visibility, investment and comparative advantage. Thus, the 2010 FIFA World Cup, the 2010 Commonwealth Games in Delhi, and indeed the 2010 Vancouver Winter Olympics are key development policy priorities for their respective governments and associated 'booster coalitions', with major implications (and often dangerously inflated expectations) for the developmental trajectories of each host.[12]

Second, development, particularly in its large-scale capitalist forms but often in community level forms as well, can be understood following the Austrian political economist Joseph Schumpeter as characteristically involving a process of 'creative destruction'.[13] The processes of change implied by development are widely presumed to be, in some respects at least, historically progressive; but also in historical terms they have frequently implied major changes to, and ultimately the destruction of, long-standing communities, social relations, and ways of life. For Canadians, one need think no further than our own history of development rooted in increasingly intensive primary commodity production which has ultimately led, in my own region of Atlantic Canada for example, to the historic demise of many of the region's rich fisheries and regional mining and manufacturing centres, and to the depopulation of many long-standing coastal communities. This experience also highlights another point: development is ubiquitous – a process that unfolds in the global 'North' as well as the global 'South', albeit with different levels of intensity and stakes. Those of us in the global North who study and work on development should be mindful, therefore, of the need to critically re-examine our own development experiences, as well as our complicity (whether directly or indirectly) in conditions of polarization and poverty in the South.

Third, and closely related to the top down/bottom up axis, is that development can be a constraining, oppressive and 'disciplining' process. This deleterious potential is highlighted both by the draconian effects of neo-liberal thinking and the structural adjustment policies it inspired in the 1980s and 1990s,[14] as well as the discursive analyses of critical 'post-development' scholars exploring the ways in which Western thinkers and agencies 'constructed' global poverty and the Third World, often with the effect of reinforcing global hierarchies and limiting the imaginative possibilities for change.[15] Yet development can also be emancipatory in both its meaning and effects, creating at its best new and unprecedented opportunities for historically marginalized people and communities.[16] Indeed at times, these emancipatory possibilities arise in and through what are widely perceived as top-down policies and institutional structures associated with official development agencies. It is this emancipatory sense of development that, I am convinced, largely explains the explosive growth of International Development Studies programmes at universities in many parts of the world, as well as the flourishing of development NGOs and indeed the mounting enthusiasm of sportspeople and sport-based organizations for international development work. It is also why, despite the fraught history and ambiguous effects of many development interventions, I am not inclined to go along with the post-development rejection of the 'development project' *in toto*, but rather to agree with John Sugden's sentiment that, given the scale, importance and interconnectedness of the global development challenges we face, 'doing nothing may no longer be an option'.[17]

Key challenges

What then are the key challenges to which this ambiguous record and idea give rise? First, there is the challenge of connecting 'top-down' and bottom-up' strategies and possibilities. It is clear that most 'grand designs' for development, whether the modernizationist projects of the early post-Second World War decades, the state-socialist designs of the East Bloc, or the neo-liberal Structural Adjustment policies of 'marketization' effectively imposed on developing countries in the 1980s and 1990s, have ultimately foundered on unanticipated consequences and damaging human effects. Consequently, so-called 'alternative development'[18] designs that arose largely in reaction to Structural Adjustment policies have stressed locality, context and responsiveness to community priorities and dynamics (captured in the 'buzzwords' of 'ownership' and 'empowerment'[19]). Often these sorts of interventions have produced promising results in the short- to medium-term, and in localized contexts; yet they are enormously difficult to sustain in the face of often-hostile regional, national and transnational political and economic conditions. In the end, neither 'top-down' nor 'bottom-up' development approaches are going to disappear, nor are they sufficient on their own to generate sustainable and broadly based improvement in development conditions. There is a need, then, for development analysts and practitioners to try to draw connections between these various levels, and/or to engage with organizations operating at different levels and in other issue areas, in a spirit of ongoing self-reflection.

Second, there is no evading the *politics* of development knowledge and development practice. Developmental ideas inevitably bear the imprint of those who have articulated them, and are therefore inclined to empower some and disempower others. Similarly development practice, as a process of far-reaching change or even 'creative destruction' at both micro and macro levels, will encounter suspicion and resistance by those who occupy positions of relative privilege and power, whether at the 'grassroots' community level or within national governments, as well as those who have been the 'victims' of misplaced development interventions in the past.

No serious sport studies scholar would any longer defend the 'myth of autonomy'[20] – the idea that sport is apolitical, 'above' or autonomous from politics. Nevertheless, it is very hard to develop the sort of contextualized understanding of the communities in and with which one is working that is necessary for successful and sustainable development interventions. This challenge may be compounded for many sportspeople, convinced as they are of the transcendent power of sport and often having been relatively disengaged from mainstream politics. It is also hard to take account of the likelihood that progressive social change will encounter resistance, both from outside and above, and from inside and 'below'. An insightful illustration of this dynamic is provided by Craig Cameron in reflecting on his experience as a DTS Programme Coordinator in a refugee camp in Benin, where at different stages he and his partner were confronted by unexpected scepticism and resistance from both the community in which they were working, and the Northern agency that had engaged them.[21] It takes careful training, as well as an adroit ability to respond constructively to unanticipated challenges and to varied sources of resistance and support within and beyond the 'partner' community, to succeed in mounting a sustainable and effective development intervention in these circumstances.

Third, the 'world of development' has become a much more complex and pluralistic place as various grand designs have foundered and both small-scale and middle-range projects and ideas have shown varying degrees of promise. Even the intellectual confidence of the major International Financial Institutions in their development prescriptions has been shaken by 'real world' events, including the global 'market meltdown' and the resulting retreat from neoliberalism, creating a new level of openness to, and reliance on, non-governmental actors. One of the difficulties this gives rise to is that the boundaries between institutions, ideas and interests have become blurry, and key development buzzwords, like empowerment, partnership, and poverty alleviation, have become profoundly ambiguous in their meanings and implications. For example, how much significance and optimism should be vested in the growing movement towards Corporate Social Responsibility (CSR) among private sector actors – a trend that bears on DTS through the role these corporate actors play in funding various initiatives? What are we to make of the requirement of large western development agencies that developing countries adopt 'participatory' Poverty Reduction Strategy Papers (PRSPs) as a prerequisite for new development support? One key practical implication of this growing overlap and complexity is that there are key strategic allies to be found in a wide range of often-unexpected places – 'mainstream', official development institutions as well as small-scale, grassroots organizations. Development thinkers and actors are being compelled to take a considerably more open and contingent view of where to look for 'progressive' agents and opportunities. It is worth noting in this context that all development organizations are increasingly populated by people who have been trained in development studies programmes with decidedly critical orientations. Many of these officials continue to seek opportunities to advance more developmentally progressive practices, and may become key supporters of important new initiatives in DTS as elsewhere.

What issues and possibilities does this raise for Development Through Sport?

This challenging landscape opens up issues and possibilities for DTS at both 'top-down' and 'bottom-up' levels. Many of these are flagged and explored in the impressive literature reviews of the Sport for Development and Peace International Working Group,[22] which is an excellent starting point for anyone interested in the current 'state of the art' in both thinking and practice concerning sport and child/youth development, health, gender, people with disabilities, and post-conflict reconciliation and the promotion of peace.

Somewhat more specifically, from the top down, one key challenge is to draw a more systematic link between major sporting events and community-level needs and interests. This is a relatively old idea,[23] but one that has rarely been effectively acted upon. There is already evidence, for example, that community-level sport and social development are being compromised by South Africa's pursuit of the trappings of externally defined and validated modernity through its hosting of the FIFA World Cup.[24] These risks may be comparably acute in the context of less high profile events and countries, such as the forthcoming 2011 All Africa Games in Lusaka, Zambia.[25] This raises the question: what would a *truly* developmental World Cup or Olympics, privileging the needs and interests of marginalized communities, look like? And how could pressure be mobilized towards this objective?

A second issue and challenge concerns the role of 'celebrity diplomats': how to draw on the celebrity of athlete-ambassadors in ways that contribute to sustainable long-term change? Organizations such as Right to Play and Athletes for Africa/Gulu Walk have made extensive use of such popular public figures,[26] and indeed in the former case much of its initial profile and success was attributable to its first lead Athlete Ambassador – Norwegian speed skater and four-time gold medalist Johann Olav Koss. The impact and effectiveness of such athletic celebrities depends in part on enlisting the 'right' ambassadors, but also on using them in ways that highlight the resilience and creativity of local communities rather than the benevolence and celebrity of these sporting heroes. This is not easy to achieve, especially given that their role is filtered through national and transnational media intent on exploiting the human interest angle of such figures. One possibility is to try to engage them much more in highlighting the need for sustained and sustainable policy change in donor governments and countries – not just on more and better aid, but on restructured trade policies, corporate social responsibility, human security interventions, and the like. It is likely, for example, that a key reason why the Canadian government has remained a major participant in the ongoing peace process in Northern Uganda is the mobilization of informed public interest and pressure through the Gulu Walks of Athletes for Africa, supported by such sport stars as former NBA Most Valuable Player Steve Nash.[27]

Particularly at more regional and local levels, there is the challenge of thinking *strategically* about the distinctive opportunities and risks associated with engaging in the politics of development from a position that is widely perceived as less *overtly political* – that is, from the position of leaders and participants in sport. In other words, how can the resilient, recreational and relatively apolitical identity of sport be drawn upon as a resource for making change? What distinctive opportunities does it provide, and what risks does it present when DTS practitioners are seen to 'stray beyond' their appropriate limits into more 'high stakes' areas of political, economic and social development? Understanding and being prepared to make use of the distinctive image of sport as 'play' demands a high level of strategic sophistication on the part of DTS practitioners, and places a very significant onus on pre- and post-departure preparation, training and de-briefing.

Similarly, how can DTS policy-makers and practitioners best use the 'convening' power of sport – what MYSA founder Bob Munro has referred to as the fact that 'every team is a mobilized youth group' – again, without compromising the recreational appeal of sport and thus undermining this mobilizing potential?[28]

Finally, and as the SDP International Working Group literature reviews highlight, there is a need to communicate and collaborate much more closely with development actors in other sectors and institutions. For, as these reviews note,[29] DTS interventions will not be successful or sustainable for most participants in the absence of a much wider range of interventions, changes and improvements. DTS practitioners must themselves be persuaded to transcend the 'myth of autonomy' to learn from, and collaborate much more systematically with, the diverse panoply of development agents, bearing in mind the earlier observation that sources of opportunity, resources and leadership can be found within a wide range of agencies up to and including some of the largest.

I want to conclude by revisiting the work of Jan Nederveen Pieterse. In his book *Development Theory*, he writes that 'Development ... is intrinsically uncertain and contested: coherence is a moving target; concertation is never fully achieved; dialogue is ever imperfect; software is never complete; learning never ends'.[30]

The paradox of development, then, is that it requires a simultaneous acceptance of contingency and contestation, which historically has discouraged risk-averse policy-makers in all sorts of organizations and has led to notoriously unstable and inconstant development priorities and policies, with the imperative need for a long-term commitment to remain engaged, build relationships and learn from mistakes as well as successes. If DTS interventions can help build and sustain such long-term commitments and relationships in the face of ongoing uncertainty and adaptation, they will have made a valuable contribution to the larger development enterprise.

Notes

[1] For useful summaries of this growing 'movement', see Kidd, 'A New Social Movement', and Beutler, 'Sport Serving Development'. Kidd notes, for example, the experience of a Canadian colleague who had more students in her sociology of sport class choose to write their research essay on Sport for Development and Peace than any other topic ('A New Social Movement', 375). I have witnessed a similar growth of interest in this area among International Development Studies students at my own university.

[2] Kidd, 'A New Social Movement', 378.

[3] Loxley, 'What is Distinctive?', 28–9.

[4] See Kidd, 'A New Social Movement', 377. For an important and impressive effort to alter this balance, see the *Literature Reviews*, commissioned by the SDP IWG.

[5] I will use Development Through Sport (DTS) in this essay in preference to Sport for Development and Peace, because it implies a broader focus not tied to the normative objectives of the SDP movement.

[6] As Kidd notes, the pursuit of social development through sport has a long history. By 'new' therefore, I am referring to the mainly post-Cold War re-emergence of interest in this relationship, marked by new athlete-activists and proliferating actors.

[7] Pieterse, *Development Theory*, 3.

[8] For an extended exploration of this distinction and its implications in the long history of development thought and practice, see Cowen and Shenton, *Doctrines of Development*.

[9] See Uvin, *Aiding Violence*.

128   D.R. Black

[10] Kidd, 'A New Social Movement', 377.
[11] It is noteworthy that the various dimensions of development discussed in the remainder of this section have interesting echoes in the world of sport. For example, 'top down' vs. 'bottom up' development can be compared with the perennial co-existence and tension between high performance and 'grassroots'/mass participation sport. Similarly sport, like development, has been both oppressive and liberating in its effects.
[12] See, for example, the Special Issue *Third World Quarterly* 25, no. 7 (2004) on 'Global Games', and *Politikon* 34, no. 3 (2007), Special Issue on 'Crafting Legacies: The Changing Political Economy of Global Sport and the 2010 FIFA World Cup'. See also Black, 'The Symbolic Politics'.
[13] On Schumpeter's 'Purpose of Development', see Cowen and Shenton, *Doctrines of Development*, 396–409.
[14] See, for example, Martinussen, *Society, State and Market*, 257–74.
[15] See, for example, Pieterse, *Development Theory*, 99–112.
[16] For an interesting instance of this potential, associated with sport, see Willis, 'Sport and Development'.
[17] Cited in the SDP IWG, *Literature Reviews*, 186.
[18] See Pieterse, *Development Theory*, 73–98. See also Parpart and Veltmeyer, 'The Development Project', esp. 48–9.
[19] See Cornwall and Brock, 'What Do Buzzwords Do?'.
[20] See Allison, 'The Changing Context', 5–6.
[21] Cameron, '"Happiness" and "Holes"'.
[22] SDP IWG, *Literature Reviews*.
[23] See, for example, Kidd, 'The Toronto Olympic Commitment', and Hiller, 'Mega-events'.
[24] See, for example, Alegi, 'The Political Economy', and van der Westhuizen, 'Glitz, Glamour, and the Gautrain'.
[25] I am indebted to Bruce Kidd for this example.
[26] See for example RTP's extensive list of 'Athlete Ambassadors': http://rtpca.convio.net/site/PageServer?pagename=athletes_map. On 'celebrity diplomacy' in international development, see Cameron and Haanstra, 'Development Made Sexy'.
[27] On Gulu Walk/Athletes for Africa, see http://www.guluwalk.com. See also Adrian Bradbury, Paul Dewar, and Alexa McDonough, 'Quiet Diplomacy or Lost Opportunity?' *Chronicle Herald (Halifax),* November 18, 2008.
[28] My thanks to Owen Willis for flagging this potential.
[29] See, for example, SDP IWG, *Literature Reviews*, 34.
[30] Pieterse, *Development Theory*, 158.

References

Alegi, Peter. 'The Political Economy of Mega-Stadiums and the Underdevelopment of Grassroots Football in South Africa'. *Politikon* 34, no. 3 (2007): 315–31.
Allison, Lincoln. 'The Changing Context of Sporting Life'. In *The Changing Politics of Sport*, edited by L. Allison, 1–14. Manchester: Manchester University Press, 1993.
Beutler, Ingrid. 'Sport Serving Development and Peace: Achieving the Goals of the United Nations through Sport'. *Sport in Society* 11, no. 4 (2008): 359–69.
Black, David. 'The Symbolic Politics of Sport Mega-Events: 2010 in Comparative Perspective'. *Politikon* 34, no. 3 (2010): 261–76.
Cameron, Craig. '"Happiness" and "Holes": Questions for the Future of Development Through Sport'. *Canadian Journal of Development Studies* 27, no. 4 (2006): 567–72.
Cameron, John, and Anna Haanstra. 'Development Made Sexy: How it Happened and What it Means'. *Third World Quarterly* 29, no. 8 (2008): 1475–89.
Cornwall, Andrea, and Karen Brock. 'What Do Buzzwords Do for Development Policy? A Critical Look at "Participation", "Empowerment" and "Poverty Reduction"'. *Third World Quarterly* 26, no. 7 (2005): 1043–60.
Cowen, Michael, and Robert Shenton. *Doctrines of Development*. London: Routledge, 1996.
Hiller, Harry. 'Mega-events, Urban Boosterism and Growth Strategies: An Analysis of the Objectives and Legitimations of the Cape Town 2004 Olympic Bid'. *International Journal of Urban and Regional Research* 24, no. 2 (2004): 439–58.

Kidd, Bruce. 'The Toronto Olympic Commitment: Towards a Social Contract for the Olympic Games'. *Olympika: The International Journal of Olympic Studies* 1 (1992): 154–67.

Kidd, Bruce. 'A New Social Movement: Sport for Development and Peace'. *Sport in Society* 11, no. 4 (2008): 370–80.

Loxley, John. 'What is Distinctive about International Development Studies?' *Canadian Journal of Development Studies* 25, no. 1 (2004): 25–38.

Martinussen, John. *Society, State and Market*. London: Zed Books, 1997.

Parpart, Jane, and Henry Veltmeyer. 'The Development Project in Theory and Practice: A Review of its Shifting Dynamics'. *Canadian Journal of Development Studies* 25, no. 1 (2004): 39–59.

Pieterse, Jan Nederveen. *Development Theory: Deconstructions/Reconstructions*. London: Sage Publications, 2001.

Sport for Development and Peace International Working Group (SDP IWG) Secretariat. *Literature Reviews on Sport for Development and Peace*, Toronto, August 31, 2007.

Uvin, Peter. *Aiding Violence: The Development Enterprise in Rwanda*. Hartford, CT: Kumarian Press, 1998.

Van der Westhuizen, Janis. 'Glamour and the Gautrain: Mega-Projects as Political Symbols'. *Politikon* 34, no. 3 (2007): 333–51.

Willis, Owen. 'Sport and Development: The Significance of Mathare Youth Sports Association'. *Canadian Journal of Development Studies* 21, no. 3 (2000): 825–49.

One day, one goal? PUMA, corporate philanthropy and the cultural politics of brand 'Africa'[1]

Michael D. Giardina

Department of Advertising, Program for Cultural Studies and Interpretive Research, College of Media, University of Illinois, Urbana-Champaign, Urbana, USA

This essay addresses lifestyle sport brand PUMA and its recent activist endeavours with respect to 'Africa'. Charting a path different from those of transaction-based philanthropic affairs such as (Product)[RED], PUMA, the author suggests, has deployed a transformation-based strategy organized around messages of peace and social justice in which supporters are charged with affecting change themselves in concrete interactions rather than impersonally or from a distance. Likewise, the author discusses the role of Cameroonian footballer Samuel Eto'o and his location to PUMA's mediated efforts with respect to PUMA's brand footprint on the continent. The essay concludes by noting that while such efforts are a step in the right direction, the story is necessarily a work-in-progress.

We can't sit around in our armchairs and expect peace to come, because it won't. We need ... to create the world we want.

Jeremy Gilley, 2004[2]

We are the change we need.

Barack Obama, 2008

Brand[ing] Africa?

The cultural anthropologist, James Ferguson, introduces his recent book, *Global Shadows: Africa in the Neoliberal World Order*, by serving up the following question and answer: 'What kind of place is Africa? The question, on the face of it, is an improbable one'. He continues, asking: 'Is there any meaningful sense in which we can speak of this as a "place" ... the unity of a thing called Africa?' The answer, he suggests, is quite simply 'no'.[3]

Yet, paradoxically, as nation-branding pioneer Simon Anholt reminds us, in the popular imagination of the West, 'Africa' is suffering from what he refers to as the continent brand effect, because, he argues, there is, generally speaking, a dearth of public awareness and knowledge of the individual countries of Africa such that every country on the continent – apart from South Africa – tends to remain grafted to the same reputation whereby 'even a relatively prosperous nation like Botswana ends up sharing perceptions of violence with Rwanda, of corruption with Nigeria, of poverty with Ethiopia, or of famine with Sudan'.[4] This is true especially in the United States, Anholt implies, where the 'simple message of ongoing catastrophe is promoted with skill, dedication, creativity and vast financial and media resources' by aid agencies, NGOs and, most prominently, by the likes of celebrity spokespersons such as Angelina Jolie and U2's Bono alongside far-reaching consumer-based projects such as (Product)ᴿᴱᴰ.[5] As a result, the branded image of Africa in the West is most assuredly *not* one of '53 individual countries in various stages of development and struggle for independent existence and identity' but rather, as Anholt puts it, 'as a uniform, hopeless basket-case'.[6]

Such an uncritical public understanding we might partially attribute to the relatively ineffectual US media, which has increasingly become consolidated around several corporate power blocs like those of News Corporation and Time-Warner, and whose news divisions operate evermore like Potter Puppet Pal theatres[7] than like serious bastions of journalistic integrity on the national stage. Indeed, most mainstream reporting of the genocide in Darfur, for example, alternates between watered-down, high school text book-level coverage on CNN or MSNBC, and childish rantings by neoconservative right-wing pundits like Rush Limbaugh, Bill O'Reilly,[8] and Glenn Beck (the latter two of whom continue to occupy prominent host positions on Fox News Channel, suggesting that irony is alive and well). And, when we look at popular media representations of 'Africa', we find, as Natilie Domeisen has chronicled, that 'In tourist offices, the most frequent images of Africa are those of safari animals; in the news, the tragedy of several conflicts linger. On film screens, conflict diamonds take centre stage in one Hollywood movie, and the latest *James Bond* includes African gunrunners.'[9]

Yet, from a cynical-if-not-relatively-successful *promotional* point of view, remaining within such a communication grid has in many ways become the accepted norm for generating charity and promoting charitable causes through the activation of feelings of pity or despair, or what Hannah Arendt might see as the deployment of a *politics of pity*.[10] Drawing from Luc Boltanski, we can understand this kind of intersubjective sentimentality as a political formulation distinguished not by activist notions of social justice but on passive, if not distant, observation: 'observation of the *unfortunate* by those who do not share their suffering, who do not experience it directly, and who, as such, may be regarded as fortunate or *lucky* people'.[11] To co-opt Lauren Berlant, the outward expression of such distant observation has forged a kind of Africa-centric philanthropic 'intimate public' within the West – an historically situated collectivity 'created by biopower, class antagonism, nationalism, imperialism, and/or the law'[12] – that frames the 'common sense' understandings of 'Africa' 'we' might hold in the first place.

In this vein, we might do well to think here of the way in which celebrities such as Jolie or Madonna have become represented vis-à-vis narratives about Africa and what many see as their role as interloping colonizers, or in numerous US-based, corporate- and/or philanthropic-oriented Public Service Announcements (PSAs) that aim to shed light on various causes, such as those related to clean water, breast cancer or HIV/AIDS. Take the case of Charity:Water, a grassroots non-profit organization that endeavours to bring clean, safe drinking water to developing nations. In perhaps its most famous television spot, we witness the collision of a maudlin musical score, distant or pensive facial expressions from those in the background, and sadness and sorrow on the part of celebrity stand-in Jennifer Connelly – who is already bound to 'Africa' via her starring turn as war correspondent Maddy Bowen alongside Leonardo DiCaprio's diamond-smuggling Danny Archer in the 2006 film *Blood Diamonds* – providing visually polluted drinking water from New York's Central Park to her children around the dinner table; the PSA concludes with a stark exhortation to contribute money to the cause.[13] The metaphoric juxtaposition of First World/Third World narratives – here placing the pond in Central Park as a stand-in for some distant, polluted African water source – is a device frequently used to forge an emotional tie to an otherwise foreign or unknown situation. And, when we follow the web address listed at the end, charitywater.org, we are delivered to a flashy-yet-minimalist site that includes links to consumer-oriented tie-ins such as one by high-end retailer Saks Fifth Avenue for Live Strong-styled black rubber bracelets available for $5, and white t-shirts with the word 'Water' printed on the front available for $25. In this instance, like much in the universe of other 'causumerist'[14] products, the branded apparel becomes a vehicle through which consumers (for a price) internally identify with a cause, and in turn make such identification a public expression of their 'activist' performativity.

Differently arrayed but with similar intent on a much grander and more ambitious scale, the much-ballyhooed, 2006-launched (Product)[RED] initiative, spearheaded by U2 frontman Bono and Bobby Shriver (one of John F. Kennedy's nephews long affiliated with philanthropic causes), explicitly moved, as Stefano Ponte and Lisa Ann Richey argue, to 'reconfigure the modalities of international development assistance' *away* from traditional notions of philanthropy and *toward* one of transaction-based global commerce.[15] Positioned as a brand identity created specifically to raise awareness and money for the Global Fund to Fight AIDS, Tuberculosis and Malaria by teaming up with iconic brands such as Apple, Converse, Gap and Dell to produce (RED)-branded, fashion-forward, identity-informing products, the campaign is akin to that of venture philanthropy, in which global corporations selling (RED) products allege to facilitate 'doing well by doing good', as Matthew Bishop and Michael Green in *Philanthrocapitalism* put it, 'conscience commerce' as Hillary Kramer terms it, or 'consumption as the mechanism for compassion', as Ponte and Richey would have it.[16]

This *business-model-first* approach is laid out in concrete terms on the (RED) website (www.joinred.com), which contains a '(RED) Manifesto' that states:

> All things being equal. They are not.
>   As first world consumers, we have tremendous power. What we collectively choose to buy, or not to buy, can change the course of life and history on this planet.
>   (RED) is that simple an idea. And that powerful. Now, you have a choice. There are (RED) credit cards, (RED) phones, (RED) shoes, (RED) fashion brands, and no, this does not mean they are all red in colour, although some are.
>   If you buy a (RED) product or sign up for a (RED) service, at no cost to you, a (RED) company will give some of its profits to buy and distribute anti-retroviral medicine to our brothers and sisters dying of AIDS in Africa.
>   We believe that when consumers are offered this choice, and the products meet their needs, they will choose (RED), and when they choose (RED) over non-(RED), then more brands will choose to become (RED) because it will make good business sense to do so. And more lives will be saved.
>   (RED) is not a charity, it is simply a business model. You buy (RED) stuff, we get the money, buy the pills and distribute them. They take the pills, stay alive, and continue to take care of their families and contribute socially and economically in their communities.
>   If they don't get the pills, they die. We don't want them to die. We want to give them the pills. And we can, and you can, and it's easy.
>   All you have to do is upgrade your choice.[17]

What we see here, as Jessica Bennett writes, is the promotion of a 'commodity context'[18] in which '[a]ctivism is the new chic, and we, the consumers, have become the new activists – saving the world one credit-card transaction at a time'.[19] In terms of (RED), its commodity context is that in which 'the thing to be exchanged is equated to the lives of African AIDS patients, *as well as* to the market price paid by consumers'.[20] Solely from the perspective of raising funds for its stated causes, the (RED) project has been unquestionably successful; according to its own press materials, the three-year campaign has thus far raised a total of USD$130 million.[21] However, Mya Frazier of *Advertising Age* magazine speculated in early 2007 that the 'collective marketing outlay by GAP, Apple, and Motorola for the (RED) campaign' for the then-one-year-old campaign had already reached close to $100 million (though others, such as Paul Vallely claimed that number was closer to USD$30 million).[22] In any event, we can submit that that campaign has at the least resulted in millions of dollars of philanthropic capital funnelled to the Global Fund, whatever the initial marketing outlay might actually have been.

But there is more to it than a simple numbers game. As Juliana Mansvelt reminds us, initiatives such as (RED) open up a space

> in which *citizenship* is produced through consumption practice with specific commodities and the social practices surrounding them providing a starting place for reflection on the regulation and surveillance of public space ... a righteous shopping community which emphasizes moral citizenship and the entrepreneurial self, while removing both real and imagined disruptive potentialities.[23]

Indeed, if we look to the '(RED) Manifesto' itself, First World/Western/neoliberal capitalism and its purveyors are positioned in a normative light vacant from any discussion of how such an enterprise itself potentially contributes negatively to the current conditions governing poverty, health or international image relative to the African continent. That is to say, following Katarina Jungar and Elaine Salo, the (RED) campaign 'employs heroic language which implies that those who support it are the "saviors" of its beneficiaries. The affective impact of this language, however, comes at the cost of recycling stereotypical images of Africa and the 'Third World' and constructing northern consumers as "good Samaritans".'[24] Not only that, but the 'samaritanization' of the West may further contribute to the formation of 'recuperative histories ... in which certain white figures come to stand for an alternative tradition of colonialism – one with which guilty white Australians, New Zealanders, North Americans and "metropolitan" Britons, among others, can identify in their attempts to disown an apparently more shameful colonial past'.[25] One major result of the above-mentioned dialectical positioning is that 'shopping for a better world' is now more than ever 'entrenched in the consumer ethic'.[26] Which is to say, writes Krishna Lalbiharie, the dominant narrative is now positioned as one in which

> buying a bottle of Starbucks Ethos water will resultantly deliver clean water to 'children of the world'; owning a pink Kitchen Aid mixer brings with it promises of a cure for breast cancer; and Ben and Jerry's 'American Pie' brand ice cream urges buyers to support its campaign to redistribute U.S. federal budget monies towards the betterment of sick children.[27]

One could argue, then, as Heather Havrilesky does, that by 'trivializing the tragic, we reduce its proportions enough to put it behind us'[28] – social activism replaced by simple consumerism, the promotion of corporate capitalism over grassroots participation. Or, as Colleen O'Manique and Ronald Labonte, writing in *The Lancet* put it, an act in which the 'seemingly just *consumer* supplants the just *citizen* and social justice itself is commodified'.[29] Samantha J. King sums it up for us:

> The significance attributed to [quick, convenient and relatively inexpensive acts of giving] stems in large part from their association with ideals of active citizenship, or from the notion that citizenship in the contemporary moment should be *less* about the exercising of rights and the fulfilment of obligations and *more* about fulfilling one's political responsibilities through socially sanctioned consumption and responsible choice.[30]

However, change *may* be afoot, with a move *away* from *transaction*-based corporate philanthropic efforts (i.e., where the purchase of products and a percentage donation of the profit is passed along to a charitable cause or initiative is considered the overriding focus, as in the aforementioned examples) and a move *toward* that of *transformation*-based efforts starting to appear more and more frequently. That is, efforts that are organized around individuals themselves becoming personally invested in, and actively participating at, the grassroots level in such efforts that aim to paradigmatically shift elements of the social order.[31] In this framework, buying a branded product isn't the first, last and only act of philanthropic citizenship engaged in by an individual. Rather, such an act might not even exist.

Although the ultimate efficacy of such a move remains unclear, it would appear that there is at least cautious reason to be optimistic (if ever such a thing could be said about placing trust in a corporate entity to 'do the right thing'). In the remainder of this essay, I outline one such brand that has endeavoured to begin moving in this direction – the lifestyle athletic brand PUMA – and explore its relationship to approaching 'Africa' not so much as a place without hope, but rather as an opportunity for revitalization. Specifically, I want to look at the intersection of three competing discourses: 1) PUMA's brand identity vis-à-vis Africa in an age of conscience commerce; 2) its sponsored association with filmmaker-activist Jeremy Gilley's 'Peace One Day' and 'One Day, One Goal' movements; and 3) its use of Cameroonian footballer Samuel Eto'o in its Africa related ad campaigns.

PUMA goes to Africa

> I believe in the responsibility to contribute to a better world for the generations to come.
>
> Jochen Zeitz, CEO, PUMA[32]

PUMA, the fourth-largest athletic apparel company in the world, has in recent years, and as part of its Phase IV long-term brand development strategy intended to 'reinforce its position as one of the leading multi-category Sportlifestyle brands'[33] in the world, implemented or adopted numerous corporate sustainability measures that seek to orient the brand as a socially conscious entity. Such moves include publicly declaring adherence to the 10 Global Compact Principles of the United Nations Global Compact – a framework for business committed to aligning their operations and strategies with ten principles in the areas of human rights, labour, the environment and anti-corruption. In line with this effort, PUMA created an internal set of standards throughout its production and supply chain, known as the SAFE Concept (which stands for Social Accountability and Fundamental Environmental Standards), and has normalized its business operations around what it refers to as its five core pillars: transparency, dialogue, evaluation, social accountability and sustainability.[34] From a business operations standpoint, these initial efforts resulted in PUMA gaining entry to the Dow Jones Sustainability Index in the United States (the first global index to track the financial performance of the leading sustainability-driven companies worldwide) and the FTSE Socially Responsible Investment Index in the United Kingdom (which performs a similar function of tracking companies that 'meet globally recognized corporate responsibility standards'[35]). Likewise, GoodGuide.com, a Certified B corporation founded by Environmental Science and Policy Professor Dara O'Rourke at the University of California-Berkeley that charts the health, environmental and social impacts and performances of corporate entities, gives PUMA generally favourable ratings in the areas of its global warming policy, energy and environmental management, workplace conditions, labour policy (non-supply chain), community engagement and corporate ethics.[36]

Recent events organized under the banner of PUMA's social responsibility engagement also include such diverse arrangements as its partnership with the US-based Soles4Souls initiative, which is oriented to provide footwear to those in need through the direct peer-to-peer giving of shoes; its scholarship programme at Central Saint Martins College of Art & Design in London; and laudable internal efforts such as Charity Cat, a volunteer organization formed by 20 PUMA employees to lend time and technical expertise to humanitarian-oriented projects.

Of particular note, and on the largest scale with respect to this public re-branding of PUMA as a *self-avowed* socially-conscious, forward-thinking corporate citizen, has been its efforts related to Africa over the last several years (since at least the run-up to the 2006 World Cup), which have been revealed most notably in its expansionary efforts toward the continent through a series of sponsorship agreements with various national teams and through endorsement deals with football stars such as Samuel Eto'o of Cameroon (who plays for Spanish *La Liga* club FC Barcelona). Somewhat remarkably, PUMA's efforts have, with some minor exceptions detailed shortly, approached Africa not as a charity case to be pitied, per se, but as an untapped marketplace and, more importantly, potential vehicle for the realization of *social change* narratives to emerge, what we might consider a transformational – rather than transactional – approach to commerce.[37]

Jochen Zeitz, CEO of PUMA, situated its brand strategy regarding Africa in this fashion:

> For us it [the Africa plan] is just part of who we are and what we do. We are about innovation and we want to look at new ways of moving the brand and our product forward and we believe there is tremendous excitement in Africa – we want to use that as part of our self-expression. It's about passion, colorfulness and diversity. To bring Africa to the rest of the world or innovation throughout Africa is an approach that no one has ever selected before. And that's why we got so heavily involved.[38]

These efforts have taken on a tripartite approach: 1) an African-themed advertising campaign featuring Eto'o combined with opening PUMA retail outlets in various African countries, such as the Accra Mall in Ghana (the first 'world class shopping centre' in the country); 2) sponsorship of various African national football clubs and the production of branded apparel of both the traditional and limited-edition charitable iterations; and 3) its involvement with Jeremy Gilley's Peace One Day campaign.

According to PUMA's own press archive, these endeavours are positioned, in the sense of media promotion, for increasing PUMA's brand footprint *in Africa*, and can be traced to efforts begun during the 2006 World Cup held in Germany. It was during that World Cup that PUMA first entered into a joint partnership with the charitable organization United for Africa to, in its own words, 'raise international awareness for the 30 aid organizations that came together in the concerted campaign United for Africa'.[39] On PUMA's part, this involved the creation of a PUMA Charity Collection complete with fashion-show launch party, a retail entertainment tram running on select routes throughout Berlin promoting United for Africa, and sponsorship of a music CD/coffee-table book collection focusing on African musicians and featuring artwork by the Nigerian fashion photographer Andrew Dosunmu. In a similar vein, numerous events and shows with celebrity artists and sportspersons took place in and around Berlin's historic Café Moskau (PUMA's de facto football headquarters during the World Cup), which further served to raise awareness for United for Africa.

It can be argued that one of the main motivating forces behind this alignment is PUMA's long-term focus on 2010, when the World Cup is to be held in South Africa. As noted in a corporate press release dated 15 June 2006, 'World Cup 2006 might not be over yet but … now, it is time for us to move on to the next project: the World Cup in South Africa'.[40] The release continued, 'PUMA will in the coming four years strive to strengthen its strong, positive position in Africa … For many this may seem to be a daunting task, but thankfully PUMA's efforts have already paid off as we are already indisputably the most visible football brand in Africa.'[41] Ghana Football Federation President Kwesi Nyantakyi later concurred with the positive effects of such a partnership, stating: 'We are proud to be partners with such a global brand that has made a commitment to football in both Ghana and the African continent on the whole.'[42]

Moving forward two years hence, to 2008, PUMA outfitted 9 of the 16 African nations competing at the Africa Cup of Nations held in Egypt. It was here that PUMA solidified its brand footprint in Africa, heavily promoting sponsorship deals with Ghana, Cameroon, Egypt, Tunisia, Senegal, Morocco and others. The result was, in PUMA's own words, that 'PUMA gained brand visibility throughout 87.5% of the tournament, showing the strongest brand visibility on the pitch of all sport apparel companies ... In the semi-finals, all teams were supplied by PUMA, making us the most prominent brand.'[43]

In fairness, the above moves represent a fairly benign approach to situating the PUMA brand in and around Africa, intended to appeal to a new wave of African consumers hoping to participate in the fruits of global capitalism at locations such as the Accra Mall in Ghana. Indeed, PUMA South Africa Managing Director, Ronald Rink, is clear on this point, stating with respect to the opening of a similar PUMA store in Cape Town's Canal Walk Shopping Centre: 'The launch of the PUMA store in South Africa is in line with PUMA's global strategy to grow it's [*sic*] presence in Africa.'[44]

However, 2008 also marked a fundamental shift *away* from the traditional sponsorship-oriented charitable foundation strategy seen in 2006, as PUMA opted instead to forge a partnership with peace activist/filmmaker Jeremy Gilley's 'Peace One Day' venture, which aims to reserve one day per year, 21 September, as a day of global cease-fire and non-violence celebration. Although PUMA once again produced *some* branded merchandise to commemorate the partnership, such as the so-called 'Peace One Day fan pack' (featuring a branded soccer ball, t-shirt, lanyard, etc.) and nation-specific shoes (i.e., PUMA shoes designed in the colours of a particular nation's flag), these efforts were seen more as ancillary promotional by-products of the overall effort rather than a primary focus.

Instead, what we saw was the lofty notion of international peace and consciousness raising activity, organized around the aptly titled 'One Day, One Goal' campaign. As part of the promotional campaign, PUMA's Zeitz explained the relationship between the two parties in this manner (filmed as part of a media-promotional package freely distributive to broadcasters and via YouTube and other online sites):

> When people play sport, when they compete, they don't fight. I think if you look into the history of sports, ever since sports have been played, the war stopped. Let's bring people together, through sport, just like we do during the European Cup, the World Cup, but let's do it for a purpose. And 'Peace Day' is a great purpose ... Peace is something that must concern all of us. And the wonderful thing about peace one day is that it's just not focusing on governments, and parties at war, or countries at war, it's something that engages everyone. That creates awareness that everyone can contribute to peace, no matter how small ... I think that's the whole idea we have together, to make sure that conflicting parties and countries play football against each other starting September 21st every year. And it's not something that we're doing in order to promote the brand, in order to promote the company, it's just using the power we have as a company to actually help make the world, make it a bit better. And therefore I believe that sport can really help achieve peace not only one day but maybe on more days also in the future.[45]

Putting aside the problematic revisioning of history[46] and the almost *too* lofty sounding sentiment concerning participation being not simply about promotion of the brand embedded in Zeitz's explication, the strategy employed by PUMA in association with the Peace One Day/One Day, One Goal movement is closely aligned with what Kate Nash, channelling Boltanski, frames as a politics of *justice*: that is, an affective mobilization of *human* capital oriented around 'the denunciation of systemic injustice, for which the appropriate emotion is indignation and the desire to bring about change'.[47] Rather than *passive* consumption geared toward raising money and awareness – as well as outward branded expressions of one's own philanthropic efforts – the aim would appear to be the much more powerful end result of 'transform[ing] national citizens into global citizens by creating *obligations* toward people ... outside the nation'.[48] In other words, to invoke Colleen O'Manique and Robert Labonte, establishing a paradigmatic order in which we as *consumers* recognize that we may not be able to 'change the course of history on the planet. But as politically engaged, informed *citizens* pushing for a just global order, we perhaps do have some agency.'[49]

* * *

At the same time as PUMA was engaged in helping to foster grassroots activism and awareness for Gilley's project, it was simultaneously employing via endorsement contracts African footballers to spread its twinned message(s) of peace and capitalism. Enlisting Cameroon's Samuel Eto'o, who starred for FC Barcelona until a 2009 move to Inter Milan, was the lynchpin of this strategy. Considered perhaps the most celebrated African footballer, Eto'o starred in a series of ads promoting PUMA products within *both* Europe and Africa, acting as a 'critical functionary performing the totemic work of Brand Aid', an 'emotional sovereign'[50] speaking as both global football star who has suffered under racist attacks (for example, his treatment by fans during an away match at Real Zaragoza in Aragon, where he was subjected to racist taunts, 'monkey-like' chants, and fans throwing peanuts at him on the pitch, quite reminiscent of the John Barnes 'banana' incident in Liverpool v. Everton in the late-1980s in the then-First Division of English football), and a politically aware spatial representative of 'Africa' (i.e., Cameroon) who has stated publicly that while he is glamorized for being a celebrity athlete: 'Away from the cameras, a black man is suffering from racism and nobody cares – and that's the problem.'[51] And, as an athlete-activist, the French-speaking Eto'o has also spoken publicly about the need to proactively use advertising and media as a catalyst for mobilizing change rather than via the use of sporadic actions or 'pity'.

Clearly, PUMA did not enter into a relationship with Eto'o unaware of his politically-aware mindset. Rather, it could be said that his extra-textual politics of representation in fact *aid* in symbolically bestowing an activist-minded imprimatur on the PUMA label. Given such an association, it is quite disappointing that PUMA has in effect fallen back on racial stereotypes of the black male athlete when deploying Eto'o in its various advertising campaigns.

Consider: In one prominent ad, titled 'My PUMAs',[52] we see a shirtless Eto'o (naked, actually, but not yet visibly so to the camera's gaze) in a locker room-type shower, presumably washing up after a hard match or practice. In the next shot, we see a light-skinned boy of about 13-years-of-age sneak into the locker room and abscond with Eto's clothes and bright red PUMA shoes. Finished showering, Eto'o emerges to find his locker empty, and goes outside to presumably look for his missing clothes. There he finds a group of six light-skinned boys kicking around a soccer ball on a dirt pitch. Seeing one of the boys wearing his shoes, the muscular Eto'o, his body dripping with water and sexual energy, lets fly with a resounding scream of 'Aarrrrgghhhhhhh!' followed by a declarative, 'My PUMAs!' The boy slowly takes off the shoes, and then he and the other five run away from Eto'o. The last scene shows a full-body shot of Eto'o, wearing only his red and white PUMAs, walking naked away from the camera, his backside clearly visible to the camera.

If this was a one-off depiction of the aggressive, black male body by PUMA, one might be able to dismiss it as clumsy creative masquerading as (a failed attempt at) playful storytelling. However, Eto'o was likewise featured in a major television advertisement for PUMA titled 'Until Then', which featured a futuristic game of football being played by half-man, half-animal combatants. Aired in heavy rotation during the 2008 Africa Cup of Nations tournament, the ad is evermore explicit about the conjoining of 'man' and 'beast' narratives, especially disturbing when we consider the long history of stereotypical media representations of black men as naturally aggressive and/or animalistic in nature. (A cousin to the 'Until Then' ad is an animated short that literally depicts Eto'o morphing into an angry puma on the pitch, complete with roaring, bestial sound effects; a similar entry in this animated series has Eto'o playing one-on-one with a lion in what appears to be the Sahara desert.)

What are we to make of the seemingly contradictory messages at play with respect to Eto'o – one that raises him up as a politically aware and socially-motivated activist-athlete on the one hand, and one that portrays him as a bestial stereotype of aggressive black masculinity on the on the other hand? Perhaps we can chalk it up to this: At the same time PUMA has endeavoured to treat Africa as an emerging market with a unique history full of untapped potential, the politics of representation governing the very same context in which it resides has not yet caught up to its (potentially) progressive promise. Thus they've only gone halfway – Africa is no longer a site to be pitied, but to become engaged with in order to produce change; its emerging markets – consumers to engage with; its communication matrix – still stuck in a Western mode of racial politics. But change *is* afoot, if slowly, and with a lot of baggage.

By way of a conclusion

Africa's participation in 'globalization', then, has certainly not been a matter of simply 'joining the world economy' ... it has instead been a matter of highly selective and spatially encapsulated forms of global connection combined with widespread disconnection and exclusion.

James Ferguson[53]

In an age in which the global corporation 'has evolved to serve the interests of whoever controls it, at the expense of whomever does not', PUMA's initial first steps toward inserting itself into discussions concerning peace and social change on a global scale are indeed laudable.[54] This is especially true when we consider some of the alternatives, such as those outlined above with respect to 'conscience commerce' and 'causumerism'. Although PUMA's efforts have at times been clumsy (sometimes overly so, such as the Eto'o campaigns), that it is seemingly trying something different at all is noteworthy. Whilst such a statement may smack of the kind of cynical times we reside in, especially here in the United States (i.e. actually being surprised when a global entity even *attempts* to act with regard to the common good instead of unleashing the ravages of global capitalism upon us all), it should not obscure those efforts undertaken by PUMA. In the concluding run-up to World Cup 2010, it will be interesting to see how PUMA acts and reacts to the changing historical present, as well as how its efforts are received in the African soccer community as well as the world community more generally. For now, however, PUMA's efforts remain an incomplete, though promising, story.

Notes

1 An earlier version of this essay was presented under a slightly different title at the 'To Remember is to Resist': 40 Years of Sport and Social Change, 1968–2008 conference, held in Toronto, Canada, in May 2008. Special thanks to Russell Field and Bruce Kidd for organizing the conference, and for their patience with me during the editorial process. The author also thanks Fiona Söderberg for lively discussions concerning this project.

2 BBC Storyline, 'Director Interview'.

3 Ferguson, *Global Shadows*, 1.

4 Anholt, 'Bono, Public Diplomacy', 1

5 Anholt, 'Branded Africa', 75.

6 Ibid., 76

7 This refers to a theatre of the absurd and is taken from the viral phenomenon of the same name, seen most notably in this clip, which has been viewed more than 60 million times on YouTube: http://www.youtube.com/watch?v=Tx1XIm6q4r4.

8 See, for example, O'Reilly's 26 January 2009 screed against President Barack Obama signing an Executive Order rescinding the so-called 'global gag rule' (a policy left over from the Bush administration) which prohibited US funding to organizations that spoke about abortions for women and girls seeking reproductive and family planning services. This policy was of particular import in debates concerning HIV/AIDS in Africa, where the de facto result was only those organizations promoting abstinence-only programmes – which don't work – could be funded.

9 Domiesen, 'Changing "Brand Africa"', 1.

10 Arendt, *On Revolution*.

11 Boltanski, *Distant Suffering*, 3.

12 Berlant, *The Female Complaint*, 8.

13 Ad available at http://www.youtube.com/watch?v=-AqlLyLeJuQ.

14 Sarna-Wojcicki, 'Refigu(red)', 14.

15 Ponte and Richey, 'Better (RED)™ than Dead', 1.

16 Bishop and Green, *Philanthrocapitalism*, 3; Kramer, *Ahead of the Curve*, 71; Ponte and Stefano, 'Better (RED)™ than Dead', 2.

17 The campaign has since altered slightly its public description and dropped the use of the word 'manifesto' on its website.

18 This is Appadurai's (1986) term.

19 Bennet, 'The Rage Over (RED)', 1.

20 Sarna-Wojcicki, 'Refigu(red)', 17, my emphasis.

21 (RED) Press Office, '(RED) Results'.

22 Frazier, 'Costly (RED) Campaign', 1. Less certain, however, is the monetary value of awareness raised for the cause itself. For a (somewhat biased) rebuttal to Frazier's claims, see Paul Vallely, 'The Big Question: Does the (RED) Campaign Help Big Western Brands More Than Africa?' *The Independent* (London), March 9, 2007, 1. http://www.independent.co.uk/news/world/ politics/the-big-question-does-the-red-campaign-help-big-western-brands-more-than-africa-439425.html.

23 Mansvelt, 'Geographies of Consumption', 106, my emphasis.

24 Jungar and Salo, 'Shop and Do Good?', 93.

25 Lambert and Lester, 'Geographies of Colonial Philanthropy', 321.

26 Lalbiharie, 'Can Bono', 1.

27 Ibid. For the definitive statement on the consumerist approach to philanthropy, see King, *Pink Ribbons, Inc.*

28 Havrilesky, 'The Selling of 9/11', 1.

29 O'Manique and Labonte, 'Rethinking (Product)RED', 1562, my emphasis.

30 King, *Pink Ribbons, Inc.*, 73.

31 The preeminent example of this shift was seen in US politics during the 2008 Presidential election campaign. Whereas such traditional campaigns as those ran by Hillary Clinton or John McCain utilized online technology primarily as a means of raising large sums of money, the campaign of Barack Obama deployed the same basic technology on hand as the means to activate and organize supporter energy to go out into the real world, knock on doors, write letters, host house parties, talk to people, and shift the dynamics of the race in meaningful ways not accessible through dollar donations alone. In short, people were charged with affecting change themselves in concrete

interactions rather than impersonally, from a distance. For more on this see Giardina, 'From Howard Dean'.

32 Cited in Margareta Pagano, 'So Hip it Hurts. Can PUMA Leave the Recession for Dead?'. *The Independent*, February 1, 2009. http://www.independent.co.uk/news/business/analysis-and-features/so-hip-it-hurts-can-puma-leave-the-recession-for-dead-1522255.html.

33 PUMA Press Office. 'PUMA Announces Strategic Directions', 1.

34 PUMA notes that this programme is accredited by the Fair Labor Association, a non-profit industry watchdog group. However, it should be pointed out that the FLA has come under recent criticism by such organizations as United Students Against Sweatshops, which calls it a 'weak code that fails to provide for women's rights, a living wage, and the full public disclosure of factory locations – in other words, more corporate cover-up than industry reform' (http://www.studentsagainstsweatshops.org/index.php?option=com_content&task=view&id=109&Itemid=9).

35 FTSE: The Index Company, 'FTSE4Good Index Series'. http://www.ftse.com/Indices/FTSE4Good_Index_Series/index.jsp.

36 GoodGuide.com, 'PUMA AG Rudolph Dassler Sport'. http://www.goodguide.com/companies/209630-puma-ag-rudolf-dassler-sport/details

37 In his revealing look at the 2004 US Presidential election, Joe Trippi, *The Revolution*, outlines the shift from the 'tyranny of transactional politics' to the progressive 'transformational politics' that governed Howard Dean's campaign for the Democratic Party nomination.

38 PUMA Press Office, 'Q&A with PUMA CEO', 1.

39 PUMA Press Office, 'PUMA Launches First South African Store', 1.

40 Ibid.

41 Ibid.

42 PUMA Press Office, 'PUMA and Ghana', 1.

43 PUMA Press Office, 'PUMA Wins', 1.

44 PUMA Press Office, 'PUMA Launches First South African Store', 1.

45 Peace One Day, Ltd, 'PUMA-POD'. Numerous PSA styled 30-second spots featuring African footballers were also produced, including one current Chelsea midfielder Michael Essien of Ghana. Spots were also produced titled 'Boy', which features a young African boy dreaming of scoring a game-winning goal, and one titled 'Soldier', which features two soldiers laying down their arms and instead kicking a ball around.

46 For example, Zeitz's statement of wars stopping for sport, where those living in Iraq whilst the 2008 Olympics were ongoing would likely take issue with such a characterization.

47 Nash, 'Global Citizenship', 174.

48 Ibid., emphasis in original.

49 O'Manique, and Labonte, 'Rethinking (Product)RED', 1563. As a side note, one could also make the argument that this 'desire to bring about change' through active civic participation was one of the key mobilizing factors driving Barack Obama's successful US presidential campaign, especially among young people who, perhaps for the first time in their lives, were energized about politics in an action-oriented way. For more on Obama's campaign, see Giardina, 'From Howard Dean'.

50 Ponte and Richey, 'Better (RED)™ than Dead'.

51 *Interview with Pierre Peyronnet*. 'Samuel Eto'o Speaks to Pierre Peyronnet'.

52 The ad in question was produced by GYRO Worldwide, directed by Londoner Jake Nava (the same director of Beyonce's famed 'Crazy in Love' music video).

53 Ferguson, *Global Shadows*, 14.

54 Duggar, *Corporate Hegemony*, 33.

References

Anholt, Simon. 'Bono, Public Diplomacy, and "Brand Africa"'. *USC Center for Public Diplomacy* May 25, 2006. http://uscpublicdiplomacy.com/index.php/newsroom/pdblog_detail/060525_bono_pub lic_diplomacy_and_brand_africa/.

Anholt, Simon. 'Branded Africa: What is Competitive Identity'. *African Analyst* 2 (2007): 72–81.

Appadurai, Arjun. 'Introduction: Commodities and the Politics of Value'. In *The Social Life of Things: Commodities in Cultural Perspective*, edited by Arjun Appadurai, 13. Cambridge: Cambridge University Press, 1986.

Arendt, Hannah. *On Revolution*. New York: Viking, 1963.

BBC Storyline. 'Director Interview: Jeremy Gilley'. September 13, 2004. http://www.bbc.co.uk/bbcfour/documentaries/storyville/jeremy-gilley.shtml.

Bennett, Jessica. 'The Rage Over (RED)'. *Newsweek* (Web Exclusive). March 14, 2007. http://www.newsweek.com/id/36192.

Berlant, Lauren. *The Female Complaint: The Unfinished Business of Sentimentality in American Culture*. Durham, NC: Duke University Press, 2008.

Bishop, Matthew, and Michael Green. *Philanthrocapitalism: How the Rich Can Save the World*. New York: Bloomsbury Press, 2008.

Boltanski, Luc. *Distant Suffering: Morality, Media, and Politics*. Cambridge: Cambridge University Press, 1999

Domeisen, Natalie. 'Changing "Brand Africa"'. *International Trade Forum* (January 2007). http://findarticles.com/p/articles/mi_hb3099/is_1/ai_n29373797/.

Duggar, William M. *Corporate Hegemony*. Westport, CT: Greenwood Press, 1989.

Ferguson, James. *Global Shadows: Africa in the Neoliberal World Order*. Durham, NC: Duke University Press, 2006.

Frazier, Mya. 'Costly (RED) Campaign Reaps Meager $18 Million: Bono & Co. Spend up to $100 Million on Marketing, Incur Watchdogs' Wrath'. *AdvertisingAge*. http://adage.com/article?article_id=115287.

Giardina, Michael D. 'From Howard Dean to Barack Obama: The Evolution of Politics in the Network Society'. In *Everyday Life in the (Post)Global Network*, edited by Grant Kien and Marina Levina. New York: Peter Lang, forthcoming.

GoodGuide.com. 'PUMA AG Rudolph Dassler Sport'. http://www.goodguide.com/companies/209630-puma-ag-rudolf-dassler-sport/details.

Havrilesky, Heather. 'The Selling of 9/11'. *Salon.com*, September 7, 2007. http://dir.salon.com/story/mwt/feature/2002/09/07/purchase_power/index.html.

Interview with Pierre Peyronnet. 'Samuel Eto'o Speaks to Pierre Peyronnet on Solidarity, Over-simplifying Racism, and Walking Off the Pitch'. *FeelFootball.com*. (2007). http://www.youtube.com/watch?v=2gSTxsN-44M.

Jungar, Katarina, and Elaine Salo. 'Shop and Do Good?' *Journal of Pan African Studies* 2 (2008): 92–102.

Kramer, Hillary. *Ahead of the Curve*. New York: Free Press, 2007.

King, Samantha J. *Pink Ribbons, Inc.: Breast Cancer and the Politics of Philanthropy*. Minneapolis, MN: University of Minnesota Press, 2006.

Lalbiharie, Krishna. 'Can Bono, Cause-related Marketing and Shopping Save the World?'. *Canadian Dimension Magazine*, (July/August 2007). http://canadiandimension.com/articles/2007/06/28/1191.

Lambert, David, and Alan Lester. 'Geographies of Colonial Philanthropy'. *Progress in Human Geography* 28 (2004): 320–41.

Mansvelt, Juliana. 'Geographies of Consumption: Citizenship, Space, and Practice'. *Progress in Human Geography* 32 (2008): 105–17.

Nash, Kate. 'Global Citizenship as Show Business: The Cultural Politics of "Make Poverty History"'. *Media, Culture, & Society* 30 (2008): 167–81.

O'Manique, Colleen, and Ronald Labonte. 'Rethinking (Product)RED'. *The Lancet* 371 (2008): 1562–3.

Peace One Day, Ltd. 'PUMA-POD'. April 7, 2008. http://www.youtube.com/watch?v=oVCJjMzAI-s.

Ponte, Stefano, and Lisa Richey. 'Better (RED)™ than Dead: "Brand Aid", Celebrities, and the New Frontier of Development Assistance'. *Danish Institute for International Studies*, Working Paper No. 2006/26 2006: 1–33.

(RED) Press Office. '(RED) Results'. January 1, 2009. http://www.joinred.com/Learn/Results.aspx.

PUMA Press Office. 'PUMA and Ghana Extend Partnership'. *BizCommunity*. February 7, 2008. http://www.biz-community.com/Article/196/48/21766.html.

PUMA Press Office. 'PUMA Announces Strategic Directions of Phase IV'. Press Release, June 27, 2005. http://about.puma.com/downloads/xraklk7ormxivxti.pdf.

PUMA Press Office. 'PUMA Launches First South African Store'. Press Release, June 11, 2006. http://www.splashpr.co.za/pressreleases/0607_puma.htm.

PUMA Press Office. 'PUMA Wins 6th Africa Cup of Nations Title and Extends Ivory Coast Partnership'. Press Release, February 11, 2008. http://about.puma.com/EN/3/23/23/?news_id=116&year=2008.

PUMA Press Office. 'Q&A with PUMA CEO Jochen Zeitz'. *Portfolio*, February 20, 2008. http://www.portfolio.com/views/blogs/fashion-inc/2008/02/20/qa-with-puma-ceo-jochen-zeitz.

Sarna-Wojcicki, Margaret. 'Refigu(red): Talking Africa and AIDS in "Causumer" Culture'. *Journal of Pan African Studies* 2 (2008): 14–31.

Trippi, Joe. *The Revolution Will Not Be Televised: Democracy, the Internet, and the Overthrow of Everything*. New York: Regan Books, 2004.

'No Olympics on stolen native land': contesting Olympic narratives and asserting indigenous rights within the discourse of the 2010 Vancouver Games

Christine M. O'Bonsawin

Department of History, University of Victoria, Canada

The Olympic movement is a powerful industry and resistance to it is often deemed unnecessary, and at times is considered to be criminal. The campaign calling for 'No Olympics on Stolen Native Land' is perceived to be a radical crusade calling for the cancellation of the 2010 Vancouver Olympic Winter Games. However, the reality is these Olympic Games will take place and they will be hosted on unceded and non-surrendered indigenous lands. The British Columbia land question remains unanswered, and the very presence of the current Olympic structure on contentious indigenous lands has the potential to temporarily silence, and perhaps permanently alter, the immediate needs of indigenous peoples within British Columbia, Canada. This essay contributes to the ongoing narrative of the 2010 Vancouver Olympics as it provides an historical framework for understanding the fragile tensions that exist between present-day Olympic programming and indigenous activism.

At present, organizing initiatives for the 2010 Vancouver Olympic Winter Games have caused tension and dissonance within local, provincial, national and international factions. As expected, the issue of indigenous rights, and the infringement on such rights, has once again come to the forefront of Olympic debates as indigenous peoples, communities, activists and scholars openly critique and resist the hosting of the XXI Olympic Winter Games in Vancouver, British Columbia – or what some consider 'Stolen Native Land'. For indigenous communities, opposition to the Games rests in the historical exploitation and, arguably, the ongoing disregard for the rights of indigenous peoples within Canada. The reality is that the 2010 Vancouver Olympic Games *will* take place, and in the midst of national celebrations there *will* be indigenous protest and activism as indigenous peoples and groups attempt to 'grapple' with the 'legacy of the past'.[1]

The purposes of this essay are threefold: (1) to conceptualize the paradox between Olympic principles and indigenous rights in Canada, and elsewhere, through an examination of previously hosted Olympic Games on contentious indigenous lands; (2) to provide a framework of indigenous/settler political history in British Columbia in the context of current opposition to the Vancouver Olympics; and (3) to offer recommendations for evaluating the suitability of Olympic bids from cities, and thus nations, which attempt to govern over indigenous populations. Accordingly, this essay contributes to ongoing debates surrounding the 2010 Vancouver Olympic Winter Games as it provides an historical framework for understanding the tensions that exist between present-day Olympic programming and indigenous activism.

Olympic principles, indigenous rights and representation: an historical overview

The Baron Pierre de Coubertin (1863–1937) a French aristocrat who was highly influenced by his memories of the Franco-Prussian War, the British Public School tradition of physical education, and the integrity of the nation-state, is the individual most often credited for the 'revival' of the modern Olympic Games. Coubertin meticulously oversaw the adoption and introduction of the Olympic principles, which eventually came to be branded as 'Olympism'. Olympism, by definition, is a 'philosophy of life' that praises a balance of body, will and mind. Through the unification of 'sport with culture and education, Olympism seeks to create a way of life based on the joy found in effort, the educational value of good example and respect for universal fundamental ethical principles'.[2] As a universal philosophy, Olympism is generally understood to be global coherent that speaks in truisms of equity, anti-discrimination, mutual recognition and respect, tolerance and solidarity. For Coubertin, the Olympic Games represented a site for world progress, diplomatic co-existence, global understanding, and for instilling social and moral values. By the early twentieth century, the philosophy of Olympism had been infused into the Olympic project, thereby entrenching a social ideology that would serve as the *raison d'être* for the movement itself. However, it remains unclear on what grounds this abstract concept serves as the marker, or 'core value', which elevates the Olympic Games above all other sport competitions. As Wamsley argues, 'in many respects the two [Olympism and the Olympic Games] are incongruous ... during the twentieth century, the nebulous concept of Olympism became the structural apologetic for the Olympic Games'.[3]

By the early years of the twentieth century, the emerging philosophy of Olympism became the structural apologetic for a deeply politicized and xenophobic Olympic movement.[4] Since its revival, the Olympic movement has renounced Olympic-like athletic competitions that embody racial, political or religious undertones. It is believed that such events have the potential to undermine Olympism and its perceived virtues of peace, brotherhood and humanity. However, the Olympic Games, on all levels, are deeply politicized. Under the moral guise of Olympism, participants (in the capacity of athlete, builder, spectator, global citizen or otherwise; in short, universal participation in the Olympics is expected) are encouraged to cast aside everyday lived experiences, which are undeniably shaped by such factors as race, gender, sexuality, religion, culture and ideology, and class. The reality for marginalized peoples is that their everyday experiences are lived not on equitable, anti-discriminatory, tolerant, respectful and harmonious terms.

In the Olympic context, spectators have to look no further than the ceremonies to appreciate the discordant historical and contemporary realities of indigenous peoples around the world. It is in this context, the ceremonies, that the allure of the Olympic spectacle is most evident. And it is in this same medium where the plight and hardships of indigenous peoples within colonial and settler societies become most sensationalized. In the opening ceremonies of both the 2000 Sydney and 2002 Salt Lake City Olympic Games, organizers followed informal tradition, thereby taking this opportunity to recount, and in many instances reinvent, national narratives. In both examples, indigenous peoples were relegated to nominal and inconsequential roles. The foundations of both nations rest heavily on the hardships and sufferings of indigenous peoples, yet their contributions to these national histories are by no means nominal or inconsequential.

For the 2000 Sydney Olympic Summer Games, Australian organizers promoted and endorsed their Games under a national campaign which called for 'Reconciliation' between aboriginal and settler Australia. Despite tense relationships at home as well as international scrutiny from abroad, the Sydney Olympics opened in celebration of national reconciliation. For example, in its media guide, the Sydney Organising Committee for the Olympic Games (SOCOG) described the opening ceremony to have been:

> A celebration of Australia that begins by the sea and returns to the harbour city after a journey through our land and history … we are taken on a journey through Australian history, environment and culture by two characters; a little girl and the traditional Aboriginal dancer, Djakapurra … her dream [the little girl, Nikki Webster] gives way to Djakapurra, Aboriginal dancers and members of tribes from all corners of the country, form circles around burning eucalyptus leaves. They conjure a giant Wandjina, a creation myth spirit symbolizing the unity of Indigenous people … a segment that takes us on a journey through European settlement … this is a cue for a series of groups to sweep into the area. This represents the successive waves of immigration that has transformed Australia into the cosmopolitan and diverse society it is today. With 2,000 people in the centre of the arena, Sydney's landmark Anzac Bridge rises, and Djakapurra and our little girl meet again amid a crescendo that celebrates the city of Sydney.[5]

As the ceremony moved forward, it was revealed that Cathy Freeman, a highly celebrated yet controversial aboriginal athlete and political figure in Australia at this time, would light the Olympic cauldron. Symbolically, the message was 'reconciliation', and the international audience was led to believe that a gesture of respect and an opportunity for healing was being offered to aboriginal Australia. However, in the years and months leading up to the 2000 Sydney Olympic Summer Games, Australia was anything but reconciled.

In the late seventeenth century, the concept of *terra nullius* – land belonging to no one – had been employed during these early years of settlement in the new colony. In 1901, at the time of Confederation, *terra nullius* was firmly embedded within the political and legal governance of Australia. It was not until 1992, in the case of *Mabo and Others* v. *The State of Queensland* that the High Court of Australia finally rejected the concept of *terra nullius* and ruled that native title – the right to exclusive use and occupation of land – had not previously been extinguished in Australia. In 1993 the Keating government responded by enacting the Native Title Act, a legislative document that established criteria for dealing with native title, particularly by validating the interests of non-indigenous land holders. In the 1996 case of *Wik Peoples* v. *The State of Queensland*, Australia's High Court once again ruled in favour of aboriginal rights, and decided that pastoral leases could co-exist with native title. In 1998, the Howard government amended the Native Title Act through its 'Ten Point Plan', which removed aboriginal rights to negotiate on pastoral leases. Consequently, in 1999, at its 54th session in March of 1999, the United Nations Committee for the Elimination of Racial Discrimination (CERD) placed Australia on an 'urgent business' priority as it brought down 'damaging findings' against the government concerning its treatment of an aboriginal population. These findings were once again supported in August of 1999 at the 55th session.[6] This was the first time in its history that CERD expressed 'serious concerns' about a Western nation going backwards on the land rights of indigenous people.

For the opening ceremony, Australian organizers altered historical and national narratives in an attempt to promote a reconciled and united Australia. Magdalinski argues that that the hosting of these Games provided the nation with an opportunity to explore:

> Australian identity and nostalgic remembering in a climate of economic restructuring and social turmoil. In a growing era of political disquiet, where right-wing fundamentalism [was] increasing, where indigenous and migrant issues [were] threatening the homogeneity of Australia's political and social landscape and where the Asian economic crisis threatened national economic security, the Olympic Games provided a useful cultural focal point around which images of the Australian nation could be generated.[7]

Magdalinski further argues that during times of rapid social change, national celebrations, such as hosting the Olympic Games, become increasingly significant as nations attempt to 'project themselves into the future' while struggling with the 'legacy of the past'. In the closing ceremony of the Sydney Games, Olympic and political officials were publicly embarrassed, and ultimately criticized, as the Australian band, Midnight Oil, took the stage wearing 'SORRY suits'. The apology was directed to aboriginal Australians. The band publically criticized Prime Minister Howard's (who was in attendance at the closing ceremony) refusal to apologize to aboriginal Australians for the treatment they had received under white rule, particularly the survivors and families of the Stolen Generations (Stolen Children).[8] An apology was eventually offered by Prime Minister Kevin Rudd in February of 2008.[9]

In many respects, the hosting of the 2002 Salt Lake City Olympic Winter Games also brought the matter of indigenous rights to the forefront of national and international politics. By comparison, indigenous opposition to the Games appeared to have been silenced, or at least overshadowed. Certainly the events of September 11th, 2001, which led to increased anxieties and considerable monies directed at security efforts, reduced adversarial response to the Games. Despite increased tensions, the festivities of the Salt Lake City Olympics thrived and the Games opened in national celebration. The opening ceremony was a celebration of the American west, with organizers seeking to feature the five tribes of Utah, including the Shoshone, Ute, Paiute, Goshute and Dine-Navajo. For this ceremony, members of these nations danced into the stadium in traditional regalia followed by drummers who were positioned on planks, which were sequenced to match the five colours of the Olympic rings. At the end of their performance, tribal representatives from the five Nations welcomed Olympians, and in return received gift bundles; however, American broadcasters failed to translate these blessings or explain the significance of indigenous gift-giving practices. Consequently, the deeper cultural meanings of the welcomes and gift exchange were lost, and viewers were left with appropriated and mythological images of 'all things Indian'. While an otherwise uninformed audience was left with messages of a fabled past, indigenous critics publically asserted their dissatisfaction.

Susan Shown Harjo, a prominent Cheyenne and Hodulgee Muscogee writer and activist, claimed that:

> [After the Indians had their moment in the spotlight], they danced back into history, making way for miners, cowboys and settlers of all races to do-se-do together (as if that ever happened in that place and time). Only the Indians were missing from the hoedown in Salt Lake ... But these are just symbols, you say? Well, yeah. Mega-bucks worth of symbols. Symbology that reaches millions of people around the world and leaves a lasting impression in place of reality.[10]

As Harjo suggests, Native representatives *should* have welcomed Olympic dignitaries. This would have served as an important contextual point that affirmed the sovereignties and rights to the lands that Natives American peoples possess today. However, the failure to do so confirmed tensions within the current relations between indigenous peoples and the American state.[11] Furthermore, Native American concerns rest with the hypocrisy of parading the tattered American flag from the September 11th bombings of the World Trade Centre. For many Americans this display provided assurance that by bravely going forward and hosting the Olympic Games, the United States was reclaiming its security in the face of terrorism. However, as Judith Lowry, a painter of Maidu and Pit River ancestry, suggests, Native Americans 'would like to live with the illusion that we are safe, but for those of Native heritage, that is impossible. The reminders stay with us from generation to generation.'[12]

In its hosting of Olympic Games, Canada has also grappled with the appropriateness of including indigenous peoples and their complementary imagery within the programming of the Games. Similar to Australia and the United States, Canadian Olympic Games organizers have appropriated indigenous imagery. In response to the contentious inclusion of indigenous imagery within the programme of the 1976 Montréal Olympic Summer Games, Forsyth notes the paradox that exists between the celebratory promotion of indigenous peoples within the Olympic context, and the everyday lived realities such populations experience in Canada. Forsyth argues that:

> Although Olympic organizers stated publicly that the Closing Ceremony was being held to honor Canada's Aboriginal peoples, the organizers did not consult with the populations who they proposed to respect in the construction of the program. From start to finish, the celebration was designed *by* Olympic organizers *for* Aboriginal peoples.[13]

The most blatant disregard for indigenous peoples occurred during the closing ceremony with the participation of nine First Nations, including the Abenaki, Algonquin, Atikamekw, Cree, Huron, Mi'gmiq, Mohawk, Montagnais and Naskapi nations. Olympic organizers invited representatives from these nations to participate in what was proposed to be a 'commemoration ceremony'. In the end, 200 representatives from the nine First Nations were escorted into the arena and led in 'traditional' dance by 250 non-indigenous performers who were painted and dressed to look like 'Indians'. Despite proposals that this performance was being held to honour indigenous peoples, the choreography was under the direction of Canadian choreographer Michel Cartier, the musical inspiration was based on the works of Canadian composer André Mathieu, which included *La Danse Sauvage*, and due to financial constraints, over half of the 'Indian hosts' were, in fact, local non-indigenous people who were painted and dressed to look like 'Indians'.

In the case of Calgary, organizing efforts attempted to appropriate indigenous imagery for the purpose of promotional gain. Wamsley and Heine identify the various ways in which the Olympiques Calgary Olympics '88 (OCO) used indigenous culture to present a 'Western' character of Calgarian hospitality. In doing so, they utilized the international prestige of the Calgary Stampede and based their cultural programming around the Stampede's symbolic use of the Mountie, the cowboy and the Indian.[14] Indigenous peoples within Alberta and throughout Canada took offence to a number of suggestions and actions taken by the OCO that involved the use of indigenous imagery for Olympic programming. For example, the composition of the Olympic medals displayed winter sporting equipment protruding from a ceremonial headdress, an enormous teepee at McMahon Stadium supporting the Olympic cauldron, and the Calgary Stampede Board's suggestion that an 'Indian attack and wagon-burning' be a part of the opening ceremony (this was ultimately rejected). For Olympic organizers, programming also encroached upon by indigenous activism, notably the Lubicon Lake Cree Nation who opposed federal, provincial and corporate funding in support of indigenous Olympic programming. The Lubicon Cree initiated boycotts of the Petro Canada sponsored torch relay run, and the Shell Canada/Federal co-sponsorship of 'The Spirit Sings' Olympic exhibit, which was hosted by the Glenbow Museum. The debate centred upon the presence of these oil corporations on contested indigenous territories, as well as the federal and provincial governments' unwillingness to engage in honourable treaty negotiations with the Lubicon Cree.

In July 2003, Jacques Rogge, the president of the International Olympic Committee (IOC), announced Vancouver's successful candidacy to host the XXI Olympic Winter

Games. Vancouver's successful bid was the result of the formation of a 500-plus-member committee, a four-year preparation effort, a multi-million dollar investment from public and private entities, the development of a 460-page Bid Book, and a municipal plebiscite vote that went in favour of the Games. Incorporated within *The Sea to Sky Games: Vancouver 2010 Bid Book* was the clear recognition of indigenous peoples. S. 1.1 of the Bid Book states, 'Canada is a living mosaic of peoples and cultures from around the world. Virtually every nation has *joined* [emphasis added] Canada's First Nations, making us a truly multicultural society.'[15] In this context, bid organizers fomented a wider confusion about indigenous peoples as an ethnic minority within Canada's multicultural milieu. Furthermore, as explained in the Vancouver 2010 Bid Book, organizers claimed that the four political institutions of Canada include the federal government, the provincial and territorial governments, the municipal/regional governments, and the 'First Nations'. However, a national policy has yet to be developed that recognizes First Nations as an official political institution within Canada. This leads one to question the integrity, or at the very least, the organizational creditability of an international movement that permits a few individuals, normally members of the political and corporate elite, to provide the IOC with an abridgment of complex national structures. In the case of Vancouver 2010, bid members positioned First Nations as an official political institution of Canada. Beyond the erroneous nature of this claim it is important to note that indigenous peoples continue to live in disadvantaged, and in many instances, desperate conditions within this very nation. This IOC process, arguably, sustains indigenousness as 'an identity constructed, shaped and lived in the politicized context of contemporary colonialism'.[16]

With its successful candidacy to host the XXI Olympic Winter Games, the bid committee quickly dissolved and the Vancouver Olympic Organizing Committee for the 2010 Olympic and Paralympic Winter Games (VANOC) was established. Throughout the entire process, organizers have made significant attempts to ensure that indigenous participation and imagery are prominent and visible expressions of the Vancouver Olympics. For example, there has been the implementation of the Four Host First Nations (FHFN) Protocol Agreement, the adoption of the inukshuk logo, indigenous representatives in the 2006 Torino handover ceremony, the inclusion of the indigenous-inspired Olympic mascots, the creation of a Sustainability and Aboriginal Participation programme, a torch relay schedule that includes stops in over 300 aboriginal communities, and significant aboriginal programming administered through 2010 Legacies Now (an official partner of VANOC).[17] VANOC has made considerable efforts to ensure indigenous visibility and economic support in the organizing and hosting of the Games. Large sums of Olympic dollars are being directed at indigenous programming and economic projects within communities; however, a troubling reality looms overhead: the Vancouver 2010 Olympic Winter Games are being hosted on unceded and non-surrendered indigenous lands.

Indigenous/settler political history in British Columbia and opposition to the Olympics

Opposition to the 2010 Vancouver Olympic Winter Games has rallied under the Olympic Resistance Network and the anti-Olympic campaign calling for 'No Olympics on Stolen Native Land'. This Olympic Resistance Network is based in Vancouver and works in solidarity with communities across British Columbia, 'particularly indigenous communities who have been defending their lands against the onslaught of the Olympics since the bid itself'.[18] This umbrella network represents the continuously growing number of groups and individuals who share common anti-colonial and anti-capitalist understandings, and work in solidarity with those negatively impacted by the 2010 Games. Some of the associate organizations and groups include 2010 Games Watch, Anti-Poverty Committee, No 2010 Olympics on Stolen Native Land, No One is Illegal, and Our Freedom.[19] The Olympic Resistance Network has been working under a common anti-Olympic campaign that calls for 'No Olympics on Stolen Native Land'. From this position, it is argued that British Columbia:

> Remains largely unceded and non-surrendered Indigenous territories. According to Canadian law, BC has neither the legal nor moral right to exist, let alone claim land and govern over Native peoples. Despite this, and a fraudulent treaty process now underway, the government continues to sell, lease, and 'develop' Native land for the benefit of corporations, including mining, logging, oil [and] gas, and ski resorts. Meanwhile, Indigenous peoples suffer the highest rates of poverty, unemployment, police violence, disease, suicides, etc.[20]

Certainly, this campaign must appear one-sided to those unaware of the histories and contemporary realities of indigenous populations whose lands make up present-day British Columbia; and no doubt, this effort must seem insulting to Olympic loyalists who perceive the Games and its virtuous ideals to be humanitarian-centred. The question arises: what do advocates mean when they petition for 'No Olympics on Stolen Native Land'?

The British Columbia land question is a complex legal issue in present-day Canada, which arises from a multifaceted political history between indigenous and settler populations. While this issue has been discussed at length and appropriately critiqued elsewhere, for the purpose of this essay it is important to provide an historical framework for the unlawful transfer of indigenous territories to Crown and provincial lands.[21] In an effort to account for the ongoing conflicts within the historic and present-day treaty process (or lack thereof), the issue of aboriginal title is discussed from two perspectives – a Western perspective and an indigenous worldview – as there is a clear contradiction between the two sides concerning ideological understandings of land ownership.

From a Western perspective, there is considerable debate as to the origins and continued assertion of aboriginal title in the province of British Columbia. Foster and Grove aptly summarize the brief history of treaty making in British Columbia.[22] Following the signings of the Vancouver Island Treaties (commonly referred to as the Douglas Treaties) in the 1850s, treaty making in the colony arbitrarily ceased. From the 1860s to 1927 the 'Indian Land Question' in British Columbia was a significant issue amongst indigenous peoples as they were resisting settler encroachment and exploitation of their lands. With the exception of a small portion of land in northeastern British Columbia, which was negotiated into Treaty 8 in 1899, land cession treaties were never made in the province during this time period, as was the case in Ontario and the Prairies. Furthermore, an amendment to the Indian Act in 1927 temporarily ceased the treaty process throughout Canada as this revision made it illegal for indigenous people to pursue legal counsel, and thus treaty. This amendment would not be overturned until 1951 in a radical rewrite of the Indian Act.[23]

A commonly held view amongst legal scholars and historians is that treaty making ceased because aboriginal title was not recognized in the colony. Rationales for this include that Sir James Douglas and his successors were not aware of the 1763 Royal Proclamation, which set up the criteria for treaty making elsewhere in Canada, and therefore did not realize that they were legally obliged to extinguish aboriginal title; that there were instructions from the Colonial Office in Britain informing Douglas that 'measures of liberality and justice may be adopted *for compensating [the Indians] for the surrender of the territory which they have been taught to regard as their own*';[24] and that

Douglas and his successors were influenced by policy and judicial decisions in the western regions, notably in the states of Washington, Oregon, Alaska, as well as significant legal decisions being made in New Zealand, which had established an alternative formula – other than treaty – for extinguishing aboriginal title.[25] Despite this rationale, the question of aboriginal title was never addressed in British Columbia. Accordingly, the lands were settled by immigrant families and laws were established to govern over those inhabiting the territories – indigenous and non-indigenous.

It was not until 1973, in the landmark decision of *Calder* v. *British Columbia* that the Supreme Court of Canada ruled in favour of indigenous rights as it was decided that aboriginal title had not been extinguished through previous means, and therefore continued to exist in British Columbia. This decision would eventually assist with the establishment of a comprehensive lands claims process in Canada, which set the stage for modern treaty making. Prominent agreements that have been negotiated under the modern treaty process include the James Bay and Northern Quebec Agreement (1975)/Northeastern Quebec Agreement (1978), the Nunavut Land Claims Agreement Act (1999), and the Nisga'a Final Agreement (2000). Furthermore, other judicial landmark decisions, including *Guerin* v. *The Queen* [1984] and *Delgamuukw* v. *British Columbia* [1997] have since ruled in favour of aboriginal title, and have made definitive statements as to the definitional meaning of this abstract concept. As Kanien'kehaka (Mohawk) scholar, Taiaiake Alfred, explains:

> The Delgamuukw decision is generally seen as progressive, expanding the notion of indigenous rights by ruling that 'Aboriginal title' – defined as 'the right to exclusive use an occupation of land' – is 'inalienable' except to the Crown (that is, such rights cannot be extinguished except by the federal government), and indigenous peoples have a constitutionally protected right to be consulted on and compensated for title infringements that affect their access to or use of the lands for purposes integral to their cultural survival.[26]

Decisions such as Calder, Guerin and Delgamuukw are often considered positive steps forward for indigenous rights in Canada; however, as Alfred further questions, what does this mean 'to people whose traditional territories have for the most part already been alienated from them by law, settled by others, or handed over to corporate interests for resource development'?[27]

From an indigenous perspective, rights to the land derive from the presence of indigenous peoples on these territories since time immemorial. The concept of aboriginal title does not exist within indigenous philosophies, at least not in the Western concept of land ownership and exploitation of resources. Concepts such as *terra nullius* and aboriginal title were manufactured and employed under Western capitalist imperialism to validate illegal land grabs and justify the subjugation, containment and mistreatment of indigenous populations. In the case of British Columbia, indigenous peoples maintain that the land was never surrendered, and in recent years, the common law legal system in Canada has supported such claims.

By the early 1990s, it became clear to provincial and federal politicians that the British Columbia land question could no longer be ignored. Beyond legal reasoning, the province was most likely prompted by external, yet interconnected, events drawing attention to indigenous issues. These events include the violent standoff at Oka in the summer of 1990; the unprecedented allocation of federal funds in 1991 to a Royal Commission that was mandated with the responsibility of investigating the historical and existing state of indigenous affairs; judicial rulings in Canada's high and supreme courts supporting aboriginal title and indigenous rights; and the fact that comprehensive/modern land claims were being negotiated elsewhere in Canada. In 1991, the British Columbia Land Claims

Task Force released its report, which recommended that the province establish a 'new relationship' with indigenous peoples through a 'made in-BC Treaty Process'. In 1993, the British Columbia Treaty Commission (BCTC) officially opened for business. However, since its inception many have questioned the dishonest characterization of this 'treaty' process.

By definition, 'A treaty is … a formal agreement between two or more recognized, sovereign nations operating in an international forum'.[28] However, one must question the sincerity of a 'treaty' process that attempts to extinguish indigenous nationhood by bringing such peoples into the Canadian political and legal structures and which refuses to employ the word 'treaty' in any of its text 'agreements'. And it should not be forgotten that the BCTC was founded upon a mistaken premise in Canadian law – that Crown title exists in British Columbia. To assert the authority of Crown title is to expose an historical intellectual framework based on racist conceptions of 'civilized' and 'uncivilized' societies. In this capacity, the concept of *terra nullius* and the application of aboriginal title are prioritized over the rights of indigenous peoples, their nationhoods and respective territories.[29] So we stand at an impasse.

Through the authority of its Charter, the Olympic Movement has the capacity to do many things, particularly contravene national policies and laws of host nations. In the case of Vancouver 2010, the most obvious imposition of IOC rule over national governance is the IOC's decision not to include women's ski jumping on the program. The decision was challenged in BC Supreme Court on the grounds that providing events for men only violated the *Canadian Charter of Rights and Freedoms*. In rejecting the challenge, the Honourable Madame Justice Fenlon ruled that while VANOC is subject to the *Charter*, the discrimination that the plaintiffs are experiencing is the result of the action of a non-party (i.e., the IOC) which is neither subject to the jurisdiction of this court nor governed by the *Charter*.[30]

A second example of IOC imposition on national policy relates to section 51 (3) of the Olympic Charter, which states, 'No kind of demonstration or political, religious or racial propaganda is permitted in any Olympic sites, venues or other areas'.[31] This IOC prohibition also conflicts with the *Canadian Charter of Rights and Freedoms* as this constitutional document guarantees freedom of expression, albeit through a limitation clause.[32] VANOC is once again abiding by IOC regulations and will be creating 'Free Speech Zones' (also referred to as 'Protest Zones'), which will provide a space for protestors and activists to engage in 'lawful protest'. However, Royal Mounted Canadian Police Assistant Commissioner Bud Mercer has recently announced that protesters are not limited to these zones as 'lawful protest is legal and lawful in Canada'.[33]

With regard to the rights of indigenous peoples, the imposition of Olympic policy and the delivery of programmes have significantly altered the treaty process and treaty making in British Columbia. Since awarding the 2010 Olympic Games to Vancouver, the BCTC has been significantly altered as a result. For example, there are currently 49 sets of negotiations with First Nations communities in British Columbia. Not surprisingly, the *only* First Nation community to reach a Final Agreement – Stage Six: Implementation of a Treaty – is Tsawwassen First Nation.[34] It is important to note that the Tsawwassen First Nation community will play an active role in the 2010 Games as the traditional territory of this Coast Salish community is not only within 30 kilometres of downtown Vancouver but also because the province of British Columbia, through B.C. Ferries, has established a major port on Tsawwassen territory. By negotiating this agreement the province has 'secured the uninterrupted functioning of the major passenger and shipping ports for the lower mainland. A disruption to either of these ports, with the eyes of the world on Canada, up to and during 2010, would have been a massive embarrassment.'[35] Furthermore, the treaty process highly encourages First Nations communities that are engaged in the treaty process to develop tourist centres with the purpose of promoting indigenous cultures and attracting local, national and international visitors. This will greatly assist the cultural programme of the 2010 Olympics as local indigenous culture will provide the city, province and country with a unique local identity.

The inclusion of colonial narratives has tacitly been enshrined within the Olympic formula, and indigenous peoples have long served the performance needs of nations whose histories rest in imperial conquest. Such storylines position the subjugation and containment of indigenous peoples within national histories, thereby removing them in time and space from present-day realities. Throughout Olympic history, most notably within the last quarter of the twentieth century and the first decade of the twenty-first century, there have been numerous incidences to support claims that indigenous peoples have been proactively, if not productively, incorporated into the cultural programmes of Olympic modules in support of colonial narratives. In this ever-growing global community, the rights of indigenous peoples are coming to the forefront of international political action (i.e. the adoption of UN Declaration on the Rights of Indigenous Peoples in 2007 and many state apologies to indigenous peoples) and as an international body with significant global influence, it is the responsibility of the IOC – in the name of Olympism – to adopt new policies that support the rights of indigenous peoples.

Recommendations for evaluating the suitability of Olympic bids

The Olympic movement has used the medium of sport to educate the youth and the people of the world about honesty, fair play and respect for self and others, despite the fact that through such educational forums cultural imperialism continues to be advanced, cultural dependency is promoted, and sport continues to be abused in order to promote nationalism, sexism, racism and xenophobia.[36] As Lenskyj suggests, there exists, 'The strong possibility of a neocolonialist agenda at work when Western sporting practices are imposed on developing countries and when recipients lack the power to negotiate and dialogue with donors'.[37] In other words, basic human needs should not be pushed aside in favour of sport, the Olympics, or what Lenskyj terms, 'circuses'.[38]

While Olympism 'seeks to create a way of life based on the joy found in effort, the educational value of good example and respect for universal fundamental ethical principles',[39] current Olympic policies do not have adequate structures in place to uphold such virtues. As mentioned in the introduction to this work, the 2010 Vancouver Olympic Games *will* take place, and in the midst of national celebrations there *will* be indigenous protest and activism as indigenous peoples and groups attempt to 'grapple' with the 'legacy of the past'. The Olympic industry is too powerful, and consequently, the interests of marginalized groups become lost in the fanfare of Olympic symbolism. It is for this reason that the IOC *must* adopt a strict process of evaluation for bid and candidate cities (and thus nations) aspiring to host the Olympic Games. As previously mentioned, *The Sea to Sky Games: Vancouver 2010 Bid Book* correctly followed Olympic bid procedures by outlining the political institutions of Canada. However, no one in Canada, indigenous or non-indigenous, would seriously contend that 'First Nations' is a recognized and official political institution of Canada. So why is it that the IOC takes such information at face value and what prevents it from seeking out truths and realities?

The answers rest within the limitations of the Olympic Charter. As is stated at the beginning of its text, 'The IOC is the supreme authority of the Olympic Movement' and 'Any person or organization belonging in any capacity whatsoever to the Olympic

Movement is bound by the provisions of the Olympic Charter and shall abide by the decisions of the IOC'.[40] S. 37 of the Olympic Charter is dedicated to the 'Election of the host city', which establishes that this process is the 'prerogative of the IOC alone'.[41] While there are specific guidelines in place that bid cities are required to follow (i.e. approval from a National Olympic Committee, timelines, and guarantees), there is no process or by-law in place that allows for external (non-IOC) review of a bid or candidate city. In many regards, the IOC has relied on the United Nations (UN) to assist with sustainability and equity procedures. However, the IOC has fallen way-short of entrenching such measures within the mandate of the Olympic movement, and thus its bid and selection process.

In 1999 the IOC enacted *The Olympic Movement's Agenda 21: Sport for Sustainable Development*. This policy was inspired by the UN's 'Agenda 21', a global action plan, which was adopted by consensus on 14 June 1992 by 182 governments represented at the UN Conference on Environment and Development (UNCED) Earth Summit in Rio de Janeiro, Brazil. With the inclusion of this global plan into its own framework, sport communities are provided with a reference tool for their respective environmental and sustainable development programmes.[42] According to this plan the Olympic Movement is dedicated to 'Strengthening the Role of Major Groups', which includes the advancement of women, promoting the role of young people, and the recognition and promotion of indigenous populations.[43] In consideration of indigenous peoples, it is stated:

> Indigenous populations have strong historical ties to their environment and have played an important part in its preservation. The Olympic Movement endorses the UNCED action in favour of their recognition and the strengthening of their role. In this context, it intends: to encourage their sporting traditions; to contribute to the use of their traditional knowledge and know-how in matters of environment management in order to take appropriate action, notably in the regions where these populations originate; to encourage access to sports participation for these populations.[44]

While this reference appears to be vague in substance, it has placed bid, candidate and host cities in fragile positions whereby they must seriously consider establishing cordial (or at least the appearance of) working relations with local indigenous populations, or be dismissed in favour of cities/nations willing to comply with Olympic standards of environmental protection, sustainable development and the promotion of major groups. On the surface, this may be viewed as a positive initiative; however, it must not be misconstrued as having the capacity to assist the very persons or entities which it proposes to advance.

The adoption of *The Olympic Movement's Agenda 21* is deeply flawed on two levels. First, since it is not entrenched within the Olympic Charter it merely serves as an invitational guide that bid, candidate, and host nations can 'take or leave'. Second, and perhaps more importantly, it does not consider the basic human needs and rights of marginalized peoples. In order for the latter to be addressed, and the former to be embedded, the IOC's evaluation process for bid and candidate cities *must* be restructured. Accordingly, the IOC needs to make room for external consultation and evaluation of potential host cities/nations. For example, the UN has implemented various committees, including CERD and the Human Rights Committee, which have both established resolutions for evaluating internal and national treatment of marginalized groups. While the decisions and resolutions of such committees are non-binding, they operate within international philosophical norms of justice. Indigenous beliefs, and the just treatment of such populations, are becoming increasingly eminent within UN and global resolution plans. If the Olympic Movement is to prosper into the twenty-first century, then it must follow suit. For instance, an amendment to S. 37 'Election of the host Nation' of the Olympic Charter could allow for external consultation or at the very least the adoption of an evaluation process, as already developed by UN Committees. Under such an assessment process, bid and candidate cities would be identified as 'suitable' or 'unsuitable' as they have either succeeded or failed to meet international norms of morality. If a bid or candidate city/nation is in fact deemed suitable, then the guiding principles of a doctrine such as *The Olympic Movement's Agenda 21* could sensibly be imposed as the indigenous peoples (recipients) are considered to be on fair terms with Olympic organizers (donors). Under such a process, we can begin to view Olympism as a philosophy that speaks in truisms of equity, anti-discrimination, mutual recognition and respect, tolerance and solidarity.

Prior to awarding the Games to this city/nation, there was no process in place to determine whether the recipients (i.e. indigenous peoples) held the power to negotiate with its donors (i.e. VANOC and the IOC), and whether or not they would benefit from a policy such as *The Olympic Movement's Agenda 21*. As it stands, indigenous programming has proven to be a clear priority for VANOC. However, this should not be misconstrued to be anything more than a reinvention of national narratives, as demonstrated in Montréal, Calgary, Sydney and Salt Lake City. A serious flaw exists within the current Olympic structure, particularly the bid process, which continues to play a part in the ongoing marginalization and exploitation of indigenous peoples. In this ever-growing global community, the rights of indigenous peoples are coming to the forefront of international political action. As an international body with significant global influence, it is the responsibility of the IOC – in the name of Olympism – to adopt new policies that support the rights and dignity of indigenous peoples. However, as history has proven itself, it would take nothing short of a World War to cancel the Olympic Games. The Olympic Movement is a powerful industry and resistance to it is often deemed unwarranted, and at times, criminal. The Olympic Resistance Network has rallied under a public campaign calling for 'No Olympics on Stolen Native Land', and its various factions have engaged in educational, resistance and activist activities to disseminate anti-colonial, anti-capitalist and anti-Olympic messages at home and abroad. However, the reality is that the 2010 Vancouver Games *will* take place, and in the midst of national celebration there *will* be indigenous protest and activism. The British Columbia land question remains unanswered, and the very presence of the current Olympic structure on contentious indigenous lands has the potential to temporarily silence, and perhaps permanently alter, the fragile state of indigenous affairs in the province.

Acknowledgements

I am extremely grateful to Adam Barker, Emma Lowman and Cheryl Suzack for their conceptual and editorial refinement of this essay.

Notes

[1] Connerton, *How Societies Remember*.
[2] International Olympic Committee, *Olympic Charter*, 12.
[3] Wamsley, 'Laying Olympism to Rest', 231.
[4] Ibid.
[5] 'Media Guide'. *Opening Ceremony of the Games f the XXVII Olympiad in Sydney*, September 15, 2000.
[6] United Nations Committee on the Elimination of Racial Discrimination, 'Decision on Australia'.
[7] Magdalinski, 'The Reinvention of Australia', 309.
[8] Lenskyj, *The Best Olympics Ever?*
[9] Government of Australia, House of Representatives, 'Apology to Australia's Indigenous Peoples', February 13, 2008.

[10] Susan Shown Harjo, 'Indians in the Opening Ceremony: Postcard from the Past'. *Indian Country Today*, February 16, 2002.

[11] Ibid.

[12] Ibid.

[13] Forsyth, 'Teepees and Tomahawks', 72.

[14] Wamsley and Heine, '"Don't Mess with the Relay"'.

[15] 'The Sea to Sky Games', 17.

[16] Alfred and Corntassel, 'Being Indigenous', 597.

[17] For clarification on some of the controversies surrounding the inclusion of indigenous imagery into the programme of the Olympics see, O'Bonsawin, 'The Conundrum of Ilanaaq'.

[18] Olympic Resistance Network, http://www.web.resist.ca/ ~ orn/blog/?page_id = 2.

[19] Furthermore, the Olympic Resistance Network works in support of an international resolution that was passed by over 1,500 indigenous representatives who attended the Intercontinental Indigenous Peoples Gathering in Sonora, Mexico in October 2007. Resolution No.2 states, 'We reject the 2010 Winter Olympic on sacred and stolen territory of Turtle Island – Vancouver, Canada'. Consequently, 2010 resistance efforts are working towards hosting a global anti-capitalist and anti-colonial convergence from 10 February to 15 February 2010. See Olympic Resistance Network.

[20] 'Why We Resist 2010'.

[21] Alfred, 'Deconstructing the British Columbia Treaty Process'; Foster, Raven, and Webber, eds., *Let Right Be Done*.

[22] Foster and Grove, '"Trespassers on the Soil"'.

[23] Ibid.

[24] Ibid., 63.

[25] Ibid.

[26] Alfred, *Peace, Power, Righteousness,* 120.

[27] Ibid.

[28] Alfred, 'Deconstructing the British Columbia Treaty Process', 3.

[29] Ibid.

[30] *Sagen v. Vancouver Organizing Committee for the 2010 Olympic and Paralympic Winter Games*, Supreme Court of British Columbia, 10 July 2009: 41, 42.

[31] International Olympic Committee, *Olympic Charter*, 99.

[32] *Canadian Charter of Rights and Freedoms, Part I of the Constitution Act,* 29 March 1982.

[33] '2010 Olympic Security Plans Include "Free Speech Areas"'. *CBC News,* July 2, 2009. http://www.cbc.ca/canada/british-columbia/story/2009/07/08/bc-olympic-security-plans-free-speech-areas.html.

[34] There are six-stages in the BCTC including Stage 1: Statement of Intent to Negotiate, Stage 2: Readiness to Negotiate, Stage 3: Negotiation of a Framework Agreement, Stage 4: Negotiation of an Agreement in Principle, Stage 5: Negotiation to Finalize a Treaty, and Stage 6: Implementation of the Treaty. Tswwassen is the only First Nation community to reach Stage 6: Implementation of a Treaty. See 'First Nations & Negotiations', BC Treaty Commission, http://www.bctreaty.net/.

[35] Barker, O'Bonsawin, and Ogilvie, 'Business as Usual?', 26.

[36] Lenskyj, *Olympic Industry Resistance*.

[37] Lenskyj paraphrases from Giulianotti, 'Human Rights'. See Lenskyj, *Olympic Industry Resistance*, 82.

[38] Lenskyj, *Olympic Industry Resistance*.

[39] International Olympic Committee, *Olympic Charter*, 12.

[40] International Olympic Committee, *Olympic Charter*, 11. In force as from 4 July 2003.

[41] Ibid., 62.

[42] This plan of action builds upon proposals put forth in the Rio Declaration on Environment and Development, and is considered to be a theoretical and practical tool for addressing problems of sustainable development concerning 'social and economic dimensions', 'the conservation and management of resources for development', 'strengthening the role of major groups', and offers a 'means of implementation'. See United Nations Department of Economic and Social Affairs – Divisions for Sustainable Development, 'Agenda 21', 14 June 1992.

[43] International Olympic Committee, *The Olympic Movement's Agenda 21*, 42–5.

[44] Ibid., 45.

References

Alfred, Taiaiake. *Peace, Power, Righteousness: An Indigenous Manifesto.* Don Mills, ON: Oxford University Press, 1999.

Alfred, Taiaiake. 'Deconstructing the British Columbia Treaty Process'. *Balayi: Culture, Law, Colonialism* 3 (2001): 37–65.

Alfred, Taiaiake, and Jeff Corntassel. 'Being Indigenous: Resurgence against Contemporary Colonialism'. *Government and Opposition* 4, no. 4 (September 2005): 597–614.

Barker, Adam, Christine O'Bonsawin, and Chiinuuks Ogilvie. 'Business as Usual? Reflections on the BC Treaty Process'. *New Socialist* 65, no. 1 (2009): 24–6.

Connerton, Paul. *How Societies Remember.* Cambridge: Cambridge University Press, 1989.

Forsyth, Janice. 'Teepees and Tomahawks: Aboriginal Cultural Representation at the 1976 Olympic Games'. In *The Global Nexus Engaged: Past, Present, Future Interdisciplinary Olympic Studies – Sixth International Symposium for Olympic Research*, edited by Kevin Wamsley, Robert K. Barney, and Scott G. Martyn, 71–5. London, ON: The International Centre for Olympic Studies, 2002.

Foster, Hamar, and Alan Grove. '"Trespassers on the Soil": United *States v. Tom* and a New Perspective on the Short History of Treaty Making in Nineteenth Century British Columbia'. *BC Studies* 138/139 (2003): 51–84.

Foster, Hamar, Heather Raven and Jeremy Webber eds. *Let Right Be Done: Aboriginal Title, the* Calder *Case and the Future of Indigenous Rights.* Vancouver: UBC Press, 2007.

Giulianotti, R. 'Human Rights, Globalization and Sentimental Education: The Case of Sport'. *Sport and Society* 7, no. 3 (2004): 355–69.

International Olympic Committee. *The Olympic Movement's Agenda 21: Sport for Sustainable Development.* Lausanne: International Olympic Committee, 1999.

International Olympic Committee. *The Olympic Charter.* Lausanne: International Olympic Committee, 2007.

Lenskyj, Helen Jefferson. *The Best Olympics Ever?* Albany, NY: State University of New York Press, 2002.

Lenskyj, Helen Jefferson. *Olympic Industry Resistance: Challenging Olympic Power and Propaganda.* Albany, NY: State University of New York Press, 2007.

Magdalinski, Tara. 'The Reinvention of Australia for the Sydney 2000 Olympic Games'. *International Journal of the History of Sport* 17, no. 2/3 (June 2000): 305–22.

No Olympics on Stolen Native Land. 'Resist the 2010 Corporate Circus'. http://www.no2010.com/node/19.

O'Bonsawin, Christine M. 'The Conundrum of Ilanaaq: First Nations Representation and the 2010 Vancouver Winter Olympics'. In *Cultural Imperialism in Action: Critiques in the Global Olympic Trust*, edited by Nigel B. Crowther, Robert K. Barney, and Michael K. Heine, 387–94. London, ON: International Centre for Olympic Studies, 2006.

'The Sea to Sky Games: Vancouver 2010 Bid Book'. VANOC, 2002.

United Nations Committee on the Elimination of Racial Discrimination. 'Decision on Australia'. Session (54) of 18 March 1999 and Session (55) of 19 August 1999.

Wamsley, Kevin B. 'Laying Olympism to Rest'. In *Post-Olympism? Questioning Sport in the Twentieth-First Century*, edited by John Bale and Mette Krogh Christensen, 231–42. Oxford: Berg, 2004.

Wamsley, Kevin B., and Michael Heine. '"Don't Mess with the Relay – It's Bad Medicine" Aboriginal Culture and the 1998 Winter Olympics'. In *Olympic Perspectives: Third International Symposium for Olympic Research*, edited by Robert K. Barney, 173–98. London, ON: University of Western Ontario, Centre for Olympic Research, 1996.

'Why We Resist 2010'. No Olympics in Stolen Native Lands: Resist the 2010 Corporate Circus. http://www.no2010.com/.

Epilogue: the struggles must continue

Bruce Kidd

Faculty of Physical Education and Health, University of Toronto, Toronto, Canada

In the epilogue to this special issue, the co-editor reflects upon recent efforts to bring about social change in and through sport, the contributions of scholarship to those efforts and the current terrain. He argues that while sport has power to effect progressive change, we should not exaggerate the extent of that power. Moreover, sport activists rarely make effective coalitions with progressive groups outside of sport, to the detriment of both. He concludes that the most pressing need today is to shore up public opportunities for sport and physical activity. To that end, he suggests four contributions scholars can make: document and publicize the contradictions between promise and reality, conduct critical research, engage students and support open source publication.

How do the lessons of the last 40 years illuminate the struggles for human rights and justice today? What are the priorities and possibilities?

What we've learned and affirmed from this volume and the conference that gave it birth is that sport has been an important site for advancing social change. It is clear that activism – whether in the form of advocacy and lobbying, astute media relations, research-based report carding, court challenges, demonstrations and sit-ins – has brought about significant changes *in sports*, and has often contributed moral and organizational force to equity and human rights campaigns *in other fields*. As just one example, the current campaign for fair labour practices in the production of athletic uniforms and sports shoes has persuaded universities, Olympic organizing committees, governments and corporations to adopt progressive procurement policies, strengthening the rights of workers in the global supply chain while increasing sportspersons' awareness of the social connections of the products they endorse.

It is also clear that a shared, critical understanding of the history of such struggles can contribute significantly to effective activism. Such knowledge has not always been available for those on the front lines. The young women who fought for gender equity in the early days of second-wave feminism did so largely in ignorance of the efforts and successes of their first-wave counterparts two generations earlier. Except for the snippets of news that they could smuggle or steal from their warders, the men who created the Robben Island football leagues were completely shut off from the outside world and the efforts of their anti-apartheid comrades and supporters in South Africa and other parts of the world. But where a sense of that history is available, whether from the oral accounts of forerunners, committed teaching, or scholarship, it can provide inspiration, instruction and energy. I think of the contributions of history to the long struggle for civil rights and against racism in so many parts of the world. 'To remember', as Lennox Farrell, the eloquent African-Canadian veteran of those campaigns, has said, gives both motivation and tutelage 'to resist'.[1]

Sport does not necessarily lend itself to progressive politics. In fact, there are just as many examples of sport teaching conformity and the acceptance of the established order as of resistance. In the 1960s, 'jockrakers' such as Jack Scott, Paul Hoch and Dave Meggyesy argued that sport had become a school of sexism, racism and militarism.[2] But under the right circumstances, with astute leadership, sport can become a favourable ground for change. In the first place, the idea of sport as a curriculum, the belief that the intrinsic, embodied discipline of learning and playing a sport teaches transferable values and habits of mind, validates it as a vehicle of social change. First popularized in the nineteenth century by the Christian Socialist Thomas Hughes in his best-selling novel, *Tom Brown's Schooldays*, the idea of sport as education has become so widely accepted (albeit with little empirical validation) that all manner of change agents have embraced it. At one point or another, it has been taken up by feminists, socialists, communists and other social reformers as well as philanthropic capitalists, middle-class educators and religious and ethnic organizations.[3] The modern Olympic Movement and most North American college and university sport programmes still preach this ideal, even though they do little to implement it in a systematic way. This deep current of what Peter Donnelly calls 'sport for good' has long predisposed the culture to the idea of sport for social change.

The structure, symbolic representation and constructed appeal of sport create other openings for progressive advocacy. Ever since the beginnings of modern sport, fashioned, elaborated, emulated and spread amid the explosive globalization of industrial capitalism and the interconnected struggles for liberal democracy, organizers and participants have proclaimed sport a meritocratic, moral order, and imbued their activities with the rules and narratives of 'the level playing field' and 'fair play'. To be sure, most sports retained the patriarchal, middle-class, heterosexist and Europeanist character of their principal organizers. But just as contradictions between the liberal promise of rights and the class and gender restrictions upon the franchise sparked the great campaigns for universal and feminist suffrage in the nineteenth and twentieth centuries, so the contradictions between the spirit of the 'level playing field' and the actual demographics of participation and leadership in sport have always provided a rallying point for those left outside the fence. The moral claims of sport legitimize it as a site of struggle. This tendency has been reinforced by the rapid extent to which sport was inscribed with representational status, so that individual athletes and teams were bestowed with/took on the characteristics and stereotypes of entire peoples. The uphill battles of female, aboriginal, black and other other-identified athletes for inclusion and athletic success were thus widely understood to symbolize the aspirations and experiences of those peoples, and lent themselves to struggles well beyond sport. With the rapid spread of sport through the mass media and the public institutions of the playground and school, so that it became one of the most accessible forms of male popular culture, it is easy to understand why sport has long been understood as a legitimate site of struggle around issues of equity and human rights.

That, of course, does not tell us much about how progressive change has actually come about, why some athletes and activists beat their heads against the wall for decades with little effect, and then a little later, someone else comes along and engineers a breakthrough. Or why some important victories have been reversed. For more than a decade before Branch Rickey integrated Major League Baseball in the United States by bringing Jackie Robinson up to the Brooklyn Dodgers, the owners and players of the black leagues, energetically supported by the black and communist media, waged an impressive campaign to integrate black and white professional baseball, but got nowhere. Rickey's and Robinson's success was the result of the former's cunning and the latter's extraordinary courage and athletic ability but it was also enabled by the mass mobilizations and social innovation in the workplace, public housing, education, recreation and the arts that briefly shook up North America at the end of the Second World War.[4]

We can trace the steps that particular actors took but it's much more difficult to unravel the broader economic, social and political changes that empowered and complicated the changes under study, and why some options were taken and others rejected. The integration of Major League Baseball contributed to the legitimacy and moral force of the post-Second World War civil rights movement. The searing indictments of racism from the Olympic Project for Human Rights in 1968, just four years after the passage of the US Civil Rights Act, in the same year as the assassination of Martin Luther King, the resulting riots in Detroit, Chicago and Los Angeles, and the youth mobilization against the US-led war in Vietnam, brought a quick end to overt discrimination in North American sport. But as Harry Edwards, the intellectual leader of the Olympic Project for Human Rights, so poignantly points out, the form that integration in baseball and the civil rights movement took had the consequence of destroying the black professional leagues and many of the associated black businesses, contributing to the split of black communities along class lines, with devastating consequences for the transmission of cultural traditions. Could it have been any different? What circumstances might have enabled that? What alternative options were open to the leaders? 'What if' questions are impossible to answer, but in drawing lessons from the histories of social change we must recognize both the choices that are possible and the array of forces buffeting the actors involved. As Marx reminds us, 'men make their own history but they do not make it just as they please; they do not make it under circumstances chosen by themselves, but under circumstances directly encountered, given and transmitted from the past'.[5]

Similar questions can be raised about the other great breakthroughs of the last 40 years addressed in this volume, including the defeat of apartheid, the achievement of equity legislation and policies in government and sports organizations, and the realization of athletes' rights in the Olympic sports. How, for example, do we assess the ultimate impact of the international campaign against apartheid sport? What has been the legacy of the heroic activism against apartheid sport within South Africa upon South African sport today? By the late 1980s, the international campaign had effectively barred athletes from the apartheid sector of South African sport from competing virtually everywhere in the world and stopped athletes and teams from other countries from travelling to South Africa to play. In New Zealand, it so bitterly divided the country during the 1981 Springboks' tour that subsequent governments agreed to stop further tours from going ahead. Each tightening of the cordon around apartheid sport was alarmingly reported in the South African media, bringing the international hostility home to the white majority on the front pages of their newspapers, while bringing hope to the repressed majority. Within South Africa, the non-racial sports movement resisted the coercion and inducements to legitimate apartheid sport, maintaining their own programmes under extremely difficult circumstances under the slogan 'No normal sport under abnormal conditions', while as Tony Suze and Chuck Korr discuss, the political prisoners on Robben Island taught themselves to be a 'government in waiting' by playing football. It was the most sustained, internationally coordinated campaign for justice in sport the world has ever seen.

In the end, was it the sports boycott that tipped the balance and brought about the end of apartheid? Or the military impasse achieved by the Cuban-reinforced Angolans against the South African Defence Force at Cuito Cuanavale in 1988, bringing about the withdrawal of South African troops and the independence of Namibia, furthering the encirclement of apartheid? Or the economic boycott, initiated by the hundreds of divestment campaigns around the world and eventually supported by western governments? Or the educational or cultural boycotts mounted by teachers and artists? Or the extraordinary mobilization of the mass democratic movement within South Africa? Could the sports boycott have been effective without these other interventions? In the New Zealand case presented by Malcolm Maclean, it was a 'perfect storm' of factors that enabled the success of the 1981 mobilization, and when under different conditions the organizers sought to renew the coalition that conducted it, they were unable to pull it off.

For sports scholars, these questions illustrate the necessity of approaches to investigation and explanation that assume contingency, dynamic complexity and the importance of history. For activists, they remind us that sport has power, but we should not exaggerate the extent of that power. These points have not always been accepted. During the 1970s and 1980s, despite the rich history of socialist and workers' sport prior to the Second World War, many on the left completely rejected sport as 'totally situated within capitalist society', while mainstream politicians and academics dismissed sport as the 'sandbox'. In this milieu, sport was considered to have the least capacity or possibility for effecting change. Even some sport activists came to believe that sport is completely over-determined by the dominant institutions and forces in capitalist societies. My answer then as now is that people should work politically where they happen to be located, where they have experience and are respected for what they contribute to a particular community, field or institution. With such experience and respect, they can gradually build a constituency for change. I also believe/d sports affect millions of people, as participants, spectators and as consumers of, and contributors to, global culture, many of whom think seriously about their engagement and experiences. To be sure, sport is profoundly caught up with, and often organized to reproduce, the dominant ideas and institutions of capitalism, but it also provides a measure of space for independent thought, even activism. That space may be tiny, but no matter how constrained, as Dino Numerato demonstrates about communist Czechoslovakia, it can still be used for subversion and advocacy.

Sportspersons committed to equity and human rights need to do better to forge coalitions with people in similar struggles, however. Perhaps it's because we tend to be competitive about everything we do. Or perhaps it's because the engrossing demands of 'sport for sport for sport's sake' shrink the horizons, the 'paradox of sport' so insightfully explored by Rick Gruneau.[6] But from my Canadian experience, few equity or rights-based campaigns have gone beyond the familiar contours of sport to create alliances. Instead, they focus on one or two sports, or just the high-performance sector, limiting their impact. While the Canadian campaigns for gender equity and athletes' rights have made important breakthroughs, as Ann Peel attests, they have drawn their support primarily from sportspersons. What else could they have achieved if they were linked organizationally to the broader women's movement, or the efforts by students, artists, workers and those in other constituencies to win collective bargaining and other protections for themselves? Moreover, the decades-long Canadian efforts for more government funding for sport and physical activity have rarely connected with similar lobbying by artists and the campaigns to revitalize the public sector in education, health and social services. As a consequence, sports advocates are often scorned as 'vested interests', even by those who should be natural allies, and efforts to rebuild the sports infrastructure though major games face community opposition. Some colleagues argue that major games are by definition incompatible with social justice.[7] In her essay, Christine O'Bonsawin challenges the legitimacy of organizing committees and host nations that have not settled aboriginal land claims. But I am optimistic that with genuine, broadly representative, needs-based consultation and negotiation, major games can realize many social priorities, not just those in sports. The memorandum of understanding between the Chicago bid committee for the 2016 Olympics and its community outreach council governing employment, contracting and procurement, housing and community enhancements is one recent example.[8]

Today, after the end of the Cold War and the breakup of the Soviet Union, the revolution in communication technologies, the resurgence of Islam, the doubling of the world's population, and other remarkable changes, the world is very different than it was 40 years ago. Despite the ambition and optimism of the youth radicalization of 1968, the world seems as plagued by conflict and war, the proliferation of guns and weapons, poverty, disease and environmental destruction as it was then. The neo-liberal globalization has exacerbated inequalities within and between societies, and governments' initial responses to the current worldwide economic crisis have exacerbated those inequalities. These conditions profoundly affect the possibilities for equity and human rights in sports. On the one hand, the advances documented in this volume have eliminated explicit discrimination against girls and women and persons of colour in many sports and jurisdictions. Campaigns to extend the protections of law and policy to lesbian, gay, bi-sexual, transgender and queer (LGBTQ), athletes from ethno-cultural, linguistic and religious minorities, and persons with disabilities are well underway. In professional and Olympic sports, athletes have won the rights to bargain collectively, elect their own representatives to decision-making bodies, and appeal unfavourable decisions to independent tribunals, such as the Sport Dispute Resolution Centre of Canada and the International Court of Arbitration for Sport (CAS). If CAS had been in existence in 1968, Tommie Smith and John Carlos would never have been expelled for their black power salute on the victory podium at the Mexico Olympics. On the other hand, the symbolic landscape of sport (re)presented by the mass media remains as unabashedly masculinist as ever. The protections of athletes' rights are rarely found in college, university, school and youth sports in the Global North, and from top to bottom in the Global South, and do not always apply to coaches and officials. Even more seriously, the immiseration of public institutions in many countries and the dramatic increase in class and regional inequalities, both a deliberate consequence of the neo-liberal ascendency, have made the promise of physical education and sport for all so much harder to realize. To be sure, the demise of opportunities is exacerbated by the systematic reduction of physical activity in daily life brought about by the accelerating transformations of work, place and time, what Frank Booth calls the 'sedentary death syndrome',[9] but the assault on public institutions and the very idea of inclusive citizenship has enabled it to grow. While we need to ensure that equitable policies and protections are in place and fully realized throughout sports, the most urgent priority is to shore up public sport and physical activity.

During the last two decades, national and international corporations, foundations, non-governmental organizations (NGOs), sports organizations and professional and Olympic athletes have responded to the inadequacy of the public schools and recreation centres that once provided accessible opportunities for sport and physical activity by creating their own organizations and programmes. Influential examples include the Nike Foundation, the UK Sport Trust and Right to Play. In North America, virtually every professional team and many individual athletes have their own foundations that raise funds and donate to local charities, community sports programmes, even public schools and municipal recreation centres. They breathe new life into Thomas Hughes' old ambition of effecting change through sports participation, and link it in new ways to the culture of spectatorship. One focus of such interventions is 'youth-at-risk'; another, girls and women. The Nike

Foundation seeks to alleviate poverty through the 'girl effect' of female empowerment. While the best invigorate community sports programmes with new ideas, energy and funds, and tackle difficult issues such as sexual violence, they often compete with each other and complicate an already confusing patchwork of public, private and voluntary opportunities. Despite their commitment to disadvantaged groups and neighbourhoods and, through statements of corporate social responsibility, to human rights, they rarely initiate or support reforms that would change the structured inequality that necessitates intervention in the first place. Increasingly, as Michael Giardina documents, such programmes are shrewdly interwoven with corporate and institutional branding and marketing. Whether intended or not, they serve to legitimate corporate and private power at the expense of the democratic state. A generation ago in Ontario, the professional sports industry used its political clout to abolish a tax on their ticket sales; the tax funded a provincial government agency that supported amateur sport. Today, the major professional teams raise funds from their fans in 50:50 draws to finance their highly publicized charitable contributions. While the source of such funds is essentially the same, i.e., the team supporters, it is now private corporations and their foundations – not the democratic state – that direct the expenditures and get the credit.[10]

How can we advance the realization of human rights in sport and society on this complex terrain? The ultimate success of any such effort will require the elimination of inequality, war and disease and the creation of much more environmentally sustainable ways of life, all urgent, complex and seemingly utopian tasks in 2010. It will take a sustained, concerted, coordinated effort in countless constituencies and places. What those of us in sport can contribute to these momentous tasks will be determined by social location, strategic choice and the interplay of social forces.

Let me conclude this brief essay by endorsing four approaches:

1. Document and publicize the contradictions

The achievement of equity and human rights in legislation and policy is an important step, but it does not guarantee that those rights are actually experienced and enforced. There are too many 'say-do' gaps between promise and reality. Some coaches and administrators still do not act as if athletes have rights; some athletes are unaware of their rights and the protections available to them. Moreover, social and cultural barriers inhibit participation among disadvantaged groups, even though they may be singled out for inclusion. In Sydney, Australia, for example, Kristine Toohey and Tracy Taylor found that while 75% of recreation providers believed that their facilities were open to all, 75% of women from the targeted ethno-cultural, religious and linguistic minorities reported that there were barriers to their participation.[11] In response, activists, scholars, social observatories, NGOs and even governments have monitored compliance and published 'report cards' as a means of measuring behaviour and creating pressure for corrective action. During the anti-apartheid struggle, the United Nations Register of Sports Contacts with South Africa, compiled from the reports of activists and sympathetic governments around the world and mailed twice yearly, enabled the international campaign to focus its efforts more strategically. In recent years, the Racial and Gender Report Card published annually by scholar activist Richard Lapchick has shone the spotlight on the hiring policies in US professional sport.[12] In Ontario, the annual tracking reports of the parent-led NGO, People for Education, have pushed the provincial government into hiring more subject specialists, especially in physical education.[13] Increasingly, governments, sports bodies, and donors require such accounting, but where it is not available, we should insist that it be produced, or do it ourselves. Where there is a patchwork of providers, with the likelihood of both gaps and duplication, jurisdiction-wide surveys and analysis are necessary. Whatever the findings, we should see that the results are publicized.

2. Critically evaluate sport for development and peace

One encouraging recent development is the emerging movement of sport for development and peace (SDP), the use of sport well beyond the competition-focused, networks of clubs and sports governing bodies to address difficult challenges in education, health and conflict resolution.[14] In the UK, for example, the focus of the new sport colleges has been school retention, academic improvement, community safety and increased physical activity, not sports performance.[15] Throughout the Global South, governments, sports organizations, private corporations and NGOs provide sports programmes to empower girls and women, combat HIV/AIDS, and reduce tension in war-torn societies. The UN's International Working Group on Sport for Development and Peace has recruited sport to the realization of the Millennium Development Goals. These interventions constitute a striking re-assertion of Thomas Hughes' nineteenth-century ideals of sport as a pedagogy of beneficial change. But despite the impassioned promise of advocates, very little is known about the determinations of the intended outcomes, i.e. the mechanisms by which sport participation helps students to attain improved math scores, girls and women to protect themselves from unwanted sexual activity, and players to develop respectful interactions with opponents from hostile groups. What we do know from the literature is that '*the evident benefits appear to be an indirect outcome of the context and social interaction that is possible in sport* rather than a direct outcome of participating in sport'.[16] The literature also indicates that leadership is key to successful programmes. We therefore need to increase our understanding of the precise circumstances under which sport may result in positive outcomes, for different groups, and what forms of leadership and leadership training are more productive. Such knowledge would strengthen the monitoring and evaluation of programmes.

3. Engage students

Those of us who teach courses about sport and society have ample opportunity to engage students in struggles for equity and human rights, by encouraging them to voice their own concerns, giving them the skills to conduct research into the circumstances and available remedies, and teaching them about the histories of activism. Such instruction can be as simple as an assignment requiring students to write a letter to the editor pointing out an inequity or violation of human rights, or as extensive as a community service internship with an NGO. It must be consistent with the principles of academic freedom and critical, open-ended inquiry, i.e. it cannot be proselytizing or recruitment for a single cause. But it can empower students in rewarding ways, and stimulate innovation and improvement, especially in your own institution. My favourite examples these days are drawn from Harry Wray, the political scientist who introduces students to urban activism on a bicycle in Chicago,[17] but many other colleagues do this well. In 2008, the North American Society of Sport History devoted a session to activist scholars and their engagement of students.

4. Contribute to open source publication and dissemination

While academic and commercial publishers have been indispensible to the production and dissemination of knowledge, the increasing commodification of copyright and the concentration of ownership have raised the price barriers to the acquisition of knowledge, especially for public libraries, students and residents of poorer countries. These are difficult issues for academics. On the one hand, as authors we support the extension of copyright and the payment of royalties as a way of fairly remunerating the producers of knowledge. On the other hand, it's disturbing to see how these practices and the increasing monopolization of ownership that seems to have gone hand in hand with them limit dissemination and readership. One response is open source access and publication, free electronic access to ebooks and journals (such as that provided by the LA84 Foundation Library and several Olympic study centres around the world), and the publication of new knowledge in open source ejournals (such as the *Canadian Journal of Sociology*). If open source publication is to give academics the peer-reviewed standard we need for career recognition, it must be supported by senior scholars and university departments.[18]

To do all this, we must strengthen the material and social conditions for critical sport studies and history. Recovering, presenting and writing the histories of social activism are no easy matters. Scholars struggle to unravel events and determinations and forge interpretation and understanding, working within different social locations, ideologies, political positions and methodologies, often with scant materials and resources, sometimes in isolation, sometimes against 'a flurry of elbows'. No matter how carefully written, history has always been potentially divisive. In recent decades, in the former Yugoslavia, in Rwanda, in Iraq and throughout the Middle East, it has been mined selectively to whip up appalling hatred and violence. In Spain, the memories of the civil war and the Franco years have been so painful that public remembrance was outlawed until very recently.[19] But history that is critical, comprehensive and informed by a respect for the humanity of all peoples is essential to the extension and realization of equity and human rights. Like Herbert Gutman, we believe that 'historical understanding ... transforms historical givens into historical contingencies. It enables us to see the structures in which we live and the inequality people experience as only one among many other possible experiences. By doing that, you free people for creative and critical thought.'[20]

Acknowledgements

I am extremely grateful for the comments of Peter Donnelly and Russell Field on a draft of this paper.

Notes

1. Farrell, 'Black Rhythms'.
2. Scott, *Athletic Revolution*; Hoch, *Rip Off*; and Meggysey, *Out of their League*.
3. Kidd, *Struggle for Canadian Sport*.
4. Lipsitz, *Rainbow at Midnight*.
5. Marx, *The 18th Brumaire*, 15.
6. Gruneau, *Sport, Class*, 23–8.
7. Lenskyj, *Olympic Industry Resistance*; Shaw, *Five Ring Circus*.
8. Chicago 2016, 'Memorandum of Understanding'.
9. Ira Dreyfuss, 'Sedentary Death Syndrome. It's Real Researchers Say'. *Associated Press*, May 31, 2001. http://www.wordspy.com/words/sedentarydeathsyndrome.asp.
10. Cf. Kidd, '"Making the Pros Pay"'; Jays Care Foundation, http://mlb.mlb.com/tor/community/tor_community_jayscare.jsp; and 'Toronto Raptors Report to Community 2007-2008', http://www.nba.com/media/raptors/0708RaptorsReporttoCom.pdf.
11. Taylor and Toohey, 'Sport and Cultural Diversity'.
12. E.g. 'The Racial and Gender Report Card', http://web.bus.ucf.edu/sportbusiness/?page=1445.
13. People for Education, http://www.peopleforeducation.com/school_survey.

[14] Kidd, 'A New Social Movement'.
[15] Youth Sport Trust, 'Know the Score 2008'.
[16] Kidd and Donnelly, *Literature Reviews*, 4. Italics in original.
[17] Wray, *Pedal Power*.
[18] Association of American Universities, 'The University's Role'; Association of Research Libraries, *Open Access*; Houghton *et al.*, 'Economic Implications'; and Lessig, *Free Culture*.
[19] MacMillan, *Uses and Abuses*.
[20] Merrill, 'Herbert Gutman', 203.

References

Association of American Universities. 'The University's Role in the Dissemination of Research and Scholarship-A Call to Action'. *Research Library Issues* 262 February 2009: 1–6. http://www.arl.org/resources/pubs/rli/.

Association of Research Libraries. *Open Access*. SPARC, Washington, DC. http://www.arl.org/sparc/bm~doc/openaccess-2.pdf.

Chicago 2016. 'Memorandum of Understanding'. http://www.chicago2016.org/Portals/0/WhyChicago_OurPlan/MOU%20FINAL.pdf

Farrell, Lennox. 'Black Rhythms in White Rituals'. http://www.timbooktu.com/lennox/rituals.htm.

Gruneau, Richard. *Sport, Class and Social Development*. Amherst, MA: University of Massachusetts Press, 1983.

Hoch, Paul. *Rip Off the Big Game: The Exploitation of Sports by the Power Elite*. New York: Doubleday, 1972.

Houghton, John, Bruce Rasmussen, Peter Sheehan, Charles Oppenheim, Anne Morris, Claire Creaser *et al.* 'Economic Implications of Alternative Scholarly Publishing Models: Exploring the Costs and Benefits. A Report to the Joint Information Systems Committee'. Loughborough: Loughborough University. http://www.jisc.ac.uk/media/documents/publications/rpteconomi-coapublishing.pdf.

John Beckwith Centre for Sport. 'Know the Score 2008'. Loughborough University, January 2008.

Kidd, Bruce. '"Making the Pros Pay" for Amateur Sport: the Ontario Athletic Commission 1920–1947'. *Ontario History* 87, no. 2 (1995): 105–27.

Kidd, Bruce. *The Struggle for Canadian Sport*. Toronto: University of Toronto Press, 1996.

Kidd, Bruce. 'A New Social Movement: Sport for Development and Peace'. *Sport in Society* 11, no. 4 (2008): 370–80.

Kidd, Bruce and Peter Donnelly, eds. *Literature Reviews on Sport for Development and Peace*. Toronto: International Working Group for Sport for Development and Peace, 2007.

Lenskyj, Helen. *Olympic Industry Resistance: Challenging Olympic Power and Propaganda*. Albany, NY: State University of New York Press, 2008.

Lessig, Lawrence. *Free Culture: How Big Media Uses Technology and the Law to Lock Down Culture and Control Creativity*. New York: The Penguin Press, 2004.

Lipsitz, George. *Rainbow at Midnight: Class and Culture in Cold War America*. New York: Praeger, 1981.

MacMillan, Margaret. *The Uses and Abuses of History*. Toronto: Viking, 2008.

Marx, Karl. *The 18th Brumaire of Louis Napoleon*. New York: International Publishers, 1964 (1852).

Meggysey, Dave. *Out of their League*. Lincoln, NE: University of Nebraska Press, 2005 (1971).

Merrill, Mike. 'Herbert Gutman'. In *Visions of History*, edited by E.P. Thompson and Henry Abelove, 185–216. New York: Pantheon Books, 1983.

Scott, Jack. *The Athletic Revolution*. New York: Free Press, 1971.

Shaw, Chris. *Five Ring Circus: Myths and Realities of the Olympic Games*. Vancouver: New Society Publishers, 2008.

Taylor, Tracy, and Kristine Toohey. 'Sport and Cultural Diversity: Why are the Women being Left Out?' In *Sport in the City: The Role of Sport in Economic and Social Regeneration*, edited by Chris Gratton and Ian Henry, 204–13. London: Routledge, 2001.

Wray, Henry. *Pedal Power: The Quiet Rise of the Bicycle in American Public Life*. Boulder, CO: Paradigm Publishers, 2008.

Youth Sport Trust. *Know the Score 2008: The Positive Impact of the Sports College Network – An Update of Evidence*. Youth Sport Trust, John Beckwith Centre for Sport, Loughborough University, January 2008.

Index

Page numbers in **Bold** represent figures.

170   *Index*

Printed in the USA/Agawam, MA
September 23, 2011

561478.036

0 1341 1431080 5